BACK TO
BAKING

BACK TO

200 Timeless Recipes
to Bake, Share, and Enjoy

Anna Olson

whitecap

Whitecap Books is known for its expertise in the cookbook market, and has produced some of the most innovative and familiar titles found in kitchens across North America. Visit our website at www.whitecap.ca.

PUBLISHER: Michael Burch
EDITOR: Sarah Maitland
DESIGNER: Mauve Pagé
FOOD PHOTOGRAPHER: Ryan Szulc
FOOD STYLISTS: Anna Olson and Lisa Rollo
PROP STYLIST: Madeleine Johari

Printed in Canada

LIBRARY AND ARCHIVES CANADA CATALOGUING IN PUBLICATION

Olson, Anna, 1968-
    Back to baking : 200 timeless recipes to bake, share, and enjoy / Anna Olson.

Includes index.
ISBN 978-1-77050-063-1

    1. Baking. 2. Desserts. 3. Cookbooks. I. Title.

TX765.O47 2011   641.8'15   C2011-904465-X

The publisher acknowledges the financial support of the Government of Canada through the Canada Book Fund (CBF) and the Province of British Columbia through the Book Publishing Tax Credit.

12 13 14 15   5

ENVIRONMENTAL BENEFITS STATEMENT

Whitecap Books Ltd saved the following resources by printing the pages of this book on chlorine free paper made with 10% post-consumer waste.

TREES	WATER	ENERGY	SOLID WASTE	GREENHOUSE GASES
10	**4,537**	**4**	**303**	**837**
FULLY GROWN	GALLONS	MILLION BTUs	POUNDS	POUNDS

Environmental impact estimates were made using the Environmental Paper Network Paper Calculator 3.2. For more information visit www.papercalculator.org.

CONTENTS

INTRODUCTION

THOSE OF US who bake understand that baking is about a sense of satisfaction, a sense of sharing. Especially these days, when time is our most valuable commodity, taking the time to make something that doesn't just feed the family but is meant as a reward is a gift that can be as gratifying for the giver as it is for the receiver. If you are ready to feel that sense of satisfaction and sharing, then it is time to get back to baking.

This book is about those extras, those treats that have a place in a balanced diet, in modest portions. Making something from scratch gives you control. You know what you are making, what is going into the dish, and how it is being prepared. And there is luxury in the fact that, because these delights are homemade, the recipes can suit those with food intolerances and allergies.

I've devoted chapters in this book to dairy-free, egg-free, gluten-free, and low-fat/low-sugar baking. Many more of these types of recipes are scattered throughout the rest of the book and designated as such.

I've also included several recipes in the book that are "foundation" recipes. These recipes are used as a base for other recipes. For example, Basic Brown Sugar Cookie Dough (see page 17) is the base for several drop cookie recipes. Foundation recipes are designated as such.

Some of the recipes in this collection are based on basic sweet treats, like Chocolate Chip Cookies, Currant Scones, and Raisin Butter Tarts. The book also includes recipes for more elaborate and formal desserts, like Chocolate Layer Cake with Caramel Frosting, Dobos Torte, and Pear, Grand Marnier, and White Chocolate Trifle. I've also introduced new techniques, such as the one for the Lemon Meringue Pie.

Whether you are a novice cook—perhaps a young person who wants to make your first batch of brownies, or a more adventurous baker—someone who is ready to tackle a wedding cake, this book has something for you. It provides fundamental formulas and guidelines as well as sophisticated advice. For some of you, this book will refresh your memory of the principles of baking and help you ease back into the art.

Over my years of baking, I've tried many different techniques; some worked, some didn't. Each experience was an opportunity for me to learn new things, and now I can share what I've learned with you. Throughout the book, I've added information based on some of the most common baking questions I've been asked. Baking is not just about the "what to make" but the "why it all works in the wonderful ways it does." I've tried to provide as many answers as I could to the "whys" so that you will be able to take these tips into the kitchen and bake with confidence.

One final note: The recipes in this book were not compiled from my other books. All of these recipes are new. I've had fun creating, making, and testing each treat and dessert, all the while asking myself: "How can I make it tastier? How can I make it simpler? Who will get the reward today?"

Bake, share, and enjoy,
Anna Olson

before you bake

BAKING RECIPES CONTAIN a number of commonly repeated ingredients, tools, and terms, and although you may be comfortable jumping right in and starting a recipe, this chapter gives you some guidelines to the phrasing used in this book.

In addition, the chapter introductions contain general advice for recipes within that chapter. These topical blurbs cover some of the most common baking questions I am asked. Specific tips, called "Notes from Anna's Kitchen," also accompany certain recipes for when you are making the recipe (not everyone reads the opening chapters to a cookbook before they begin!).

Baking actions are movements made to produce specific results. Here are definitions of some of the most commonly used actions in baking:

. . . .

BEAT To stir with a vigorous motion (by hand with a spoon or spatula, or by machine, which will usually be specified) with the expectation that some air may get worked into the batter.

BLEND To combine ingredients to a homogeneous consistency. The level or speed of blending will be specified if it is important.

CREAM To work one or more ingredients, usually butter and sugar, together in a way that aerates the ingredients by spreading them along the side of the mixing bowl with a wooden spoon or spatula or by using beaters on a medium to high speed until the mixture is light and fluffy. Butter and sugar that have been well creamed give structure to cookies in particular. Creaming is typically called for in recipes with equal amounts of sugar and butter, or those with more sugar than butter. Recipes with greater amounts of butter are typically beaten to aerate the batter.

DOCK To pierce a pastry dough with a fork in an even pattern. This is typically done to shortbread cookies and to pie or tart shells that are pre-baked. The holes allow hot air to escape from within and underneath the dough, thus preventing any bubbles forming. Docking also allows room for expansion during baking, so the pastry again remains flat as it bakes and then cools. The docking holes do fill in as the pastry bakes so that, once filled, a pie or tart will not leak.

FOLD To gently incorporate ingredients while maintaining the air in the lighter ingredient. A lighter ingredient like whipped egg whites or whipped cream is usually incorporated into a heavier base. The motion should be a gentle circular action, with the spatula reaching right to the bottom of the bowl to lift the heavier base until incorporated. There is no benefit to folding too slowly—on occasion, folding too deliberately gives the whipped ingredient more time to break down and collapse. If whipped cream or egg whites are being folded in multiple additions, as a recipe would typically state, the first addition does not need to be fully incorporated before adding the next addition since you will be folding again. By the final folding, the mixture should be homogeneous.

MIX To combine ingredients by the easiest means possible. The term *mix* implies that nothing technically significant need be considered (compared to beating, whisking, etc.).

SIFT To gently push dry ingredients through a sieve or strainer to aerate and combine them.

STIR To combine ingredients in a circular motion, usually with a spoon or spatula, to create a homogeneous mixture with an even consistency.

WHIP To use a whisk, electric beaters, or a stand mixer with the whip attachment to aerate ingredients and create the volume specified in the recipe.

WHISK To use a whisk or electric beaters to blend or lighten a single ingredient, or to blend fluid ingredients easily to reach an even consistency. Whisking does not need to be vigorous—whipping is the faster version of whisking.

Using your intuition and tasting as you cook can take you far in the world of savoury cooking, but these methods are not always possible in the world of baking since a raw batter tastes and looks nothing like its finished, baked result. Success in baking is largely reliant on accurate measuring. Chefs in professional baking kitchens use weights to measure all ingredients for the prime reason of infallible accuracy, and this technique is used in both professional and home cookbooks from Europe, Asia, Australia, and elsewhere.

In North America we are still committed to measuring by volume, and this cookbook reflects that. Some ingredients, like chocolate, should always be measured by weight since volume is too hard to calculate—it depends on how coarsely or finely you chop the ingredients. Measuring nuts is the same. See the table on page 5 for a chart of volume to weight conversions.

Here are some other basic tips for accurate volume measuring:

WET VS. DRY Use dry measuring cups (typically cups with a handle where the measure is met by filling right to the top) for solid ingredients, and liquid measures (glass, plastic, or metal cups where the measure is marked on the side of the cup in increments) for wet ingredients. Chopped fresh fruits, dried fruits, and nuts can be measured in a glass liquid measure so the volume can be better seen, and because the volume size of liquid measures is often large (i.e., a 4-cup/1 L measure would be used to measure apples for a pie).

BROWN SUGAR Always spoon the brown sugar into a dry measuring cup, pack it up to the lip, then level it with a knife.

FLOUR Stir the flour in the canister before loosely spooning it into a dry measuring cup. Do not tap the measure on the counter, as this settles the flour and you risk adding too much to the recipe. Quickly level the measure with a knife, and always measure *before* sifting.

HONEY, MAPLE SYRUP, AND MOLASSES These should be measured in a liquid measuring cup. Unless the liquid will be folded into whipped egg whites, rub the inside of the cup with a little oil before adding the honey, maple syrup, or molasses so that all of the liquid will pour out easily, ensuring accuracy.

SPOONS Measure dry ingredients by dipping the spoon into the ingredient and then leveling it. Clean the measuring spoon between uses. Measure wet ingredients over a small dish near your mixing bowl, not directly over your mixing bowl in case too much of the ingredient drips in by accident (for example, a few extra drops of almond extract can overwhelm a cookie recipe).

TESTING YOUR MEASURES

The most common mistake in baking is mismeasuring, and it happens to novices and professionals alike. To build baking confidence, know that your measuring tools are accurate.

Many people find it surprising that you can't assume accuracy in volume measuring tools (dry measuring cups, liquid measuring cups, and measuring spoons), but I've fallen victim to this myself, having discovered that some of my favourite sets are not truly accurate. A supposed 1-tablespoon (15 mL) measure that is actually ¼ teaspoon (1 mL) less or more may not seem like a big deal, but it can greatly impact a recipe, especially with ingredients like baking powder and salt.

When I purchase a new set of measuring cups or spoons, I use my kitchen scale to confirm their precision (a kitchen scale is an indispensable tool). To do this, simply:

1. Place a bowl on the kitchen scale and "tare" it (the scale will set itself to zero to factor out the weight of the bowl).
2. Fill your 1-cup (8 fluid ounces/236.56 mL) measure with water and pour the water into the bowl on the scale. If your measuring cup is accurate, the scale should read 8 ounces (236.56 g) since the volume of water is identical to the weight of water (8 ounces/236.56 mL by volume equals 8 ounces/236.56 g by weight).
3. To double check, empty the bowl, dry it, and refill it with 8 ounces (236.56 g) of water by weight. Carefully pour this water into your 1-cup (8 fluid ounces/236.56 mL) measuring cup. If accurate, all of the water should either

fill the cup right to the top for a dry measure or to the line for a liquid measure.

If there is any variation, then you shouldn't use the set of measuring cups for baking. I've had to toss out more than a few measures and relegate the pretty sets for display. Basically, you get what you pay for. Quality names are more reliable than discount brands or decorative sets.

For tips on how to best measure your ingredients, see Measuring (page 4).

VOLUME TO WEIGHT CONVERSION TABLE

This table converts North American cup volume measures for some common ingredients to metric rather than Imperial weights, since grams allow more precision than ounces.

Note that Australian volume measures for cups and spoons are different from North American ones, so if you're baking in Australia, follow the metric measures provided within each recipe.

The weights have been rounded to the nearest 5-gram measure and are based on Canadian ingredients.

Butter
¼ cup (60 mL) = 60 g
⅓ cup (80 mL) = 75 g
½ cup (125 mL) = 115 g
1 cup (250 mL) = 225 g

Flour—All-Purpose, Whole Wheat
¼ cup (60 mL) = 35 g
⅓ cup (80 mL) = 50 g
½ cup (125 mL) = 75 g
1 cup (250 mL) = 150 g

Rolled Oats
¼ cup (60 mL) = 25 g
⅓ cup (80 mL) = 35 g
½ cup (125 mL) = 50 g
1 cup (250 mL) = 100 g

Granulated Sugar
¼ cup (60 mL) = 50 g
⅓ cup (80 mL) = 65 g
½ cup (125 mL) = 105 g
1 cup (250 mL) = 210 g

Packed Brown Sugar
(Slight variations between brown sugar styles may occur.)
¼ cup (60 mL) = 50 g
⅓ cup (80 mL) = 70 g
½ cup (125 mL) = 105 g
1 cup (250 mL) = 210 g

Nuts
GROUND NUTS
¼ cup (60 mL) = 30 g
⅓ cup (80 mL) = 40 g
½ cup (125 mL) = 60 g
1 cup (250 mL) = 120 g

WHOLE ALMONDS
¼ cup (60 mL) = 40 g
⅓ cup (80 mL) = 50 g
½ cup (125 mL) = 75 g
1 cup (250 mL) = 150 g

WHOLE HAZELNUTS
¼ cup (60 mL) = 40 g
⅓ cup (80 mL) = 50 g
½ cup (125 mL) = 80 g
1 cup (250 mL) = 155 g

LARGE WALNUT PIECES
¼ cup (60 mL) = 30 g
⅓ cup (80 mL) = 40 g
½ cup (125 mL) = 60 g
1 cup (250 mL) = 115 g

LARGE PECAN PIECES
¼ cup (60 mL) = 30 g
⅓ cup (80 mL) = 40 g
½ cup (125 mL) = 60 g
1 cup (250 mL) = 115 g

MASTERING MIXING

There are some times when using electric beaters or a stand mixer yields the best results, and other times when a little elbow grease is best. So how do you decide?

HAND MIXING This is the best method for muffins and quick breads, not merely because it is simplest and produces few dirty dishes. Stirring such batters by hand is a gentle method that creates tender muffins and loaves. Using electric beaters or a food processor for such a wet batter can overwork the glutens (proteins) in the flour, making muffins peak in the centre and seem spongy or chewy.

ELECTRIC BEATERS Electric beaters are good for anything that needs a smooth, strong mixing, such as cake batter or cheesecake. Depending on the style of the beaters, they can also work well for whipping cream or egg whites. Avoid using electric beaters for drier or tougher dough, like scones or some yeast doughs (unless you have the dough-hook beaters)—the motor may not be able to keep up.

STAND MIXER A stand mixer is an asset for the regular baker. While it may take up space on the counter, a stand mixer has a strong motor and can take on just about any baking task, sometimes in double or triple batches.

FOOD PROCESSOR This multipurpose tool has an important place in baking. It can grind nuts to a perfect fine texture, and it can cut butter into scone dough or a pie crust in no time. Avoid the food processor for cakes and muffins, as the fast blade action may overwork the dough, and if using it for cheesecake, be sure to scrape the bowl right to the very bottom to avoid lumps. It's best to use only the pulse feature when baking. The friction of the blade can heat up butter and over process, which is less likely to happen if you are simply pulsing the blade.

BAKING PAN CHOICES

There is much debate over how much, or even whether, the material of your baking pans impacts your results. Here is a summary of the basic baking pan choices, along with the darts and laurels of each one.

Ultimately, any pan can be used for any purpose, and the difference between the materials is so minimal that you do not have to adjust the oven temperature or baking time of a recipe. The ingredients in the recipe and the formula of that recipe have a greater impact on how the treats bake than the baking pan itself. For example, a square with a high sugar and fat content is more susceptible to overbrowning than one with less of these ingredients.

CERAMIC Ceramic dishes absorb and conduct heat slower than metal and glass, and coffee cake or anything with leavening takes longer to bake in ceramic, and risks baking inconsistently. That said, the slower conduction makes ceramic a great choice for custard desserts, and for cobblers and crisps, because ceramic dishes cook the custard or fruit filling gently (standard ramekins are a prime example). Ceramic dishes chip more easily than glass ones, so wash and store them carefully.

GLASS Glass baking dishes can make oven-to-table presentations nicer than other dishes, and cleaning and maintenance are simple, but keep in mind that glass conducts heat moderately faster than metal, so it does not suit recipes like fruit crisps and crumbles. I prefer baking pies using a glass pie plate so that the crusts brown nicely, and I can also check the bottom of the crust to see that it has baked through. Glass dishes usually have rounded corners, so they can make awkward corners or edges for brownies or squares, and you may have to trim part of the square to make them all the same.

METAL Metal baking pan materials include aluminized steel, stainless steel, aluminum, and nonstick and other coated metals. This family of pans is the most commonly available, so most recipes in this book were tested using this style of pan. These pans are often quite affordable, too. The heavier the gauge of the pan, the slower it is to heat up in the oven, and the longer it takes to cool coming out. Keep in mind that metal conducts heat, so items will brown, which is a desirable feature in many coffee cakes and squares. Dark metals do not promote browning significantly more than light metals—the thickness of the metal has the greatest impact. Nonstick pans make for easy removal of baked goods and quick cleanup, but be sure not to scratch the finish, or rust could develop.

SILICONE The most recent in baking pan options, silicone takes the most getting used to. Silicone does not become hot in the oven, so it does not promote browning. Items like muffins can be unexpectedly soft, and even seem steamed—a crust on the outside of the muffins to keep them from falling apart might be desired. Silicone pans are good for other recipes for that same reason. For a Bundt cake that has to spend 60 to 80 minutes in the oven, a silicone pan ensures it won't overcolour. Since silicone does not stick and is so flexible, it makes cakes easy to remove from the pan—simply peel the pan off. When using silicone, remember to place the flexible pan onto a metal baking tray (which will conduct the heat through the bottom of the silicone pan, by the way), before filling it and lifting it to the oven, and be wary of very fluid batters, as they may bulge the pan, resulting in an oddly shaped loaf or cake.

PREPPING YOUR PANS

Different baking methods often determine how to prepare your pans for baking to achieve the best result as well as ease in removing the cooled baked goods from the pan. Here is the inside scoop:

UNGREASED PANS Angel food cakes and chiffon cakes require ungreased pans. As the cake bakes and the whipped eggs rise and set, the ungreased surface offers something for the eggs in the cake to cling to, allowing the cake to "climb" and hold as it bakes. A greased pan would cause the batter to slide down, resulting in a flat and dense cake. Pies and tarts are typically baked in ungreased pans so that the pastry does not slide or shrink down the pan. Sprinkle a little flour on the bottom of a pie plate or tart shell before lining it with pastry to help slices come away easily.

GREASED PANS Simply greasing the pan works for basic, quick cakes and muffins—typically any batter that has a great deal of moisture.

GREASED AND FLOURED PANS This process is for delicate and tender cake batters, and for cakes that need to climb up the pan but would stick if the pan were ungreased. It is important to grease the pan evenly, ensure that all surfaces are coated with flour, and tap out any excess flour so that it doesn't gum up the cake at the edges.

GREASED AND PARCHMENT-LINED PANS This method most often replaces the need for flouring cake pans, but you must ensure that the entire pan surface is covered with parchment. Greasing the pan here serves only one purpose—to allow the parchment to stick to the pan evenly. Squares and brownies benefit from a pan that is greased and lined with parchment paper so that you can remove the whole square recipe from the pan and then slice it into individual squares outside the pan. Sometimes a very wet or delicate batter can cause the parchment lining the sides of the pan to buckle, making for uneven sides to a cake. Because of this buckling effect, recipes will often call for the bottom of the pan to be lined with parchment but the sides to be greased and coated with flour. Cookies are best baked on parchment paper since greasing the pan can sometimes scorch the pan or promote too much browning on the bottom. Room-temperature butter and food-release spray are the best products to use for greasing. Avoid using flavoured sprays, as the cake recipe itself should be the dominant taste.

When should you use convection heat and when should you use still heat for baking?

A convection oven uses a fan that is usually located at the back of the oven to circulate warm air within it. Moving the warm air around can accelerate cooking, and in some cases, this is a good thing, especially with food like roasted chicken and potatoes. In the case of baked goods, this is not always the case.

The challenge of baking with convection heat is that the outside of baked items can brown quickly (due to the high sugar or fat content), before the inside is baked through. And the increased air current can promote eggs to soufflé within recipes like cheesecake, causing cracking after they cool. As well, with very fluid or fluffy batter, the convection current can actually move the batter, causing a lopsided cake!

As a general rule, or if in doubt, it's best to bake without convection to achieve control. If you decide you wish to use a convection current, then set your oven temperature to 25°F (10°C) less than stated in the recipe (unless it specifically calls for convection heat). Some ovens have a "convection bake" setting that has a gentler fan and does not require a temperature compensation, although your goodies may bake a few minutes sooner than the recipe states.

Here's a breakdown to help you:

Essential to Bake in a Still Oven (No Convection)

›› All custards (crème brûlée, crème caramel, etc.)
›› Cheesecake
›› Delicate tarts
›› Shortbread
›› Brownies
›› Most cakes

Carefully Bake with Convection

›› Cookies
›› Squares
›› Pies
›› Muffins
›› Quick breads
›› Sticky buns
›› Butter tarts

Best Baked with Convection

›› Yeast Breads

Finally, do bear in mind that over-crowding your oven can impact how long or how evenly your goods take to bake and that different spots in your oven can hold or vary their temperature. As a general rule, try to bake things in the centre of your oven, so that the air can move evenly around your tray or pan.

CHOCOLATE 101

Chocolate is a beautiful thing, and when you are comfortable working with it, all the desserts you bake will be beautiful things as well. To build this comfort level, here are some basics:

COUVERTURE VS. CHIPS The chocolate used in all baking recipes should be couverture, also known as baking chocolate. Couverture chocolate has been formulated to melt and incorporate into other ingredients, to yield lusciously rich taste and texture. Chocolate chips and chocolate candy bars are NOT made for melting into the body of recipes like brownies and cakes. They have added (though natural) ingredients that are designed to keep them stable and hold their shape in chocolate chip cookies, which is good, but it means they will not melt smoothly into other recipes. Buy the best-quality chocolate available to you, as the quality of your dessert is only as good as the quality of chocolate you use. The recipes in this book were tested using basic grocery store chocolate, so you know they will work and be delicious, but if you can upgrade, so much the better!

PERCENTAGE What does that number on your chocolate mean? Chocolate is made up of cocoa solids (also known as the liquor), which give chocolate its taste; cocoa butter, which makes it creamy; milk; sugar; vanilla; and sometimes lecithin, which keeps the ingredients emulsified. The percentage number on the chocolate tells you the proportion of cocoa solids that is in the chocolate, which serves as a guide to the intensity of taste. Milk chocolate has about 35 percent cocoa solids, giving it a mild taste. Semisweet chocolate can be anywhere from 51 percent to 65 percent cocoa solids, and bittersweet chocolate is usually 68 percent to 72 percent. Unsweetened chocolate has no percentage listed because it is virtually 100 percent cocoa solids, and white chocolate has no cocoa solids, so has a 0 percent value.

The higher the percentage of cocoa solids, the more intense the chocolate tastes, the more stable and easier the chocolate is to handle, and the higher the temperature must be to melt the chocolate.

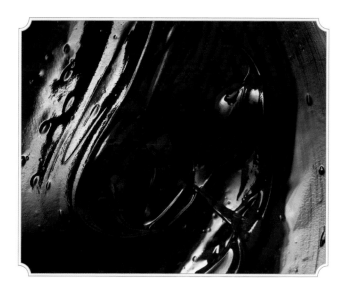

MELTING CHOCOLATE

Chocolate is a delicate ingredient, but it doesn't have to be difficult to handle if it's treated with a gentle hand. Here are a few tips:

1. The best way to melt chocolate is in a metal bowl placed over a pot of water that is just barely simmering (bubbles barely breaking the surface of the water). The bowl should not touch the water directly; it is merely the steam heating the bowl that melts the chocolate.

2. Stir the chocolate with a spatula or wooden spoon in a slow and gentle motion. Using a whisk or stirring too vigorously could cause the chocolate to seize.

3. Since chocolate with a high percentage of cocoa solids is more stable, unsweetened chocolate (practically 100 percent cocoa solids) can be melted over direct, albeit low, heat.

4. Chocolate with higher cocoa-solids content requires a higher melting temperature, too. Bittersweet chocolate melts between 92°F (33°C) and 94°F (34°C), milk chocolate melts at 90°F (32°C), and white chocolate melts at 88°F (31°C). When melting white chocolate, it's best to remove the chocolate from the heat before it has fully melted. A gentle stirring will distribute the warmth to completely melt all of the white chocolate.

5. If your chocolate happens to seize, usually the result of too drastic a temperature change or too much vigorous

stirring, it will lose its shine and seem to solidify and turn granular. All is not lost. Add a few drops of tepid water to the chocolate and stir where the water was added in a small circular motion. Widen the circular motion and add another drop or two of water, and the chocolate should return to its smooth and glossy state.

6. You can melt chocolate in the microwave, but take care. It is best melted on medium heat and should be stirred at 10-second intervals so that it does not scorch. Once scorched, there is no saving it.

COCOA POWDER: REGULAR VS. DUTCH PROCESS

Cocoa powder is made solely of the finely ground cocoa solids from the cocoa bean, without any fat or cocoa butter. Some recipes call for regular powder, some specify Dutch process. What is the difference?

REGULAR COCOA This cocoa is sometimes referred to as "natural," and it is untreated cocoa that can have a slightly reddish hue to it. Its use is specified in some recipes because its low pH (high acidity) level may be needed to quickly activate baking soda to achieve a desired result.

DUTCH PROCESS COCOA This cocoa has been alkalized, lowering the acidity and giving you finer leavening control than with regular cocoa. The alkalizing process also darkens the colour of the cocoa, making it visually appealing, and mellows the flavour, lessening the sharpness of its taste to some measure. "Dutch process" does not refer to superior quality, but merely the treatment of the cocoa and the expected result.

The most obvious example to illustrate the difference is chocolate brownies. Using regular cocoa powder, the brownies may be somewhat light in colour but have a sharp chocolate taste. Using Dutch process cocoa, the brownies will have a richer colour and a milder (but still intensely chocolate) taste.

In this book, if a recipe calls for one or the other type of cocoa, then you should use that type, but if no preference is specified, you can assume that either would work.

EXPLAINING EGGS

Eggs are a fundamental part of baking, and understanding them helps you know how to best work with them.

1. Most recipes (and all recipes that use eggs in this book) call for large eggs. Eggs are sorted by weight, and a large egg weighs 2 ounces (60 g)—the yolk is 1 ounce (30 g) and the white is 1 ounce (30 g).

2. Brown eggs differ from white eggs because of just one thing—the shell colour. You can use brown or white eggs interchangeably in a recipe, just make sure you use the same size.

3. Although water accounts for more than 90 percent of an egg's makeup, egg yolks also contain fat and give tenderness and richness to recipes. The white has protein, giving batters structure and strength so that they hold up and rise.

4. In a recipe that calls for room-temperature butter, it's also best to use room-temperature eggs since ingredients of like temperatures incorporate more effectively, producing the ideal texture in the batter and the end result.

5. Warm eggs whip to a fuller volume than cold eggs. The easiest way to warm eggs is to immerse them, in their shells, in hot tap water. Within 3 minutes, they will have warmed to room temperature, and in 6 minutes they will be warm enough for whipping.

MILK AND CREAM

It's amazing what a few little percent numbers can do to change a recipe—in a custard dessert particularly, since a custard's set and texture are primarily determined by its ratio of eggs to cream or milk. And since eggs can be used only as yolks, whites, or whole, the choice of milk, cream, or a combination is really how we can tailor taste and texture.

Here are the basics:

WHIPPING CREAM Whipping cream earns its name. With a 35 percent butterfat content, it is the only cream that can whip up and hold its volume (for a great tip on how to stabilize whipped cream so that it holds its shape for a long time, check out page 11). It is unctuous and rich, suiting crème brûlée, but can weigh down cake batters, so milk is typically used there. Recipes that have some form of acidity, such as lemon juice or wine, will call for whipping cream since any dairy above 30 percent will not curdle. If you substitute whipping cream with a lower-fat alternative in a recipe that uses an acidic ingredient you'll end up with a clotted, curdled mess.

TABLE CREAM Sometimes known as cereal cream or pouring cream, table cream has an 18 percent fat content. It is not often called for in recipes because you can achieve similar results by simply using a combination of whipping cream and milk, or half-and-half (though it makes for a really rich cup of coffee).

HALF-AND-HALF CREAM This cream has 10 percent fat and is readily available for purchase in different volumes. It adds nice richness to recipes but is not too heavy or greasy.

LIGHT CREAM This cream has its place between cream and milk, with 5 percent fat. Although it's now a preferred cream for coffee, it hasn't fully made its way into the world of baking.

WHOLE MILK With 3 percent fat or higher, whole milk used to be the milk of choice in baking, though it's not so much anymore. It adds a pleasing richness and tenderness to cakes, so it can be used in place of 2% milk in baking.

2% MILK It doesn't have a pretty name, but 2% milk is now the most common milk used in baking and cooking, and it is the milk that all the recipes in this book have been tested with. It has enough fat in it to give richness, tenderness, and structure to most baked goods.

1% MILK You might not think that reducing the fat content in milk by just 1 percent would make much of a difference in baking, but you do lose some structure, tenderness, and richness when you use 1%. It is possible to substitute 1% for 2% milk in recipes like muffins and loaves, but you may find that the muffins made with 1% are a little more crumbly and aren't quite as moist. I have designed some recipes that use 1% milk in the Low-Fat/Low-Sugar chapter, but I balanced it out with other ingredients to achieve tasty results.

SKIM MILK I've heard skim milk referred to as "the ghost of milk" because of its almost-transparent blue hue. With virtually no fat, you might as well use water in your baked goods. That last percent of butterfat in 1% milk is the difference between a tender, moist, delectable treat and a crumbly, dry, tasteless one. If you enjoy drinking skim milk, continue to do so, but use 2% milk in your baked goods.

BUTTERMILK Although "butter" is part of the name, buttermilk is low in fat, with just 1 percent butterfat. Buttermilk gets its name because it is the liquid left from the butter-making process. It has a thick texture (and it's a good idea to shake the carton well before pouring) and a tangy acidity to it, making it a perfect ingredient to activate leavening in cakes. It is typically not used in custards since it curdles once heated.

STABLE WHIPPED CREAM

Whether whipping cream to top a trifle, frost a cake, or simply serve alongside a bowl of fresh berries, we've all had the same issue—you whip the cream ahead of time and put it in the fridge for later, then what happens? It weeps, leaving a puddle of liquid at the bottom of the bowl, and as soon as you stir the whipped cream, it deflates.

Although the cream can easily be rewhipped and used right away, I have a great trick for stabilizing whipped cream so that you can whip it a full day ahead of when you need it and it will hold its body, including every swirl or dollop you make.

When whipping, I add 1 tablespoon (15 mL) of instant skim milk powder to every 1 cup (250 mL) of fluid whipping cream. The powder can be added at any point while whipping, and it does not impart any taste or texture. It will make the mixture hold its shape, whether in a serving bowl, or on a cake or a cupcake.

SALT IN BAKING . . . WHY?

The majority of baking recipes call for salt, but why in the world of sweets is it there? Quite simply, salt seasons everything, whether savoury or sweet. It heightens the chocolate taste in cakes and brownies, and brings out the vanilla in a simple shortbread cookie. Salt also tempers or balances out taste in highly sweetened desserts. Just look at the popularity of salted caramel desserts—that salty/sweet contrast is so appealing. Without the salt, desserts could taste flat or bland.

So, should you wish to, you could eliminate salt from baking for dietary reasons without impacting the science behind a baked item, but it would impact the taste. However, salt measurements in baking aren't typically so great that they significantly raise our sodium levels. For notes on adjusting salt in recipes if using salted butter, see pages 12–13.

The one place where salt *does* serve a scientific function is in recipes that call for yeast, such as bread and sticky bun recipes. Salt works to slow and control the function of yeast, which helps yeast dough develop flavour and texture.

In terms of choosing which salt to bake with, I recommend a fine sea salt. Sea salt is untreated and natural, but the fine grind is the most important point. Fine salt melts easily into baked goods. Chocolate chip cookies spend only 10 minutes in the oven—a coarse or kosher salt may not melt evenly in that short time. Using fine salt also ensures an accurate measurement. Coarse salt's larger granules mean you get less salt by measure since the granules don't sit as compactly as those of finely ground salt. You can use a tender, flaked salt, such as Maldon salt flakes, but crush the salt in your fingers before measuring.

SUGAR 101

There are so many choices in the world of sugar, without even touching on liquid forms of sweetening. While granulated sugar is the most commonly used, recipes are designed using particular sugars in particular quantities for reasons beyond mere sweetness.

As desserts bake, the sugar within them turns fluid, and the quantity of sugar in a recipe can impact the timing of how something bakes. Once cooled, that choice of sugar and measure can determine if a cookie is going to be soft (like a molasses cookie), crisp yet tender (like a cinnamon cut-out cookie), or straight-up tender (like a shortbread). Sugar also lends structure to desserts, giving egg whites body and strength as they whip and then cook, keeping textures light and fluffy. Sugar also extends the shelf life of many desserts, keeping items fresh and moist for a long time.

As a general rule, sugar varieties can *not* be substituted on a measure-for-measure basis, but with experimentation, you may find some pleasing results. Nor can sugar be reduced in a recipe without impacting the taste and the texture, moisture, and shelf life of a dessert. Refer to the Low-Fat and/or Low-Sugar Desserts chapter for some recipes designed with less sweetening.

Here are some sugar basics:

BROWN SUGAR Originally brown sugar was partly refined sugar and the process was halted to keep some of the molasses in it, but now it is composed of refined sugar with molasses added back to it. Brown sugar is sold as light brown (or golden) and dark brown. The difference is in the strength of the molasses taste, which can impact recipes. It is important to pack the measuring cup with brown sugar for an accurate measure.

DEMERARA SUGAR This sugar is made from sugarcane, like turbinado sugar, but it typically has a darker colour and a bit of moisture. In most cases, demerara sugar can be used to replace dark brown sugar in the same measure.

GRANULATED SUGAR Granulated sugar is the most common sugar, and can be refined from sugarcane, sugar beets, or corn.

ICING SUGAR Sometimes known as confectioners' sugar or powdered sugar, icing sugar is finely ground and granulated, with a small percent of cornstarch to keep it from clumping due to moisture. This fine texture lends density to cookie dough and keeps it tender at the same time.

MOLASSES This is the by-product of the sugar refining process. It can be purchased as "fancy," the most commonly used and mildest version, or "blackstrap," which is stronger and has a bit of bitterness (usually used in bread baking).

MUSCOVADO SUGAR Muscovado is an unrefined brown sugar from sugarcane. It has a more intense caramel flavour compared to dark brown sugar due to the larger quantity of molasses in it, but it can be used to replace dark brown sugar if that strength of taste is desired.

PALM SUGAR From the coconut or sago palm, palm sugar has the same sweetness level as granulated sugar but it has been recognized to register lower on the glycemic index. It typically comes in a solid block form and can be grated into desserts using a box grater or zester, though ground palm sugar is becoming more available.

TURBINADO SUGAR This coarsely granulated sugar is made from sugarcane and can be found in organic form. It is the colour of light brown sugar, but is dry like granulated sugar and has a coarse grind. It is often used for sprinkling overtop of cookies or muffins to create crunch. If you wish to use turbinado sugar in baking, it is best to grind it in a food processor first, making it finer and more easily beaten into recipes.

UNSALTED BUTTER . . . WHY?

This is likely the question I'm asked most often about baking, and it is certainly a logical one to ask: since most recipes call for salt, why use unsalted butter in baking?

Here are the three main reasons:
1. Brand by brand, the salt content in salted butter can vary, and ultimately you want to be the one in control of the salt in your baking.
2. Recipe by recipe, the butter measurements vary from as little as a teaspoon to up to a pound. And recipe by recipe, the salt measurements vary, too. The only way to truly control butter and salt proportions is to keep the salt and butter measurements separate.

3. Salt is a natural preservative, and it extends the shelf life of butter both in the grocery refrigerator and in your own. That said, with a longer shelf life comes a greater opportunity for butter to pick up "fridge taste." While you may not taste the age of your butter when you spread half a teaspoon of it on your toast in the morning, you will taste it when you use a cup in a shortbread cookie recipe. Unsalted butter is fresher and sweeter tasting.

If you like to use salted butter for your everyday use but wish to use unsalted butter for occasional baking, simply wrap and freeze any unused unsalted butter for up to 4 months for your next baking session. And if you prefer using salted butter in your baking, or can't get to the store to buy unsalted, then you should generally reduce the salt in a recipe by ¼ teaspoon (1 mL) for every 1 cup (250 mL) of butter used.

SOUR CREAM AND YOGURT

Sour cream and yogurt are tasty ways to add moisture and richness to coffee cakes and muffins, but using full-fat versions is the key to successful baking. The sour cream you use should be 14 percent fat and the yogurt should be a minimum of 3 percent, ideally 6 percent. The reason for these high percentages is that lower-fat options are set with other thickeners such as guar gum, starch, or even gelatin. Once heated, the thickening agents dissolve and the lower-fat sour cream or yogurt turns watery. Therefore baked items could be dense and heavy coming out of the oven, and crumble easily after cooling.

VANILLA: ANYTHING BUT PLAIN

Vanilla is a foundation ingredient in many dessert recipes. It is often used to amplify other flavours, so it is sometimes relegated as a background note, although it really does round out sweet flavours, whether chocolate, caramel, or fruit. But vanilla on its own is anything but ordinary or bland. If I am testing out a new ice-cream shop or *gelateria*, I always try vanilla ice cream first to assess the quality of the place. As with using chocolate, the quality of the ingredient counts, and although good vanilla comes with a premium price tag, a little goes a long way, so your investment does last.

Here are some basic vanilla forms:

- BEANS   The cured beans of the vanilla orchid plant are a pastry chef's staple. A fresh bean should be shiny, have almost an oily feel to the outside, and be very pliable. The seeds scraped from the inside of the bean need contact time with a hot liquid or a good length of baking time to draw out their flavour, so they are suited to recipes like crème brûlée and cheesecake. The vanilla bean shell also has a great deal of flavour, even after the seeds have been scraped out. Place your scraped vanilla bean pod into a jar with sugar, and within 2 weeks you'll have a fragrant sugar to use in desserts or to stir into your coffee.
- EXTRACT   Alcohol is the liquid base for vanilla extract, which is why when you make a recipe that is simmered the extract is added at the end, otherwise the alcohol would evaporate and weaken the vanilla taste. Because of the alcohol, vanilla extract does not spoil or expire, although the intensity of the vanilla taste may fade after a year. Always use pure vanilla extract, not the artificial stuff.
- PASTE   A newer creation, vanilla paste is made when vanilla bean seeds are suspended in extract thickened with sugar and a little natural gum. This product saves you the effort of scraping the seeds out of the vanilla bean, does not require lengthy heat extraction, and is often a better value than buying the whole beans. You can substitute the bean paste for extract measure for measure in virtually any recipe where you'd like to see the pleasing speckles of seeds, and 1 tablespoon (15 mL) of vanilla bean paste is equal to the contents of 1 vanilla bean.

Here are some basic vanilla varieties:

- BOURBON MADAGASCAR VANILLA   This is the most commonly used and most familiar tasting vanilla. This vanilla extract is suited to virtually all baking, from cookies and cakes to custards and tarts.
- MEXICAN VANILLA   This more robust vanilla has subtle spice notes and is best suited to chocolate desserts since it can stand up to and heighten the complexity in chocolate.
- TAHITIAN VANILLA   This prized vanilla has a thicker pod and a more intense perfume. It is best suited to desserts where vanilla is the lead or key flavour, such as crème brûlée, vanilla cheesecake, or ice cream. In intensely spiced desserts or in chocolate desserts, the delicate flavour can get lost.

cookies

TO FREEZE OR NOT TO FREEZE

We all like getting ahead of baking, particularly around the holidays, but as you've likely discovered, some baked cookies freeze better than others.

As a guideline, cookies that have a low amount of sugar, such as shortbread, freeze very well, and cookies with a great deal of sugar, such as lace cookies, freeze poorly. Once frozen and thawed, the sugar in cookies becomes fluid, making cookies seem soft or even sticky. The more sugar in the cookies, the softer the cookies are once they're thawed.

My preference is to freeze raw cookie dough as opposed to baked cookies.

Raw cookie dough maintains its quality and texture for up to 6 months when frozen. Simply thaw the dough in the refrigerator if the cookies are an icebox style (like Cinnamon Roll Pinwheels, page 29), or thaw on the counter if the cookies are a drop style (like Chocolate Chip Cookies, page 18).

Raw cookie dough takes up less room in the freezer than tubs of baked cookies do. Simply label and date the dough. You can even write the baking instructions on the label so you don't have to look up the recipe again once the dough is thawed.

You can bake as many cookies as you need. For instance, before you freeze your chocolate chip cookie dough, scoop it into cookies using an ice-cream scoop, then chill in the refrigerator until firm, pack in a resealable bag, and freeze. Then you can pull out just a few or a full batch, as needed.

For holiday baking, making cookie dough and freezing it is ideal, since most of the effort (and mess) in holiday cookies is in making the dough. Come December, I simply pull out my cookie dough; slice, roll, or scoop, and bake; and fill the house with festive fragrances and have fresh cookies on hand all month.

BASIC BROWN SUGAR COOKIE DOUGH
• *Makes enough dough for 2 to 3 dozen cookies* •

foundation
RECIPE

THIS COOKIE DOUGH is the base for the favourites of the drop cookies: Chocolate Chip, Oatmeal Raisin, Molasses, and Peanut Butter. After a couple of batches, you'll likely have these proportions memorized and be able to whip off a batch of cookies with your eyes closed. Before making any of the cookies for which this dough serves as a base, read the specific cookie recipe itself to see if additions need to be made to this basic dough recipe.

½ cup (125 mL) unsalted butter,
   at room temperature
½ cup (125 mL) packed light brown sugar
¼ cup (60 mL) sugar
1 egg, at room temperature
1 tsp (5 mL) vanilla extract
1¼ cups (310 mL) all-purpose flour
2 Tbsp (30 mL) cornstarch
½ tsp (2 mL) baking soda
½ tsp (2 mL) salt

1. Cream the butter, brown sugar, and sugar together until fluffy.
2. Beat in the egg and then the vanilla.
3. In a separate bowl, stir the flour, cornstarch, baking soda, and salt.
4. Add the flour mixture into the butter mixture and stir until evenly blended.
5. Follow instructions to make Chocolate Chip (page 18), Oatmeal Raisin (page 20), Molasses (page 20), or Peanut Butter (page 22).

notes from anna's kitchen

1. The cornstarch is the secret to this dough. Regardless of which cookie variation you choose to make with this recipe, the cookies stay soft in the centre and are delectably tender.

2. Ever run out of brown sugar? You can re-create light brown sugar by using granulated sugar and adding 1 tablespoon (15 mL) of fancy molasses to a recipe for every 1 cup (250 mL) of brown sugar called for. The molasses creates the taste and the moisture that the brown sugar would add to a recipe.

CHOCOLATE CHIP COOKIES
• *Makes about 2½ dozen cookies* •

*I*T DOESN'T GET more homespun than this: a good, basic cookie dough and lots of chocolate chips.

1. Preheat the oven to 350°F (175°C), and line 2 baking trays with parchment paper, or lightly grease.
2. Prepare the cookie dough recipe as on page 17 and then stir in the chocolate chips.
3. Drop the dough by tablespoonfuls onto the prepared baking trays, leaving 1½ inches (4 cm) between cookies.
4. Bake for about 10 minutes, until the cookies are golden brown. Let the cookies cool on the tray for 5 minutes, then transfer the cookies to a rack to cool completely. The cookies can be stored in an airtight container for up to 3 days.

1 recipe Basic Brown Sugar Cookie Dough (page 17)
1 cup (250 mL) chocolate chips

note from anna's kitchen
It is the size of the bowl of the spoon that essentially shapes the cookie. Although measuring ingredients is important in baking, the measures of the dough you scoop are allowed to be a little more flexible. When scooping dough by teaspoonfuls (5 mL), the cookies are really about a tablespoon (15 mL) by measure, and when scooping tablespoonfuls (15 mL) of cookie dough, you are really scooping almost 2 tablespoons (30 mL) of dough. Baking times are given a range based on variables that occur when scooping dough.

Shaping dough into drop cookies

OATMEAL RAISIN COOKIES
• *Makes about 2½ dozen cookies* •

*T*HESE COOKIES ARE chewy and satisfying, and can be tailored to anyone's taste by switching the raisins for the same measure of chocolate chips or walnut pieces.

1 recipe Basic Brown Sugar Cookie Dough (page 17)
½ cup (125 mL) packed dark brown sugar
1 cup (250 mL) regular rolled oats (not quick cook
　　or instant)
½ cup (125 mL) raisins
½ tsp (2 mL) ground cinnamon

1. Preheat the oven to 350°F (175°C), and line 2 baking trays with parchment paper, or lightly grease.
2. In step 1 of the Basic Brown Sugar Cookie Dough, add the additional ½ cup (125 mL) of dark brown sugar with the other sugars.
3. Complete step 2 of the cookie dough. Stir in the oats, raisins, and cinnamon until evenly incorporated.
4. Drop the dough by tablespoonfuls onto the prepared baking trays, leaving 1½ inches (4 cm) between each cookie.
5. Bake the cookies for 10 to 12 minutes, until evenly browned (the cookies will be very soft coming out of the oven). Let the cookies cool for 5 minutes on the tray before removing to cool completely. The cookies can be stored in an airtight container for up to 3 days.

note from anna's kitchen
Baking with regular rolled oats gives the best texture and taste in baking, as well as adding more fibre than other oats. Since quick-cook and instant oats have been precooked and then dried, they absorb moisture faster, whether for your morning oatmeal or in baking, so your cookies, muffins, and other treats may turn out dry or crumbly. Regular oats provide a great chew, and these cookies stay moist.

MOLASSES COOKIES
• *Makes about 2½ dozen cookies* •

*T*HESE COOKIES ARE a childhood favourite of mine, and they make an excellent cookie for ice-cream sandwiches.

1 recipe Basic Brown Sugar Cookie Dough (page 17)
¼ cup (60 mL) fancy molasses
2 tsp (10 mL) ground ginger
½ tsp (2 mL) ground cinnamon
⅛ tsp (0.5 mL) ground cloves
⅓ cup (80 mL) sugar, for rolling cookies

1. Preheat the oven to 350°F (175°C), and line 2 baking trays with parchment paper, or lightly grease.
2. Prepare step 1 of the Basic Brown Sugar Cookie Dough, and after creaming the butter and sugars, beat in the ¼ cup (60 mL) of molasses.
3. Follow step 2 of the dough recipe, stirring the additional spices into the flour mixture.
4. Spoon out tablespoonfuls of dough and roll them in the sugar to coat, then place the cookies onto the prepared baking trays, leaving 1½ inches (4 cm) between them.
5. Bake the cookies for 10 to 12 minutes, until lightly browned around the edges. Cool the cookies for 10 minutes on the baking trays before removing to cool completely. The cookies can be stored in an airtight container for up to 3 days.

Oatmeal Raisin Cookies (page 20),
Chocolate Chip Cookies (page 18),
Peanut Butter Cookies (page 22), and
Molasses Cookies (page 20)

Oatmeal
Raisin

Chocolate
Chip

Peanut
Butter

Molasses

PEANUT BUTTER COOKIES
• Makes about 2½ dozen cookies •

MAKING THE FAMILIAR criss-cross pattern on peanut butter cookies actually serves a function: to flatten down the cookies since the cookies wouldn't flatten on their own.

1 recipe Basic Brown Sugar Cookie Dough (page 17)
½ cup (125 mL) peanut butter, any kind you prefer

1. Preheat the oven to 350°F (175°C), and line 2 baking trays with parchment paper, or lightly grease.
2. Prepare step 1 of the Basic Brown Sugar Cookie Dough. Stir in the peanut butter, then complete the remaining steps of the dough recipe.
3. Drop tablespoonfuls of the dough onto the prepared baking trays, leaving 1½ inches (4 cm) between the cookies. Using a fork dipped in flour, press the cookie down and make criss-crosses on the top of each cookie.
4. Bake the cookies for 12 to 14 minutes, until they are lightly browned. Let the cookies cool for 5 minutes before removing them from the tray to cool completely. The cookies can be stored in an airtight container for up to 3 days.

note from anna's kitchen
If you use natural (unsweetened) peanut butter in this recipe, be sure to let it come to room temperature first, and stir it well before measuring to work in the oils that have naturally separated out.

BASIC WHITE SUGAR COOKIE DOUGH
• Makes enough dough for 2 to 3 dozen cookies •

foundation
RECIPE

THIS COOKIE DOUGH is the base for Snickerdoodles, Toffee Softies, and Double Ginger Wonders. A classic and simple drop cookie can be so satisfying, whatever its variation (though Snickerdoodles, on page 23, seem to be the universal favourite.) Before making any of the cookies for which this dough serves as a base, read the specific cookie recipe itself to see if additions need to be made to this basic dough recipe.

1 cup (250 mL) unsalted butter, softened but still cool
1 cup (250 mL) sugar
2 eggs, taken directly from the fridge
1 tsp (5 mL) vanilla extract
2½ cups (625 mL) all-purpose flour
1 tsp (5 mL) cream of tartar
½ tsp (2 mL) salt

1. Cream the butter and sugar until fluffy and light.
2. Add the eggs one at a time, blending well after each addition. Stir in the vanilla.
3. In a separate bowl, stir the flour, cream of tartar, and salt to combine, then add to the butter mixture, blending well.
4. Follow instructions to make Snickerdoodles (page 23), Toffee Softies (page 23), or Double Ginger Wonders (page 24).

note from anna's kitchen
For tips on using vanilla in your baking, review the notes on page 13, Vanilla: Anything but Plain.

SNICKERDOODLES
• *Makes about 3 dozen cookies* •

*T*OSSED WITH CINNAMON sugar, these tender cookies melt on the tip of your tongue.

1 recipe Basic White Sugar Cookie Dough (page 22)
½ cup (125 mL) sugar
1 tsp (5 mL) ground cinnamon

1. Preheat the oven to 350°F (175°C) and line 2 baking trays with parchment paper.
2. Prepare the Basic White Sugar Cookie Dough.
3. Stir the sugar and cinnamon together in a small bowl.
4. Portion the prepared cookie dough by tablespoonfuls and drop into cinnamon sugar. Gently roll each cookie to coat it with the sugar and to shape it into a ball, and place the balls onto the prepared baking tray, leaving 1½ inches (4 cm) between them. Before baking, gently press the cookies with your palm to flatten them.
5. Bake for 12 to 14 minutes, until the cookies are just lightly browned on the bottom. Cool the cookies for 2 minutes before removing to a rack to cool completely. Snickerdoodles can be stored in an airtight container for up to 3 days.

TOFFEE SOFTIES
• *Makes about 3 dozen cookies* •

*A*DDING TOFFEE BITS to the Basic White Sugar Cookie Dough adds a butterscotch flavour, and while the toffee bits have a nice crackle once cooled, the cookie still remains tender and soft.

1 recipe Basic White Sugar Cookie Dough (page 22)
¾ cup (185 mL) SKOR Toffee Bits
½ cup (125 mL) turbinado sugar

1. Preheat the oven to 350°F (175°C) and line 2 baking trays with parchment paper.
2. Prepare the Basic White Sugar Cookie Dough.
3. Stir the toffee bits into the cookie dough.
4. Portion the dough by tablespoonfuls and drop into the turbinado sugar. Gently roll each cookie to coat it with the sugar and to shape it into a ball, and place them onto the prepared baking tray, leaving 1½ inches (4 cm) between them. Before baking, gently press the cookies with your palm to flatten.
5. Bake for 12 to 14 minutes, until the cookies are just lightly browned on the bottom. Cool the cookies for 2 minutes before removing to a rack to cool completely. The cookies can be stored in an airtight container for up to 3 days.

note from anna's kitchen
If you do not have turbinado sugar, you can use regular granulated sugar to achieve a crunchy exterior to the cookies.

DOUBLE GINGER WONDERS
• *Makes about 3 dozen cookies* •

*T*HESE COOKIES HAVE a nice spicy nip to them but are softer compared to a traditional crunchy gingersnap cookie.

1. Preheat the oven to 350°F (175°C) and line 2 baking trays with parchment paper.
2. In step 1 of the Basic White Sugar Cookie Dough, stir the 1 tablespoon fresh ginger in with the butter and sugar. Prepare the dough following the rest of the steps.
3. Stir the candied ginger into the prepared dough.
4. Shape tablespoonfuls of the cookie dough into balls. Roll the cookies into the ⅓ cup (80 mL) of sugar and place them on the prepared baking tray, leaving 1 inch (2.5 cm) between them.
5. Bake the cookies for about 12 minutes, until just lightly browned around the edges. The cookies can be stored in an airtight container for up to 3 days.

1 recipe Basic White Sugar Cookie Dough (page 22)
1 Tbsp (15 mL) finely grated fresh ginger
2 Tbsp (30 mL) finely diced candied ginger
⅓ cup (80 mL) sugar

TRADITIONAL SHORTBREAD
• *Makes 36 shortbread squares* •

egg-
FREE

THESE SHORTBREAD COOKIES have all the characteristics of a classic shortbread: they are buttery and tender, and improve when they sit for a few days in the cookie tin.

1. Preheat the oven to 375°F (190°C) and grease an 8-inch (20 cm) square pan.
2. Beat the butter for 2 minutes to make it fluffy and light. Add the icing sugar and sugar, and beat again for 2 minutes, until fluffy, then beat in the vanilla.
3. Sift the flour, rice flour, and salt, then add to the wet ingredients, stirring until evenly blended.
4. Scrape the dough into the prepared pan and press it flat into the bottom of the pan (the dough will be quite firm and easy to press, but if your fingers stick, dust them with a little flour). Use a fork to dock the shortbread at 1-inch (2.5 cm) intervals.
5. Bake the shortbread for about 25 minutes, until the outside edges have browned a little.
6. Let the shortbread cool for 10 minutes, then cut it into squares. Allow the cookies to cool completely before lifting them out of the pan to store. The shortbread will keep in an airtight container for up to 10 days.

1 cup (250 mL) unsalted butter,
at room temperature
½ cup (125 mL) icing sugar, sifted
¼ cup (60 mL) sugar
1 tsp (5 mL) vanilla extract
2¼ cups (560 mL) all-purpose flour
¼ cup (60 mL) brown or white rice flour
¼ tsp (1 mL) salt

notes from anna's kitchen

1. When making shortbread, beating the butter thoroughly before adding the sugar is a key step. Since shortbread has no eggs or baking powder, making the butter fluffy keeps the cookies tender and light, even though they rise when baked.
2. To dock shortbread, pierce the dough with a fork, right through the depth of the dough. This prevents air bubbles that would push the dough up and allows the dough room to expand and to bake evenly.

VANILLA CORNMEAL WEDGES
• *Makes 32 shortbread cookies* •

*V*ISIBLE VANILLA BEAN seeds fleck these triangular cookie wedges, and the cornmeal enhances their buttery yellow colour, adds a delicate crunch that delights the mouth, then easily melts away.

1 cup (250 mL) unsalted butter, at room temperature
⅔ cup (160 mL) sugar
2 tsp (10 mL) vanilla bean paste or vanilla extract
⅓ cup (80 mL) cornmeal
2 Tbsp (30 mL) cornstarch
¼ tsp (1 mL) salt
1⅔ cups (410 mL) all-purpose flour

1. Preheat the oven to 350°F (175°C). Lightly grease two 9-inch (23 cm), removable-bottom, fluted tart pans and set the pans in a baking tray.
2. Beat the butter for 2 minutes, then add the sugar and beat for another 2 minutes. Stir in the vanilla.
3. Stir in the cornmeal, cornstarch, and salt. Add the flour in 2 additions, blending evenly.
4. Divide the dough between the 2 pans (the dough will be soft), and press the dough using floured fingers so that it covers the bottom of the pans. Cut each pan of dough into 16 wedges.
5. Bake for about 20 minutes, until just the edges of the shortbread begin to brown. Remove the pans from the oven and while still warm, cut each pan of shortbread into wedges again and cool completely in the pan before serving or storing. The shortbread will store for up to a week in an airtight container.

note from anna's kitchen
If you're wondering why baking recipes call for unsalted butter but also require salt, see page 12.

DEMERARA SHORTBREAD WEDGES
• *Makes 16 wedges* •

*D*EMERARA SUGAR LENDS these shortbread wedges a nice caramel richness, perfect alongside a bowl of vanilla ice cream.

1 cup (250 mL) unsalted butter, at room temperature
½ cup (125 mL) packed demerara dark brown sugar
¼ tsp (1 mL) salt
⅛ tsp (0.5 mL) ground nutmeg
2 cups (500 mL) all-purpose flour
Turbinado sugar, for sprinkling

1. Preheat the oven to 325°F (160°C) and grease a 9-inch (23 cm) pie plate.
2. Beat the butter for 2 minutes, until it is fluffy and light. Beat in the demerara sugar for 2 more minutes. Stir in the salt and nutmeg, then add the flour, blending until evenly combined.
3. Press the dough into the prepared pie plate, coating your fingers with flour if they stick. Sprinkle the shortbread with turbinado sugar, then cut through the dough to make 16 wedges.
4. Bake the shortbread for 50 to 60 minutes, until the edges of the shortbread have browned. Let the shortbread cool for 10 minutes, then cut through where the 16 wedges were previously cut. Let the cookies cool completely in the pan before removing to store. The shortbread will keep in an airtight container for up to 10 days.

note from anna's kitchen
You can use an alternate to demerara sugar in the recipe— dark brown sugar will work just as well. For more tips on sugar, refer to pages 12–13.

PISTACHIO SNOWBALL COOKIES
• *Makes about 4 dozen cookies* •

THE RICHNESS OF pistachios complements the buttery, melt-in-your-mouth tenderness of these dainty cookies.

2⅓ cups (580 mL) all-purpose flour
1 cup (250 mL) shelled, roasted, unsalted pistachios
⅓ cup (80 mL) sugar
¼ tsp (1 mL) salt
1¼ cup (310 mL) cold unsalted butter, cut in pieces
1 tsp (5 mL) vanilla extract
Icing sugar, for coating

1. Preheat the oven to 325°F (160°C) and line 2 baking trays with parchment paper.
2. Using a food processor, pulse the flour, pistachios, sugar, and salt until the pistachios are finely ground into the mixture.
3. Add the butter and vanilla, and pulse until the dough comes together.
4. Roll teaspoonfuls of dough into balls about 1 inch (2.5 cm) across and place them 1 inch (2.5 cm) apart on the prepared baking trays.
5. Bake the cookies for 15 to 18 minutes, until the bottoms just begin to colour. Cool the cookies completely on the baking trays, then roll them in icing sugar to coat. The cookies can be stored in an airtight container for up to a week.

note from anna's kitchen

Tender nuts like pistachios, pecans, walnuts, and pine nuts can typically be interchanged in recipes, so you can tailor your cookies to suit your tastes or what you may have on hand.

The oils in these nut varieties are quite delicate and can quickly turn rancid. If you do not plan on using your stock of nuts within 2 months, it's best to store them, well wrapped, in the freezer.

CHOCOLATE SHORTBREAD MELTAWAYS
• *Makes about 5 dozen small cookies* •

THESE COOKIES HAVE a chocolate intensity that balances with their buttery richness, and when piped onto a baking tray, they look like chocolate kisses. Like all of the shortbread cookies in this chapter, they are a good addition to a holiday cookie tin.

1 cup (250 mL) unsalted butter, at room temperature
1 cup (250 mL) icing sugar, sifted
1 Tbsp (15 mL) vanilla extract
1½ cups (375 mL) all-purpose flour
⅓ cup (80 mL) Dutch process cocoa powder, sifted
2 Tbsp (30 mL) cornstarch
½ tsp (2 mL) salt

1. Preheat the oven to 325°F (160°C) and line 2 baking trays with parchment paper.
2. Cream the butter and icing sugar together until smooth. Beat in the vanilla extract.
3. Add the flour, cocoa, cornstarch, and salt, and beat until evenly incorporated.
4. Spoon the soft cookie dough into a piping bag fitted with a large plain tip, and pipe 1-inch (2.5 cm) "kisses" onto the baking trays, leaving a 2-inch (5 cm) space between the cookies.
5. Bake the cookies for 12 to 14 minutes, until they lift away from the parchment paper without sticking. Let the cookies cool completely on the tray before removing. The cookies will keep in an airtight container for up to 3 days.

note from anna's kitchen

Alternatively, the cookie dough can be shaped into 2 logs, each 1 inch (2.5 cm) in diameter, and chilled for 2 hours before slicing into ¼-inch (6 mm) slices and baked as above.

LIME COCONUT MEDALLIONS
· *Makes about 2½ dozen cookies* ·

*T*HE PREPARATION OF these cookies is similar to an icebox cookie, but they qualify as shortbread because the recipe does not contain any eggs (the egg white used to hold the coconut on the outside doesn't count). The slice-and-bake style makes the dough a good one to make ahead and freeze, thawing in the fridge before slicing and baking.

1 cup (250 mL) unsweetened,
  shredded coconut
1 cup + 2 Tbsp (280 mL) all-purpose flour
¼ cup (60 mL) sugar
2 tsp (10 mL) finely grated lime zest
¼ tsp (1 mL) salt
½ cup (125 mL) unsalted butter,
  at room temperature and cut in pieces
1 egg white, lightly whisked

1. Preheat the oven to 350°F (175°C). Spread ½ cup (125 mL) of the coconut onto an ungreased baking tray and toast for 10 minutes, stirring once. Allow to cool.
2. Pulse the flour, sugar, lime zest, and salt in a food processor to combine.
3. Add the butter and pulse just until the dough is crumbly. Add the ½ cup (125 mL) of cooled, toasted coconut, and pulse until the dough comes together. Shape the dough into 2 logs about 1¼ inches (3 cm) across and 6 inches (15 cm) long, wrap in plastic, and chill until firm, about 2 hours.
4. Preheat the oven to 350°F (175°C) and line 2 baking trays with parchment paper. Pull the dough out of the refrigerator 20 minutes before slicing.
5. Place the remaining ½ cup (125 mL) of untoasted coconut onto a plate. Unwrap the dough and lightly brush each log with the whisked egg white, then roll them in the coconut to coat. Slice the cookies into medallions about ¼ inch (6 mm) thick and place them on the baking trays, leaving 1 inch (2.5 cm) between them.
6. Bake the cookies for 10 to 12 minutes, until they brown just lightly on the bottom. Cool the cookies on the tray before removing. The cookies will keep in an airtight container for up to 3 days.

egg-free
VARIATION

To make an egg-free version, use 2 tablespoons (30 mL) of melted butter in place of the egg white to get the coconut to stick, or skip the coconut coating altogether.

CINNAMON ROLL PINWHEELS
• Makes about 6 dozen cookies •

egg-
FREE

*J*UST LIKE THEIR yeast-risen, sticky bun counterparts, these cookies are great companions to a hot cup of coffee (but maybe not for breakfast).

1. For the cookie dough, pulse the flour, sugar, and salt in a food processor to combine (or use electric beaters). Add the butter, and pulse or blend in until the dough is a rough, crumbly texture. Add the cream, and pulse or blend until the dough comes together.

2. Divide the dough into 2 pieces, wrap them, and set aside while preparing the filling (do not refrigerate the dough).

3. For the filling, stir all the ingredients to combine.

4. On a lightly floured work surface, roll out 1 piece of the dough into an 8-inch (20 cm) by 12-inch (30 cm) rectangle. Spread the filling evenly over the entire surface of the dough. Roll up the cookie dough in the style of cinnamon rolls, starting at the longer side. Repeat with the second piece of dough, wrap each, and chill for 2 hours.

5. Preheat the oven to 350°F (175°C) and line 2 baking trays with parchment paper.

6. Unwrap and slice the cookie rolls into $\frac{1}{4}$-inch (6 mm) slices, and lay the cookies 1 inch (2.5 cm) apart on the baking trays.

7. Bake the cookies for about 15 minutes, until they barely start to turn golden. Cool the cookies completely on the trays before removing. The cookies can be stored for up to 5 days in an airtight container.

COOKIE DOUGH:

2 cups + 4 tsp (520 mL) all-purpose flour
½ cup (125 mL) sugar
¼ tsp (1 mL) salt
¾ cup + 2 Tbsp (215 mL) unsalted butter, cool but not cold, cut in pieces
2 Tbsp (30 mL) whipping cream

FILLING:

1 cup (250 mL) packed light brown sugar
2 Tbsp (30 mL) unsalted butter, at room temperature
2 Tbsp (30 mL) pure maple syrup
1 Tbsp (15 mL) all-purpose flour
1¼ tsp (6 mL) cinnamon

SALTED ORANGE TOFFEE SLICES
• *Makes about 4 dozen cookies* •

*I*N MY HOME, these cookies have become the household favourite—sophisticated and elegant, but ultimately a comfort-food cookie.

1. Beat the butter, sugar, brown sugar, and orange zest together until smooth. Add the egg and beat until combined.
2. Sift in the flour and baking soda, and stir until blended, then stir in the toffee bits.
3. Shape the dough into 2 logs about 9 inches (23 cm) long and 2 inches (5 cm) across, and wrap each in plastic wrap. Once wrapped, gently flatten the dough on all 4 sides to create a square shape. Chill the dough for at least 2 hours before baking.
4. Preheat the oven to 350°F (175°C) and line 3 baking trays with parchment paper.
5. Slice the logs into cookies that are ¼ inch (6 mm) wide and place them onto the prepared trays, leaving 2 inches (5 cm) between each cookie (these do spread as they bake). Sprinkle the top of each cookie with a little bit of sea salt.
6. Bake the cookies for about 13 minutes, until they have browned just lightly on the bottom. Cool the cookies on the tray and then store them in an airtight container. The cookies will keep for up to a week.

¾ cup (185 mL) unsalted butter, at room temperature
½ cup (125 mL) sugar
½ cup (125 mL) packed dark brown sugar
2 tsp (10 mL) finely grated orange zest
1 egg, at room temperature
2 cups (500 mL) all-purpose flour
½ tsp (2 mL) baking soda
½ cup (125 mL) crunchy toffee bits, such as SKOR bits
Fine sea salt, for sprinkling

GREEN TEA SESAME GINGER WAFERS
• *Makes about 4 dozen cookies* •

THE TOASTED SESAME seeds that coat the outside of these cookie slices add a nice look and depth of flavour. These cookies make a lovely garnish to a simple dish of ice cream or bowl of fresh berries.

1. Cream the butter, icing sugar, and ginger until smooth. Beat in the egg and vanilla extract.
2. Sift the flour, green tea powder, cream of tartar, and salt over the butter mixture, and stir until well blended.
3. Divide the dough into 3 equal pieces and shape them into round logs, 10 inches (25 cm) in length and about 1 inch (2.5 cm) in diameter. Wrap and chill until firm, at least 3 hours.
4. Preheat the oven to 325°F (160°C) and line a baking tray with parchment paper.
5. Sprinkle the sesame seeds onto a plate, unwrap the chilled dough, and roll the logs into the sesame seeds to coat the outsides. Cut rounds of cookie dough as thinly as possible, about 1/8 inch (3 mm) thick, and place them 1 inch (2.5 cm) apart on the baking tray.
6. Bake for 8 to 10 minutes, just until the outside edges of the cookies begin to colour. Let the cookies cool on the tray before removing. The cookies can be stored in an airtight container for up to 5 days. Any unbaked dough can also be wrapped airtight and then frozen for up to 3 months.

1 cup (250 mL) unsalted butter,
    at room temperature
1 cup (250 mL) icing sugar, sifted
1 Tbsp (15 mL) finely grated fresh ginger
1 egg
1 tsp (5 mL) vanilla extract
2⅔ cups (660 mL) cake and pastry flour
1 tsp (5 mL) matcha green tea powder
¾ tsp (4 mL) cream of tartar
¼ tsp (1 mL) salt
¼ cup (60 mL) sesame seeds

note from anna's kitchen

Matcha green tea powder can be found at some grocery stores but most often at franchised coffee or tea shops. Try using a little of this green tea powder in other recipes, such as ice cream and cheesecake, for a familiar green tea colour and taste.

BLUEBERRY OAT SLICES
• *Makes 4 to 5 dozen cookies* •

WHILE SOME PEOPLE see icebox cookies as "retro" (as retro as the term *icebox*), these cookies are quite a contemporary version. Dried blueberries contribute a concentrated hit of fruitiness, and oats add a subtle nutty taste and a sense of virtue that there's fibre in this little treat.

1. Pour 2 cups (500 mL) of boiling water over the dried blueberries and let them soak for 15 minutes. Then drain the blueberries and spread them out to dry on a paper towel.

2. Beat the butter, icing sugar, and sugar together until fluffy, then beat in the egg and vanilla. In a separate bowl, stir the flour, oats, baking powder, and salt, and stir this into the butter mixture until incorporated. Stir in the blueberries. Shape the dough into 3 logs, each about 1 ½ inches (4 cm) in diameter, wrap each in plastic, roll them to round out their shape, and chill until firm, about 2 hours.

3. Preheat the oven to 350°F (175°C) and line 2 baking trays with parchment. Slice the chilled dough into ¼-inch (6 mm) slices and arrange them on the prepared trays, leaving 1 inch (2.5 cm) between them (you may have to bake them in a couple of batches). Bake the cookies for about 10 minutes, until they turn a light golden brown on the bottom. While warm, move the cookies onto a rack to cool and repeat step 3 with any remaining dough. The cookies can be stored in an airtight container for up to 4 days.

1 cup (250 mL) dried blueberries

1 cup (250 mL) unsalted butter, at room temperature

½ cup (125 mL) icing sugar, sifted

½ cup (125 mL) sugar

1 egg, at room temperature

2 tsp (10 mL) vanilla extract

2¼ cups (560 mL) all-purpose flour

⅔ cup (160 mL) regular rolled oats

½ tsp (2 mL) baking powder

¼ tsp (1 mL) salt

TUILE COOKIES
• *Makes about 3 dozen wafer cookies* •

Tuile IS THE French word for tile. These thin wafer cookies were originally shaped to resemble roof tiles, similar to those that are visible on French rooftops. Now they are made into almost any shape and bent in many directions, garnishing plated desserts with character, but they are also delicate and tender on their own.

¼ cup (60 mL) unsalted butter
2 egg whites, at room temperature
⅔ cup (160 mL) icing sugar, sifted
½ cup (125 mL) all-purpose flour
1 tsp (5 mL) finely grated orange zest
2 tsp (10 mL) orange juice or brandy

1. Preheat the oven to 375°F (190°C) and line 2 baking trays with parchment paper. To create a template to make a particular tuile shape, use the lid of a plastic container. Cut away the edges of the lid. Trace the shape you want (such as a heart shape for Valentine's Day or an oak leaf shape for autumn) onto the centre of the lid, and cut a hole in the lid in this shape.

2. Melt the butter and set aside to cool.

3. Whip the egg whites until they are foamy, then add the icing sugar and whip (starting at a slow speed to incorporate the icing sugar) until the whites hold a medium peak (the whites will curl just slightly when the beaters are lifted). Whisk in the flour by hand, along with the orange zest and orange juice (or brandy, if using). Whisk in the cooled, melted butter.

4. Place the template onto the parchment-lined baking tray and evenly spread a thin layer of the cookie batter over it. Lift the template to reveal the shape, place the template close to the first cookie without touching it, and repeat until you have made as many cookies as you can fit.

5. Bake the cookies for 3 to 6 minutes, rotating the baking trays halfway through cooking. Once the cookies are golden brown around the edges, remove the tray from the oven. To add a curve to the cookies, immediately lift them with a spatula while they are still warm, and place them on a rolling pin until they cool and set to the curve of the pin. Once cooled, remove carefully (they are delicate) and store in an airtight container. The tuiles will keep for 1 to 3 days.

note from anna's kitchen
Delicate cookies like tuiles and lace cookies are sensitive to humidity, so they need to be stored in a tightly sealed container. They are best consumed on the day they are made, but the batter freezes very well.

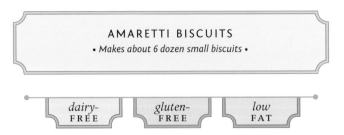

AMARETTI BISCUITS
• Makes about 6 dozen small biscuits •

dairy-
FREE

gluten-
FREE

low
FAT

*T*RADITIONAL AMARETTI BISCUITS are wrapped, two at a time, in colourful papers. You can do the same for presentation or gifting, and they can be used to crumble over ice cream, or even stirred into yogurt.

1. Preheat the oven to 300°F (150°C) and line 3 baking trays with parchment paper.
2. Whip the egg whites at high speed until foamy, then slowly pour in the sugar while whipping, continuing to whip until the whites hold a medium peak.
3. In a separate bowl, stir the ground almonds, icing sugar, and cornstarch. Add half of the almonds to the whipped whites and fold in, then repeat with the remaining half. Stir in the almond extract.
4. Spoon the batter into a piping bag fitted with a large, plain tip, and pipe 1-inch (2.5 cm) cookies onto the prepared trays, leaving 1 inch (2.5 cm) between each cookie.
5. Let the cookies sit for 10 minutes to air-dry, then bake them for about 20 minutes, until they just start to brown. Let them cool completely on the tray before storing in an airtight container. The amaretti biscuits will keep for up to 2 weeks.

2 egg whites, at room temperature
⅓ cup (80 mL) sugar
1⅓ cups (330 mL) ground almonds
1 cup (250 mL) icing sugar, sifted
1 Tbsp (15 mL) cornstarch
¾ tsp (4 mL) almond extract

ALMOND SPRITZ COOKIES
• *Makes about 4 dozen cookies* •

USING ALMOND BUTTER makes this cookie batter smooth and easy to pipe. Be certain that your almond butter is at room temperature before stirring and measuring.

5 Tbsp (75 mL) unsalted butter, at room temperature
½ cup (125 mL) room-temperature, well-stirred, pure almond butter
⅓ cup (80 mL) icing sugar, sifted
1 egg yolk
½ tsp (2 mL) vanilla extract
½ tsp (2 mL) almond extract
½ cup (125 mL) all-purpose flour
¼ tsp (1 mL) salt

1. Preheat the oven to 325°F (160°C) and line 2 baking trays with parchment paper.
2. Using electric beaters, cream the butter, almond butter, and icing sugar until fluffy. Beat in the egg yolk and extracts.
3. Reduce the speed to medium low and add in the flour and salt, mixing until evenly blended (the dough will be soft).
4. Spoon the cookie dough into a piping bag fitted with a small star tip, or into a cookie press, and pipe cookies about ¾ inch (2 cm) across and with a 1 inch (2.5 cm) space between them.
5. Bake for 10 to 12 minutes, until the cookies are just lightly browned around the edges. Cool the cookies on the trays and store them in an airtight container. The cookies will keep for up to 5 days.

LANGUES DE CHAT
• *Makes about 2 dozen cookies* •

CAT'S TONGUES *(langues de chat)* are in the same family as tuiles, and they are used as a garnish on desserts or served alongside a coffee in place of biscotti.

1 recipe Tuile Cookies batter (page 33)

1. Prepare steps 1 to 3 of the tuile cookie batter recipe.
2. Preheat the oven to 375°F (190°C) and line 2 baking trays with parchment paper.
3. Spoon the batter into a piping bag fitted with a plain tip. Pipe fingers about 2 inches (5 cm) long and 1 inch (2.5 cm) apart on the baking trays.
4. Bake for 5 to 8 minutes, until golden brown on the bottom and edges. Cool the cookies completely before storing in an airtight container. The langues de chat will keep for 1 to 3 days.

PECAN LACE COOKIES
• Makes about 2 dozen large cookies •

egg-
FREE

*T*HESE COOKIES ARE very close in style to Florentine cookies, and can be shaped or rolled while warm.

1. Preheat the oven to 350°F (175°C) and line 3 baking trays with parchment paper.
2. Place the sugar, butter, cream, and honey in a saucepot, and bring to a boil, stirring often. Once a boil is reached, stop stirring and cook the mixture, occasionally brushing down the sides of the pot with water, until it reaches 239°F (115°C) on a candy thermometer. Remove the pot from the heat and stir in the oats, pecans, and cranberries.
3. Dip a teaspoon into water and use it to drop teaspoonfuls of batter onto the trays, being certain to leave 4 inches (10 cm) between them, as the cookies spread a great deal as they bake (you will likely fit only 8 cookies per tray). With wet fingers, gently press the cookies to flatten them a little, then bake them for 8 to 10 minutes, until they are a rich golden brown. See the note below to shape the cookies, or completely cool the cookies on the trays before removing. The cookies will keep for up to 3 days in an airtight container.

¾ cup (185 mL) sugar
½ cup (125 mL) unsalted butter
⅓ cup (80 mL) whipping cream
2 Tbsp (30 mL) honey
1 cup (250 mL) rolled oats
1 cup (250 mL) chopped pecans (chopped to the size of oats)
½ cup (125 mL) coarsely chopped dried cranberries

note from anna's kitchen
To shape lace cookies, let them cool for about 2 minutes once they are out of the oven. Then lift the cookies with a spatula and place them on a rolling pin to create a curl, or on the underside of a muffin tin cup to create a dish that can hold ice cream, or roll them up into a cigarette-like cylinder to be a garnish for a custard or cake.
This cookie batter can be made ahead and chilled for up to a week before baking, or it can be frozen for up to 3 months and thawed in the refrigerator before baking.

CHOCOLATE-DIPPED ORANGE MADELEINE COOKIES
• *Makes about 2 dozen cookies* •

*T*HESE COOKIES ARE almost like little cakes and do require a madeleine pan, notable by its shell indentations. This recipe uses a whole orange, peel and all, to add a zesty kick.

1. Preheat oven to 350°F (175°C). Grease and flour a madeleine pan, tapping out excess flour.
2. Roughly chop the whole orange, removing any seeds, and place in a small saucepot. Cover the orange with water and simmer until almost all the liquid has evaporated, about 8 minutes. Remove from the heat, cool, then purée in a blender (a blender works better than a food processor). Measure ½ cup (125 mL) of the puréed orange to use for the madeleines (the volume you cooked and blended should be close to this measurement).
3. Beat the butter and sugar until fluffy, then beat in the eggs.
4. In a separate bowl, combine the flour, ground almonds, baking powder, and salt, and add this to the butter mixture, stirring just until incorporated. Stir in the measured orange purée.
5. Spoon the batter by tablespoonfuls into the prepared madeleine pan, and bake for about 20 minutes, until golden brown. Let the madeleines cool before gently removing them from the pan.
6. Melt the chocolate chips by stirring them in a metal bowl placed over a pot of barely simmering water. Dip each madeleine halfway into the melted chocolate, shake off excess, and place each on a sheet of parchment paper to set. The madeleines will keep up to 4 days in an airtight container.

1 medium-sized navel orange
½ cup (125 mL) unsalted butter, at room temperature
¾ cup (185 mL) sugar
2 eggs, at room temperature
½ cup (125 mL) all-purpose flour
½ cup (125 mL) ground almonds
½ tsp (2 mL) baking powder
¼ tsp (1 mL) salt
¾ cup (185 mL) chocolate chips

TWO-BITE CHOCOLATE ALMOND BISCOTTI
• *Makes about 6 dozen biscotti* •

dairy-
FREE

low-
FAT

*T*HESE BISCUITS ARE light and crunchy at the same time. Because the eggs and sugar are whipped together until frothy, these cookies have an almost meringue-like quality to them, but they still have a rich chocolate taste.

4 eggs, at room temperature
¾ cup (185 mL) sugar
1 tsp (5 mL) vanilla extract
1 cup (250 mL) all-purpose flour
½ cup (125 mL) cocoa powder
¼ tsp (1 mL) baking powder
⅛ tsp (0.5 mL) salt
½ cup (125 mL) sliced almonds

1. Preheat the oven to 350°F (175°C) and line 2 baking trays with parchment paper.
2. Using electric beaters or a stand mixer fitted with the whip attachment, whip the eggs and sugar on high speed until they hold a ribbon when the beaters are lifted, about 3 minutes. Beat in the vanilla.
3. In a separate bowl, sift the flour, cocoa, baking powder, and salt, then fold this into the whipped eggs.
4. Scrape this batter (which will be the consistency of cake batter) into a piping bag fitted with a large plain tip, and pipe 3 rows of batter, about 12 inches (30 cm) long and 1 ½ inches (4 cm) across, onto each tray, leaving 2 inches (5 cm) between each row. Sprinkle the biscotti batter with the sliced almonds.
5. Bake for about 16 minutes, until the tops of the biscotti appear dry (the cookies will still feel soft) and remove. Allow the cookies to cool on the tray almost to room temperature and reduce the oven temperature to 325°F (160°C).
6. On a cutting board, use a chef's knife to slice the biscotti into individual cookies that are ¾ inch (2 cm) wide and return the biscotti to the baking tray.
7. Bake the biscotti for about 20 minutes (the cookies may still feel a touch soft directly from the oven, but they will dry once cooled). If they are still soft at room temperature, return them to the oven for an additional 5 minutes. Once cooled, pack the biscotti into an airtight container. The biscotti will keep for up to 3 weeks.

Pecan Lace Cookies (page 36), *Two-Bite Chocolate Almond Biscotti* (page 38), *Almond Spritz Cookies* (page 35), and *Coconut Hazelnut Biscotti* (page 40)

COCONUT HAZELNUT BISCOTTI
• Makes about 3 dozen biscotti •

dairy-
FREE

*T*HESE BISCOTTI ARE very much of the coffee-shop style, just like the ones sold in the glass jar or packaged to take home. The subtle licorice taste of the anise seed really does cleanse the palate after a coffee.

1. Preheat the oven to 325°F (160°C) and line 2 baking trays with parchment paper.
2. Whisk the oil, sugar, egg, egg white, and extracts together until evenly blended (you can do this by hand or with electric beaters). Stir in the hazelnuts, coconut, and anise or fennel seed.
3. In a separate bowl, stir the flour, baking powder, and salt to combine, then add to the egg mixture, blending well (the dough will be sticky). Divide the batter evenly between the 2 prepared trays and, with floured hands, shape the dough into 2 logs the length of the baking tray. Mix the egg and water to form an egg wash and brush the surface of the dough with it.
4. Bake for about 30 minutes, until the cookie logs are evenly browned (they will have spread out). Allow the cookie logs to cool for 15 minutes.
5. While the logs are still warm, use a chef's knife to slice the biscotti into ½-inch (1 cm) wide slices on a cutting board, then return the biscotti to the baking trays, laying them flat and with just a small space between them. Return the biscotti to the oven and bake them for about 25 minutes, until they just begin to brown around the edges. Cool the biscotti on the tray. The biscotti can be stored in an airtight container for up to a month.

½ cup (125 mL) vegetable oil

¾ cup (185 mL) sugar

1 egg

1 egg white

1 tsp (5 mL) vanilla extract

¼ tsp (1 mL) almond extract

1 cup (250 mL) whole hazelnuts, toasted and peeled

½ cup (125 mL) sweetened, flaked coconut

1 Tbsp (15 mL) whole anise seed or fennel seed

1½ cups (375 mL) all-purpose flour

1½ tsp (7 mL) baking powder

½ tsp (2 mL) salt

FOR BRUSHING:

1 egg

1 Tbsp (15 mL) water

LEMON MACADAMIA BISCOTTI
• *Makes about 4 dozen biscotti* •

THESE BISCOTTI ARE a more traditional style than the Two-Bite Chocolate Almond Biscotti (page 38). They have a nice crunch, but they are still quite tender.

1. Preheat the oven to 350°F (175°C) and line 3 baking trays with parchment paper.
2. Beat the butter, sugar, and lemon zest together, then add the eggs one at a time, beating well after each addition.
3. In a separate bowl, stir the flour, cornmeal, and baking powder, and add this to the butter mixture, stirring until evenly blended. Stir in the macadamia nuts.
4. Spread the batter into 3 logs, one on each pan. The batter is very soft, so use floured hands to shape the logs to about 14 inches (35 cm) in length.
5. Bake for 25 to 30 minutes, until the surface of the logs is evenly golden in colour, and remove. Let the biscotti cool for 15 minutes and reduce the oven temperature to 325°F (160°C).
6. On a cutting board, use a bread knife to slice each of the logs into biscotti that are ½ inch (1 cm) wide, and place them back on the baking trays. Bake the biscotti for 10 to 15 minutes, until they just begin to brown at the edges. Let them cool completely on the trays and then store them in an airtight container. The biscotti will keep for up to 3 weeks.

½ cup (125 mL) unsalted butter, at room temperature

1 cup (250 mL) sugar

1 Tbsp (15 mL) finely grated lemon zest

2 eggs, at room temperature

1¾ cups (435 mL) all-purpose flour

½ cup (125 mL) cornmeal

1½ tsp (7.5 mL) baking powder

1 cup (250 mL) dry-roasted, salted macadamia nuts

HAZELNUT RASPBERRY LINZER COOKIES
• *Makes about 2½ dozen cookies* •

*T*HIS TENDER AND delicate sandwich cookie can be cut to just about any shape, for any season or occasion.

1. In a food processor, pulse the hazelnuts with ½ cup (125 mL) of the flour until the hazelnuts are finely ground, then pulse in the remaining ½ cup (125 mL) of flour. Add the sugar, cocoa, cinnamon, cloves, and salt, and pulse to combine.

2. Add the butter and pulse until the mixture has a sandy texture. Add the egg yolk and vanilla, and pulse until the dough comes together.

3. Shape the dough into 2 discs, wrap each, and chill them until the dough is firm, at least 1 hour.

4. Preheat the oven to 375°F (190°C) and line 2 baking trays with parchment paper.

5. Lightly flour a rolling surface and roll out the first disc of dough (you can knead the dough for 10 seconds to make it easier to roll without cracking) to a thickness of just under ¼ inch (6 mm). Using a 2-inch (5 cm) cookie cutter, cut out as many cookies as you can, then reroll the dough and continue cutting, and place these cookies on one baking tray (these will be the bottoms). Repeat this with the second disc of dough, but then, using a 1-inch (2.5 cm) cutter, cut a hole in the centre of each cookie (these will be the tops). Place these cookies on the second baking tray. Continue rolling and cutting cookies until all the dough is used, but keep count so that you have the same number of tops and bottoms.

6. Bake the cookies with the holes for about 10 minutes and the bottom cookies for about 12 minutes, until each style is just lightly golden. Let the cookies cool completely on the trays.

7. To assemble, dust the top cookies with icing sugar while they are still on the tray. Stir the raspberry jam to loosen it, then spread a little jam (about ¾ teaspoon/4 mL on each cookie. Gently press a top cookie onto the jam and let them set for an hour before storing. The cookies will store in an airtight container for up to 4 days.

1 cup (250 mL) whole, unpeeled hazelnuts
1 cup (250 mL) all-purpose flour
½ cup (125 mL) sugar
1 Tbsp (15 mL) cocoa powder, sifted
¼ tsp (1 mL) ground cinnamon
⅛ tsp (0.5 mL) ground cloves
⅛ tsp (0.5 mL) salt
½ cup (125 mL) cool unsalted butter,
   cut in pieces
1 egg yolk
1 tsp (5 mL) vanilla extract

ASSEMBLY:
Icing sugar, for dusting
½ cup (125 mL) raspberry jam

CHOCOLATE MARSHMALLOW LINZER COOKIES
• Makes about 2 dozen cookies •

W**HAT MAKES A** cup of hot cocoa so scrumptious? The marshmallows, of course! These sandwich cookies have powdered hot chocolate mix in the dough to lend authentic hot cocoa flavour, while the marshmallow fluff filling is the real reason I love these cookies.

¾ cup (185 mL) unsalted butter, at room temperature

¾ cup (185 mL) icing sugar

½ cup (125 mL) Dutch process cocoa powder

1 tsp (5 mL) vanilla extract

1 egg

1¾ cups (435 mL) all-purpose flour

¼ tsp (1 mL) salt

ASSEMBLY:

¾ cup (185 mL) marshmallow fluff (found near the ice-cream toppings in many grocery stores)

1. Beat the butter until fluffy, then sift in the icing sugar and cocoa powder, and beat to combine well. Add the vanilla and egg.
2. Stir in the flour and salt, and keep stirring until the dough comes together. Shape the dough into 2 discs, wrap each, and chill them for at least an hour.
3. Preheat the oven to 350°F (175°C) and line 2 baking trays with parchment paper.
4. On a lightly floured surface, roll out the dough to ¼ inch (6 mm) in thickness, cut out circles using a 2½-inch (6 cm) cookie cutter. Scraps of dough can be rerolled to make more cookies. With a 1-inch (2.5 cm) cutter, cut out a hole in half of the cookies. Place the cookies on the prepared baking trays ½ inch (1 cm) apart, the cookies with the cutout centres on one tray and the complete cookies on the other.
5. Bake for 10 to 12 minutes (cookies with the holes take 10 minutes; those without take 12 minutes), until they easily lift off of the baking tray. Let cool.
6. To assemble, spoon a teaspoonful of marshmallow fluff onto the base cookie and top with the cookie with the cutout, pressing gently to adhere. Let the cookies sit for 2 hours to dry before storing. The cookies will keep for up to a week in an airtight container.

CURRANT TEA FINGERS WITH LEMON CREAM
• Makes 27 cookies •

*I*T MAY SEEM funny that this recipe yields 27 cookies, but since you roll, measure, and cut these to get perfect finger cookies, that's how the math adds up. If you prefer cookies by dozens, as many bakers do, simply eat three and don't tell anyone.

1. Preheat the oven to 350°F (175°C) and line 2 baking trays with parchment paper.
2. Beat the butter and sugar together until fluffy and light. Beat in the egg yolks, sour cream, vanilla, and lemon zest. Sift in the flour and salt, and stir until blended (the dough will be crumbly). Stir in the currants and then turn the dough onto a work surface to gently knead it to bring it together. Shape the dough into 2 discs, wrap each in plastic, and let the dough rest for 15 minutes.
3. On a lightly floured surface, roll out the first disc of cookie dough into a square about 11 inches (28 cm) across. Use a ruler and trim away the rough edges to leave a square that is 9 × 9 inches (23 cm × 23 cm). Cut the square into "fingers"—rectangles that are 3 inches (8 cm) long by 1 inch (2.5 cm) across—using your ruler as a guide. Use a small spatula to lift these onto the prepared baking trays, leaving 1 inch (2.5 cm) between the cookies. Repeat with the second disc of dough. Any scraps can be rerolled and cut for extras.
4. Bake the cookies for about 15 minutes, until the bottoms turn golden brown. Cool the cookies while preparing the lemon cream filling.
5. For the filling, beat the butter with ½ cup (125 mL) of the icing sugar until fluffy. Beat in the lemon zest, lemon juice, and vanilla, then beat in the remaining 1 cup (250 mL) icing sugar.
6. To assemble the sandwich cookies, spread a generous teaspoonful of the filling on the bottom side of one cookie finger and press the bottom side of a second finger over the filling. Repeat this until all the cookies are sandwiched. The cookies can be stored in an airtight container for up to 3 days.

COOKIES:

¾ cup (185 mL) unsalted butter, at room temperature

¾ cup (185 mL) sugar

5 egg yolks

2 Tbsp (30 mL) sour cream

1 tsp (5 mL) vanilla extract

1 tsp (5 mL) finely grated lemon zest

3¼ cups (810 mL) all-purpose flour

¼ tsp (1 mL) salt

¾ cup (185 mL) dried currants

LEMON CREAM FILLING:

½ cup (125 mL) unsalted butter, at room temperature

1½ cups (375 mL) icing sugar, sifted

2 tsp (10 mL) finely grated lemon zest

¼ cup (60 mL) lemon juice

1 tsp (5 mL) vanilla extract

Chocolate
Marshmallow
—
Rugelach
—
Tea Fingers
—
Apricot
Thumbprint

Chocolate Marshmallow Linzer Cookies (page 43), Raspberry, Lemon, and White Chocolate Rugelach (page 46), Currant Tea Fingers with Lemon Cream (page 44), and Apricot Walnut Thumbprint Cookies (page 47)

RASPBERRY, LEMON, AND WHITE CHOCOLATE RUGELACH
• Makes 16 large cookies •

CREAM CHEESE IS the secret to a tasty and flaky rugelach cookie. Because the pastry is just barely sweetened, it balances the sweetness of the jam and white chocolate.

1. Beat the butter and cream cheese until smooth. Beat in 2 tsp (10 mL) of the lemon zest and the sugar.
2. Add the flour and salt, and stir until the dough evenly comes together.
3. Shape the dough into 2 discs, wrap each in plastic wrap, and chill for at least an hour.
4. Preheat the oven to 350°F (175°C) and line a baking tray with parchment paper.
5. On a lightly floured surface, roll out the first disc of dough into a circle about 12 inches (30 cm) across and just shy of $\frac{1}{4}$ inch (6 mm) thick. Trim away the rough edges.
6. Stir the raspberry jam to soften it, then stir in the remaining 1 tsp (5 mL) of lemon zest. Spread half of the jam over the surface of the dough, right to the edges. Sprinkle half of the white chocolate over the jam.
7. Cut the dough into 8 wedges, and roll up each cookie from the large edge to its point, very much like a croissant, and place the cookies 1 inch (2.5 cm) apart on the baking tray. Repeat steps 6 and 7 with the remaining disc of dough.
8. Whisk the egg white until it is very foamy and brush each cookie with it. Sprinkle the cookies generously with sugar.
9. Bake the rugelach for 20 to 25 minutes, until they are an even golden colour. Let the cookies cool on the tray before removing to store. The cookies will keep in an airtight container for up to 3 days.

¾ cup (185 mL) unsalted butter, at room temperature
½ pkg (4 oz/125 g) cream cheese, at room temperature
2 tsp (10 mL) finely grated lemon zest
1 Tbsp (15 mL) sugar, plus extra for sprinkling
2 cups (500 mL) all-purpose flour
¼ tsp (1 mL) salt
⅔ cup (160 mL) raspberry jam
2 oz (60 g) white chocolate, cut in chunks, or ½ cup (125 mL) white chocolate chips

FOR BRUSHING:
1 egg white

egg-free
VARIATION

To make these cookies egg-free, simply brush the tops of the rolled cookies with milk in place of the egg white.

note from anna's kitchen
To make smaller cookies, shape the dough into 4 discs instead of 2 and follow the same method. You will get 32 smaller cookies that bake in 16 to 20 minutes.

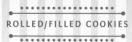
APRICOT WALNUT THUMBPRINT COOKIES
• Makes about 3 dozen cookies •

My MOM USED to make thumbprint cookies dipped in walnut crumbs every Christmas, and these remind me very much of my childhood.

1. Preheat the oven to 350°F (175°C) and line 2 baking trays with parchment paper.
2. By hand, with electric beaters, or using a standup mixer fitted with the paddle attachment, beat the butter and brown sugar until smooth. Beat in the egg yolk, zest, and vanilla.
3. Add the flour and salt, and mix until evenly blended. Spoon out table-spoonfuls of the dough and shape each into a ball. Whisk the remaining egg white in a small bowl. Dip each cookie into the egg white and then roll completely in the walnut crumbs. Place the cookies on the prepared trays, leaving 1 inch (2.5 cm) between them. Once all the cookies are on the trays, use the knuckle of your index finger to make an impression in the centre of each (they may be called thumbprint cookies, but it's easier to use your knuckle).
4. Bake the cookies for about 15 minutes, until the walnut crumbs and the bottoms of the cookies are lightly browned.
5. While still warm, press the centre of the cookies down again to make more room for the jam, stir the jam to soften, then spoon a little into each cookie. Let the cookies air-dry for about 2 hours, then store. The cookies will keep in an airtight container for up to 5 days.

1 cup (250 mL) unsalted butter,
   at room temperature
½ cup (125 mL) packed light
   brown sugar
1 egg, separated
2 tsp (10 mL) finely grated orange zest
1 tsp (5 mL) vanilla extract
2 cups (500 mL) all-purpose flour
¼ tsp (1 mL) salt
¾ cup (185 mL) walnut crumbs
   (finely chopped walnut pieces)
⅓ cup (80 mL) apricot jam

MAPLE GINGERBREAD CUTOUT COOKIES

• Makes about 5 dozen cookies •

MAPLE ADDS A gentle sweetness to these cookies, which are a little milder than traditional molasses gingerbread cookies.

½ cup (125 mL) unsalted butter, at room temperature

½ cup (125 mL) packed light brown sugar

½ cup (125 mL) pure maple syrup

1 egg

1 Tbsp (15 mL) finely grated fresh ginger

1 tsp (5 mL) finely grated lemon zest

2⅓ cups (580 mL) all-purpose flour

¾ tsp (4 mL) ground allspice

½ tsp (2 mL) ground cinnamon

½ tsp (2 mL) baking soda

½ tsp (2 mL) salt

1. By hand, with electric beaters, or in a mixer fitted with the paddle attachment, beat the butter with the brown sugar and maple syrup until light and fluffy. Beat in the egg, ginger, and lemon zest.

2. In a separate bowl, sift the flour with the allspice, cinnamon, baking soda, and salt. Add the flour to the butter mixture in 3 additions at low speed, mixing well after each addition (it will be very soft). Scrape the dough onto 3 pieces of plastic wrap, cover, and press into 3 discs. Chill until firm, about 2 hours.

3. Preheat the oven to 350°F (175°C) and line 2 baking trays with parchment paper.

4. On a lightly floured surface, roll out the first piece of cookie dough to ⅛ inch (3 mm) thick and cut with a 2-inch (5 cm) cookie cutter of any desired shape. Arrange the cookies on the prepared baking tray, leaving a gap of ½ inch (1 cm) between them, and repeat rolling and cutting the remaining 2 discs. Leftover scraps from cutting out the cookies can chill for 10 minutes and then be rerolled.

5. Bake the cookies for 12 to 14 minutes, until lightly browned. Cool the cookies on the trays before transferring them to an airtight container. The cookies will keep for a week and can be decorated with icing or simply dusted with icing sugar.

CINNAMON SUGAR CUTOUT COOKIES
• *Makes about 3 dozen cookies* •

THIS IS A variation on a traditional sugar cutout cookie. The addition of cinnamon is subtle both in taste and in colour, but if you'd like to make classic sugar cookies, you can simply omit it.

1. Beat the butter and ²⁄₃ cup (160 mL) of the sugar until fluffy and light. Beat in the egg yolks and vanilla. In a separate bowl, sift the flour, baking powder, ½ teaspoon (2 mL) of the cinnamon, and salt. Add this to the butter mixture and combine until the dough comes together. Shape the dough into 2 discs, wrap each in plastic wrap, and rest the dough for 20 minutes at room temperature.

2. Preheat the oven to 350°F (175°C) and line 2 baking trays with parchment paper.

3. On a lightly floured surface, roll out the first disc of dough to just over ¼ inch (6 mm) thick. Use a 2 ½-inch (6 cm) round cookie cutter, or other desired shape, and cut out cookies. Use a small spatula to lift the cookies onto the baking tray, leaving a 1-inch (2.5 cm) gap between them. Repeat this with the second disc of dough. Any scraps can be rerolled after they have rested for 15 minutes.

4. Whisk the egg white to loosen it and brush it overtop of the cookies. Stir the remaining 2 tablespoons (30 mL) of sugar with the remaining ⅛ teaspoon (0.5 mL) of cinnamon, and sprinkle this over the cookies.

5. Bake the cookies for 12 to 15 minutes, until the edges turn slightly golden. Cool the cookies on the tray before removing. The cookies can be stored in an airtight container for up to 4 days.

²⁄₃ cup (160 mL) unsalted butter, at room temperature

²⁄₃ cup (160 mL) + 2 Tbsp (30 mL) sugar

2 egg yolks

1 tsp (5 mL) vanilla extract

2 cups (500 mL) all-purpose flour

1 tsp (5 mL) baking powder

½ tsp (2 mL) + ⅛ tsp (0.5 mL) ground cinnamon

¼ tsp (1 mL) salt

1 egg white

note from anna's kitchen

These cookies and the Maple Gingerbread Cutout Cookies (page 48) are very suitable for decorating with icing. Simply omit the step of brushing the cookies with egg white and sprinkling them with cinnamon sugar, and prepare a batch of Royal Icing (page 252) instead. Spoon the icing into a piping bag and decorate the cookies as you wish.

squares and bars

SLICING PERFECT SQUARES AND BARS

Here are some tips for slicing your squares and bars easily, with precision, and with a minimal amount of waste:

1. Line your baking pan with parchment paper so that it comes up the sides of the pan. Once your recipe has set, you can lift out the squares or bars as a whole onto a cutting board so that slicing evenly is simple, and you won't scratch your pan.

2. Use a ruler to mark where you want to slice by notching at equal intervals along each of the four edges of the baked item.

3. Use a chef's knife to line up the measured markings and make a clean slice.

4. If cutting squares or bars of a recipe that is topped with chocolate or has a dense filling, insert your knife into a pitcher of hot tap water for a minute. Dry off the knife and let the heat do the work of softening the square or bar, allowing you to cut clean slices and not crack the chocolate top.

5. If you wish to dust your squares or bars with icing sugar for garnish, slice them first, then dust them. (But note that icing sugar melts when it is refrigerated.)

DELECTABLE FUDGE BROWNIES
• *Makes one 9- × 13-inch (3.5 L) pan* •
Cuts into 24 squares

THE KEY TO these rich and fudgy basic brownies is mayonnaise, of all things. The mayonnaise takes the place of butter and really keeps this recipe moist. The biggest-yielding recipe for brownies in this book, this is the brownie recipe to make when you need to have a large inventory on hand (and they freeze well).

4 oz (125 g) unsweetened chocolate, chopped
⅔ cup (160 mL) boiling water
2 cups (500 mL) sugar
⅔ cup (160 mL) mayonnaise
3 eggs, at room temperature
1 tsp (5 mL) vanilla extract
1 cup (250 mL) all-purpose flour
½ cup (125 mL) cocoa powder, sifted
½ tsp (2 mL) salt
1 cup (250 mL) chocolate chips

1. Preheat the oven to 350°F (175°C). Grease and line a 9- × 13-inch (3.5 L) baking pan with parchment paper so that the paper hangs over the sides slightly.
2. Place the chopped chocolate in a large bowl and pour the boiling water overtop. Let the chocolate mixture sit for 1 minute, then whisk to melt. Whisk in the sugar, then add the mayonnaise and the eggs, one at a time. Stir in the vanilla.
3. With a wooden spoon or spatula, stir in the flour, cocoa, and salt until evenly blended. Stir in the chocolate chips.
4. Scrape the batter into the prepared pan and spread evenly. Bake for about 30 minutes, until a tester inserted in the centre of the brownies comes out clean. Cool to room temperature. Once sliced, you can store the brownies in an airtight container for up to 5 days.

note from anna's kitchen
These brownies slice best when chilled but taste best at room temperature.

For great tips on cocoa powder and which cocoa to use in which recipes, refer to page 10.

PEANUT BUTTER BLONDIES
• *Makes one 8-inch (20 cm) square pan* •
Cuts into 25 squares

BLONDIES EARN THEIR name because they showcase white chocolate, or even no chocolate at all. This peanut butter version is chewy and moist, but not over-the-top sweet.

½ cup (125 mL) unsalted butter, at room temperature
½ cup (125 mL) sugar
½ cup (125 mL) packed light brown sugar
⅔ cup (160 mL) peanut butter, any kind you prefer
2 eggs, at room temperature
1 tsp (5 mL) vanilla extract
1 cup (250 mL) all-purpose flour
1 tsp (5 mL) baking powder
¼ tsp (1 mL) baking soda
¼ tsp (1 mL) salt
1 cup (250 mL) white and/or dark chocolate chips

1. Preheat the oven to 350°F (175°C). Grease an 8-inch (20 cm) square pan and line it with parchment paper so that the paper hangs over the sides slightly.
2. Cream the butter, sugar, and brown sugar together. Beat in the peanut butter. Add the eggs one at a time, stirring well after each addition. Stir in the vanilla.
3. In a separate bowl, stir the flour, baking powder, baking soda, and salt to combine, then add this to the butter mixture, stirring until evenly blended. Stir in the chocolate chips, then scrape the batter into the prepared pan.
4. Bake for about 30 minutes, until the edges are golden brown (expect it to soufflé a little in the oven and then fall once removed). Cool in the pan completely before removing to slice. The blondies will keep for up to 3 days stored in an airtight container.

FROSTED MOCHA WHOLE WHEAT BROWNIES
• *Makes one 8-inch (20 cm) square pan* | *Cuts into 25 squares* •

WHOLE WHEAT FLOUR offers a nutty taste that complements the walnuts in this recipe (and offers you a little sense of virtue, too). These brownies have a robust chocolate taste and are definitely for walnut lovers. The recipe is convenient, too, because the batter can be fully stirred together in the pot you melt the chocolate in. A great dessert and fewer dishes—a magical combination!

1. Preheat the oven to 350°F (175°C). Grease an 8-inch (20 cm) square pan and line it with parchment paper so that the paper hangs over the sides slightly.
2. Melt the butter, chocolates, and instant coffee in a medium saucepot over low heat, stirring constantly. Remove the pot from the heat.
3. Stir in the sugar, then add the eggs one at a time, stirring well after each addition. Stir in the vanilla.
4. Stir the flour, baking soda, and salt into the chocolate mixture, mixing just until blended. Stir in the walnut pieces and then scrape the batter into the prepared pan, spreading evenly.
5. Bake the brownies for about 35 minutes, until the top of the brownies takes on a dull finish. Cool the brownies completely in the pan before frosting.
6. To make the frosting, melt the chocolate, butter, and instant coffee in a metal or glass bowl over a pot of barely simmering water, stirring until melted. Beat the cream cheese to soften, pour in the melted chocolate, and beat until blended. Add the icing sugar and blend. Remove the brownies from the pan (using the edges of the parchment paper to lift out) and ice the top of the entire brownie. Let the frosting set for an hour before slicing. The brownies will keep in an airtight container for up to 3 days.

BROWNIES:

½ cup (125 mL) unsalted butter

4 oz (120 g) semisweet or bittersweet chocolate, chopped

3 oz (90 g) unsweetened chocolate, chopped

1 Tbsp (15 mL) instant coffee granules

1 cup (250 mL) sugar

2 eggs, at room temperature

1 tsp (5 mL) vanilla extract

⅔ cup (160 mL) whole wheat flour

¼ tsp (1 mL) baking soda

¼ tsp (1 mL) salt

1 cup (250 mL) lightly toasted walnut pieces

FROSTING:

3 oz (90 g) semisweet or bittersweet chocolate, chopped

2 Tbsp (30 mL) unsalted butter

1 tsp (5 mL) instant coffee granules

½ pkg (4 oz/125 g) cream cheese, at room temperature

1 cup (250 mL) icing sugar, sifted

note from anna's kitchen

For recipes such as this, where the nuts within the recipe are not exposed directly to the heat of the oven, I like to pre-toast the nuts before adding them to the recipe. Toasting adds depth of flavour to the nuts and gives them a nice crunch. Simply spread the nuts on an ungreased baking tray and bake them at 350°F (175°C) for about 10 minutes until they are golden brown.

Frosted Mocha Whole Wheat Brownies
(page 54) and *Delectable Fudge
Brownies* (page 53)

FULLY LOADED CRANBERRY COCONUT MARSHMALLOW BROWNIES

• *Makes one 8-inch (20 cm) square pan | Cuts into 25 squares* •

THESE BROWNIES ARE for those who love lots of stuff in their cookies, ice creams, and other treats. These brownies bake with that familiar shiny, crackly top, and with all the fillings, there's really no need for frosting.

1. Preheat the oven to 350°F (175°C). Grease an 8-inch (20 cm) square pan and line it with parchment paper so that the paper hangs over the sides slightly.
2. Melt the butter and bittersweet and unsweetened chocolates in a medium saucepot over low heat, stirring constantly. Remove the pot from the heat and stir in the sugar, then add the eggs one at a time, stirring well after each addition. Stir in the vanilla.
3. Sift the flour, cocoa, and salt together, and stir this into the chocolate mixture. Fold in the coconut, cranberries, and mini marshmallows, ensuring that everything gets fully coated with brownie mix.
4. Scrape the batter into the prepared pan and spread evenly. Bake the brownies for 25 to 30 minutes, until a tester inserted in the centre of the brownies comes out clean. Cool the brownies in the pan before removing them to slice.
5. The brownies will keep up to 3 days in an airtight container.

½ cup (125 mL) unsalted butter

3 oz (90 g) bittersweet chocolate, chopped

3 oz (90 g) unsweetened chocolate, chopped

1 cup (250 mL) sugar

3 eggs, at room temperature

1 tsp (5 mL) vanilla extract

½ cup (125 mL) all-purpose flour

¼ cup (60 mL) cocoa powder, sifted

½ tsp (2 mL) salt

½ cup (125 mL) sweetened, flaked coconut

½ cup (125 mL) dried cranberries, soaked in hot water for 5 minutes and then drained

2 cups (500 mL) mini marshmallows

note from anna's kitchen

Using room-temperature eggs is very important when making brownies. Cold eggs can cool the melted chocolate, making it seize (become firm and hard to work with), which results in a dry, crumbly brownie. Should the chocolate accidentally seize, gently stir 2 to 3 tablespoons (30 to 45 mL) of warm water into the brownie mix after the eggs have been added. This should fix the batter without having to make any other adjustments.

CREAMY LEMON SQUARES
• *Makes one 8-inch (20 cm) square pan* •
Cuts into 25 or 36 squares

CREAM CHEESE IS the real secret behind these refrigerated lemon squares—it lends richness and a tang that enhances the tart lemon. It also gives the lemon filling structure so that it doesn't leak into or underneath the shortbread base. And making the recipe in a food processor keeps the work time to a minimum.

1. Preheat the oven to 350°F (175°C). Grease and line an 8-inch (20 cm) square pan with parchment paper so that the paper comes up the sides.
2. To prepare the base, pulse the flour and sugar in a food processor to combine. Add the butter and pulse until the mixture is an even, crumbly texture, but the dough should not come together. Press this into the prepared pan.
3. Bake for 15 to 18 minutes, until the base turns golden around the edges. Prepare the lemon layer while the crust cools.
4. In the food processor, pulse the cream cheese with $\frac{1}{2}$ cup (125 mL) of the sugar until smooth. Add the remaining 1 cup (250 mL) of sugar, the flour, lemon zest, and baking powder, and blend. Add the lemon juice and eggs, and blend until smooth, scraping down the sides of the processor once or twice. Pour the filling over the cooled crust.
5. Bake for 35 to 40 minutes, until the edges are set and just show signs of souffléing (rising a touch higher than the centre), but the centre should still have a bit of a jiggle to it. Cool the squares to room temperature and then chill for at least 3 hours before slicing. The square can be kept refrigerated for up to 3 days.

BASE:

1 cup (250 mL) all-purpose flour
¼ cup (60 mL) sugar
½ cup (125 mL) cold unsalted butter, cut in pieces

LEMON LAYER:

½ pkg (4 oz/125 g) cream cheese, at room temperature
1½ cups (375 mL) sugar
¼ cup (60 mL) all-purpose flour
2 tsp (10 mL) finely grated lemon zest
½ tsp (2 mL) baking powder
½ cup (125 mL) lemon juice
4 eggs

notes from anna's kitchen

1. A key to successful shortbread-based squares is to not overwork the shortbread crumb mixture. A typical shortbread base should be quite dry, loose, and crumbly when being pressed into the pan—it will set once baked. If you try to work in the butter to make the crust like dough, the base may shrink as it bakes, leaving a gap for liquid filling to seep in and under the crust.
2. If you fear you may have overworked the base, press the dough slightly up the sides of the pan (just ¼ inch/6 mm) and let the crust rest for 20 minutes before baking. This will relax the proteins (glutens) in the flour that can cause shrinking.

TANGY LEMON WALNUT SQUARES
• Makes one 8-inch (20 cm) square pan | Cuts into 16 or 25 squares •

WHILE THE CREAMY Lemon Squares (page 57) are more akin to the traditional, they must be stored in the refrigerator and are delicate. This version of lemon squares stores safely at room temperature and can survive in a cookie tin or on a dessert plate when layered or stacked with other treats.

1. Preheat the oven to 350°F (175°C). Lightly grease an 8-inch (20 cm) square pan and line the bottom and sides with parchment paper so that the paper hangs over the sides by a few inches.

2. For the base, combine the flour and walnut pieces in a food processor and pulse until the walnut pieces are finely ground. Add the icing sugar, lemon zest, and salt, and pulse. Add the cold butter, and pulse the mixture until it is a rough, crumbly texture. Pour the crumb mixture into the prepared pan and press down, pushing the crumbs just slightly up the edges of the pan (1/4 inch/6 mm).

3. Bake for about 25 minutes, until lightly browned. Cool before filling.

4. For the lemon layer, whisk the eggs and corn syrup until smooth. In a small bowl, whisk the lemon juice and cornstarch together. Stir in the zest and baking powder, and quickly whisk this into the egg mixture. Pour the filling overtop of the cooled crust.

5. Bake until set, with just a little jiggle in the centre, about 25 minutes. Cool to room temperature, remove from the pan, slice, then dust with icing sugar. The squares can be stored in an airtight container in a cool place for up to 3 days, or frozen, in a single layer, for up to 2 months.

BASE:

1½ cups (375 mL) all-purpose flour

¾ cup (185 mL) coarsely chopped walnut pieces

⅓ cup (80 mL) icing sugar

½ tsp (2 mL) finely grated lemon zest

¼ tsp (1 mL) salt

½ cup (125 mL) cold unsalted butter, cut in pieces

LEMON LAYER:

2 eggs, at room temperature

¾ cup (185 mL) white corn syrup

½ cup (125 mL) fresh lemon juice

2 Tbsp (30 mL) cornstarch

1 tsp (5 mL) finely grated lemon zest

½ tsp (2 mL) baking powder

Icing sugar, for dusting

Tangy Lemon Walnut Squares, top left (page 58) and *Creamy Lemon Squares*, top centre (page 57)

MAPLE PECAN CHOCOLATE SQUARES
• *Makes one 8-inch (20 cm) square pan* | *Cuts into 25 or 36 squares* •

*T*HESE SQUARES ARE very much like butter tart squares, but the addition of chocolate makes them easy to slice and store.

1. Preheat the oven to 350°F (175°C). Grease and line an 8-inch (20 cm) square pan with parchment paper so that the paper comes up the sides.
2. Prepare the base by stirring the flour, icing sugar, and salt together. Cut in the butter until the mixture is an even, crumbly texture (this can be done by hand, with beaters, or in a food processor). Press this mixture into the prepared pan.
3. Bake for 15 minutes, just until the edges start to turn golden. Cool the crust while preparing the filling.
4. Stir the brown sugar with the cornstarch, baking powder, and cinnamon in a large bowl. Whisk in the eggs, maple syrup, butter, vanilla, and vinegar or lemon juice. Stir in the pecan halves and chocolate chips, and pour this over the cooled crust.
5. Bake for about 25 minutes, until the outside edges of the filling are bubbling and the centre has a little jiggle to it when the pan is moved. Cool to room temperature, then chill completely before slicing. The squares can be stored in the refrigerator for up to 5 days.

BASE:

1¼ cups (310 mL) all-purpose flour
½ cup (125 mL) icing sugar, sifted
¼ tsp (1 mL) salt
½ cup (125 mL) cool unsalted butter

FILLING:

½ cup (125 mL) packed dark brown sugar
1 Tbsp (15 mL) cornstarch
½ tsp (2 mL) baking powder
¼ tsp (1 mL) ground cinnamon
2 eggs
½ cup (125 mL) pure maple syrup
¼ cup (60 mL) unsalted butter, melted
1 tsp (5 mL) vanilla extract
1 tsp (5 mL) white vinegar or lemon juice
2 cups (500 mL) pecan halves
1 cup (250 mL) chocolate chips

note from anna's kitchen

As you well know, measuring is important in baking, but quite often we assume our measuring cups and spoons are correct when in fact they might not be. For tips on how to assess the accuracy of your measuring tools, check out pages 4–5.

Maple Pecan Chocolate Squares,
top (page 60) and *Caramel
Walnut Shortbread Squares,*
bottom (page 62)

CARAMEL WALNUT SHORTBREAD SQUARES
• Makes one 8-inch (20 cm) square pan | Cuts into 25 or 36 squares •

THESE SQUARES ARE sinfully delightful, and very different from the butter tart–inspired filling of the Maple Pecan Chocolate Squares (page 60). These squares are assembled with a truly homemade caramel that envelops chunky walnut pieces in almost a candy-like fashion.

1. Preheat the oven to 350°F (175°C). Grease and line an 8-inch (20 cm) square pan with parchment paper so that the paper comes up the sides of the pan.

2. Stir the flour, sugar, and salt together. Cut in the butter until the mixture is a rough, crumbly texture (it should not come together as a dough). Press this mixture into the prepared pan and bake for about 15 minutes, until it just begins to brown at the edges. Cool while preparing the filling.

3. Place the sugar, cream of tartar, and water in a small saucepot and bring to a boil on high heat, uncovered and without stirring, occasionally brushing the sides of the pot with water until the sugar caramelizes to a rich amber colour, about 4 minutes. Remove the pot from the heat, and, watching out for the steam, whisk in the cream and butter until it is blended and looks like caramel (which it is, in fact). If the sugar sticks to the whisk or pot, return the pot to low heat and stir until evenly melted. Allow the caramel to cool for 10 minutes.

4. Whisk the egg in a medium bowl, then whisk in the brown sugar and vanilla. Gently whisk in the caramel, then stir in the walnut pieces. Pour this mixture into the prepared pan and spread the walnut pieces evenly. Bake for 20 minutes, until the outside edges are bubbling. Cool the squares to room temperature before slicing. The squares can be stored in an airtight container for up to 6 days.

BASE:

1 cup (250 mL) all-purpose flour
¼ cup (60 mL) sugar
¼ tsp (1 mL) salt
½ cup (125 mL) cool unsalted butter, cut in pieces

FILLING:

½ cup (125 mL) sugar
½ tsp (2 mL) cream of tartar
2 Tbsp (30 mL) water
¼ cup (60 mL) whipping cream
2 Tbsp (30 mL) unsalted butter
1 egg
½ cup (125 mL) packed light brown sugar
1 tsp (5 mL) vanilla extract
1½ cups (375 mL) walnut halves

note from anna's kitchen

Some squares freeze better than others, and the rule that applies to freezing cookies applies here: the more sugar a square contains, the softer it will be when it thaws after being frozen.

Squares like the Maple Pecan Chocolate Squares (page 60), these Caramel Walnut Shortbread Squares, and the other candy-style bars become very sticky when taken out of the freezer, but the cake-style squares and the crumble squares freeze very well.

APPLE-RAISIN WALNUT BARS
• Makes one 8-inch (20 cm) square pan | Cuts into 24 bars •

*T*HIS RECIPE MAKES a tall bar cake—it stands about 1½ inches (4 cm) high. It might seem very close to a coffee cake, but its little bit of extra sweetness makes it more of a dessert sweet than a morning treat.

1. Preheat the oven to 350°F (175°C). Grease and line an 8-inch (20 cm) square pan with parchment paper so that the paper hangs over the sides.
2. Beat the butter and sugar together and then add the eggs one at a time, beating well after each addition. Stir in the applesauce and vanilla.
3. In a separate bowl, stir the flour, oats, baking powder, cinnamon, baking soda, allspice, and salt to combine, and add this to the butter mixture, stirring until blended. Stir in the grated apple, raisins, and walnut pieces, and scrape the batter into the prepared pan. Bake for about 40 minutes, until a tester inserted in the centre of the pan comes out clean. While the bars are baking, prepare the glaze.
4. For the glaze, stir all the ingredients except for the vanilla together in a small saucepot and bring up to a simmer, stirring often. Once the mixture comes to a simmer, continue to cook and stir it for 2 minutes, then remove the pan from the heat to cool slightly. Stir in the vanilla.
5. Once the cake comes out of the oven, pour the glaze over the hot cake and let it cool completely in the pan before removing it to slice into bars. The bars will keep for up to 4 days in an airtight container.

BASE:

½ cup (125 mL) unsalted butter,
    at room temperature

1 cup (250 mL) packed light brown sugar

2 eggs, at room temperature

½ cup (125 mL) unsweetened applesauce

1 tsp (5 mL) vanilla extract

1 cup (250 mL) all-purpose flour

½ cup (125 mL) rolled oats

1 tsp (5 mL) baking powder

¾ tsp (4 mL) ground cinnamon

¼ tsp (1 mL) baking soda

¼ tsp (1 mL) ground allspice

¼ tsp (1 mL) salt

1 large apple, peeled and coarsely grated

½ cup (125 mL) raisins

½ cup (125 mL) walnut pieces

GLAZE:

⅓ cup (80 mL) packed light brown sugar

3 Tbsp (45 mL) whipping cream

3 Tbsp (45 mL) unsalted butter

1 tsp (5 mL) lemon or apple juice

½ tsp (2 mL) vanilla extract

ICED DATE CAKE SQUARES
• *Makes one 8-inch (20 cm) square pan | Cuts into 25 or 36 squares* •

*T*HE SIMMERED DATES that are the foundation for this recipe create a bar that is very much like a sticky toffee pudding in taste and texture, which makes for a nice autumn or wintertime treat.

1. Preheat the oven to 350°F (175°C). Grease and line an 8-inch (20 cm) square pan with parchment paper so that the paper comes up the sides.
2. In a small saucepot, bring the dates and apple cider (or juice) to just below a simmer. Shut off the heat and let the date mixture cool to room temperature. Purée the dates with the cider and transfer this mixture to a large bowl.
3. Whisk the sugar, oil, egg, and ginger into the date mixture.
4. In a separate bowl, sift the flour, cocoa, baking powder, cinnamon, salt, nutmeg, and allspice, and add to the date mixture, stirring until blended. Spread the batter into the prepared pan.
5. Bake for 35 to 40 minutes, until a tester inserted in the centre of the cake comes out clean. Cool the cake completely before icing.
6. For the icing, beat the butter and ½ cup (125 mL) of the icing sugar until smooth. Add the milk and vanilla, and beat in. Add the remaining ½ cup (125 mL) of icing sugar and beat until smooth. Spread the icing over the surface of the cooled cake and let it set for at least an hour before slicing into squares. The squares will keep in an airtight container for up to 3 days.

BASE:

¾ cup (185 mL) chopped pitted dates

¾ cup (185 mL) apple cider or apple juice

¾ cup (185 mL) sugar

¼ cup (60 mL) vegetable oil

1 egg

2 tsp (10 mL) finely grated fresh ginger

1 cup (250 mL) all-purpose flour

1 Tbsp (15 mL) cocoa powder

¾ tsp (4 mL) baking powder

½ tsp (2 mL) ground cinnamon

½ tsp (2 mL) salt

¼ tsp (1 mL) ground nutmeg

¼ tsp (1 mL) ground allspice

ICING:

2 Tbsp (30 mL) unsalted butter, at room temperature

1 cup (250 mL) icing sugar, sifted

1 Tbsp (15 mL) milk

½ tsp (2 mL) vanilla extract

For a dairy-free version, omit the frosting entirely or use margarine in it instead of butter and replace the milk with almond or soy milk.

dairy-free
VARIATION

Frosted Banana Nut Bars, left
(page 66) and *Iced Date Cake
Squares*, centre (page 64)

FROSTED BANANA NUT BARS

• Makes one 8-inch (20 cm) square pan | Cuts into 18 bars •

THESE BARS ARE different from banana bread—they are sweeter and denser, and slice easily into little bites. The orange zest gives a nice nuance to the bars and the frosting dresses them up a bit.

1. Preheat the oven to 350°F (175°C). Lightly grease and line an 8-inch (20 cm) baking pan with parchment paper so that the paper comes up the sides.
2. Cream the butter and sugar together, then beat in the egg, followed by the vanilla and orange zest. Stir in the banana and orange juice.
3. In a separate bowl, sift the flour, baking powder, and salt, and add this to the butter mixture, stirring until blended. Add the walnut pieces and stir in. Scrape the batter into the prepared pan and spread it evenly.
4. Bake for 25 to 30 minutes, until a tester inserted in the centre of the pan comes out clean. Cool the cake to room temperature in the pan.
5. For the frosting, beat the butter with 1 cup (250 mL) of the icing sugar until smooth. Stir in the orange juice, zest, and vanilla, then beat in the remaining ½ cup (125 mL) of icing sugar. Remove the banana cake from the pan and peel away the parchment paper. Frost the top of the cake and sprinkle it with walnut pieces. Let the frosting set, uncovered, for an hour before slicing it into 18 bars. Store the bars in an airtight container for up to 3 days.

BASE:

¼ cup (60 mL) unsalted butter, at room temperature
½ cup (125 mL) light brown sugar
1 egg, at room temperature
1 tsp (5 mL) vanilla extract
1 tsp (5 mL) finely grated orange zest
⅔ cup (160 mL) mashed ripe banana (about 1 large or 2 small)
2 Tbsp (30 mL) orange juice
1 cup (250 mL) all-purpose flour
½ tsp (2 mL) baking powder
¼ tsp (1 mL) salt
½ cup (125 mL) lightly toasted walnut pieces, plus extra for sprinkling

FROSTING:

3 Tbsp (45 mL) unsalted butter, at room temperature
1½ cups (375 mL) icing sugar, sifted
1 Tbsp (15 mL) orange juice
1 tsp (5 mL) finely grated orange zest
½ tsp (2 mL) vanilla extract

PEANUT BUTTER NANAIMO BARS
• Makes one 8-inch (20 cm) square pan | Cuts into 25 or 36 bars •

Nanaimo bars started as a winning dessert in a baking contest in Nanaimo, BC, and have evolved into a treat that we regard as a part of Canadian food culture. A peanut butter twist takes this Canadian classic to the next level.

1. Preheat the oven to 325°F (160°C). Grease and line an 8-inch (20 cm) square pan with parchment paper so that the paper comes up the sides.
2. To prepare the base, stir the cookie crumbs, sugar, cocoa, and coconut together. Stir in the melted butter, then stir in the egg and vanilla. Add the peanuts, and press the mixture into the bottom of the prepared pan. The crust will be soft, so you can use dampened fingers to press it in evenly. Bake the crust for 15 minutes, then cool while preparing the filling.
3. For the filling, beat the butter with the icing sugar and custard powder until it forms a thick paste. Add the peanut butter, cream, and vanilla, and beat until smooth. Spread this over the cooled crust, cover with plastic wrap (you can press the plastic wrap directly onto the peanut butter filling and rub it to make it really even), and chill until firm, about 2 hours.
4. For the topping, place the chocolate and butter in a metal or glass bowl over a saucepot of barely simmering water and stir until melted. Spread this mixture overtop of the chilled peanut butter filling and chill again until set, about an hour, before slicing into bars. The bars will keep refrigerated for up to 6 days.

BASE:

2 cups (500 mL) chocolate cookie crumbs
¼ cup (60 mL) sugar
⅓ cup (80 mL) cocoa powder, sifted
1 cup (250 mL) sweetened, flaked coconut
½ cup (125 mL) unsalted butter, melted
1 egg
1 tsp (5 mL) vanilla extract
½ cup (125 mL) roughly chopped, dry-roasted, salted peanuts

FILLING:

3 Tbsp (45 mL) unsalted butter, at room temperature
⅔ cup (160 mL) icing sugar, sifted
2 Tbsp (30 mL) custard powder
⅓ cup (80 mL) peanut butter, any kind you prefer
2 tsp (10 mL) half-and-half cream
1 tsp (5 mL) vanilla extract

TOPPING:

6 oz (175 g) semisweet chocolate, chopped
2 Tbsp (30 mL) unsalted butter

note from anna's kitchen
The custard powder in the filling is one of the key ingredients that qualify a Nanaimo bar as such, but you can actually omit it from this version without compromising the taste and texture.

D'ARTAGNAN BARS

• *Makes one 8-inch (20 cm) square pan | Cuts into 25 or 36 bars* •

---

*T*HIS IS A homemade version of a 3 Musketeers bar, a childhood favourite of mine. That super-sweet chocolate filling is, in fact, a variation on divinity, a soft and chewy meringue candy.

A candy thermometer is recommended for this recipe to ensure that the divinity candy layer achieves just the right melt-in-your-mouth result.

1. Preheat the oven to 350°F (175°C). Grease and line an 8-inch (20 cm) square pan with parchment paper so that the paper comes up the sides.

2. Prepare the crust by stirring the cookie crumbs, icing sugar, cocoa, and flour together. Add the melted butter and stir until fully combined. Press this mixture into the bottom of the prepared pan and bake the crust for 10 minutes. Cool the crust while making the filling.

3. For the filling, melt the chocolate in a metal or glass bowl resting over a saucepot of barely simmering water, stirring until melted. Set aside to cool. Whip the egg whites and salt in a large bowl until they just begin to hold a soft peak, and set aside.

4. Pour the water into a medium saucepot, then add the sugar and corn syrup. Without stirring, bring the mixture to a boil and continue to boil over high heat while brushing the sides of the pot with water until the sugar reaches a temperature of 255°F (124°C). Remove the sugar from the heat and carefully pour it into the whipped egg whites while beating at medium-high speed until fully added. Continue whipping the mixture until it cools almost to room temperature, about 7 minutes. Beat in the chocolate and vanilla, and quickly spread this over the cooled crust (you can use a lightly greased spatula to spread the candy evenly) and chill for an hour.

5. To prepare the topping, melt the milk chocolate in a metal or glass bowl placed over a saucepot of barely simmering water, stirring until melted. Pour the fluid chocolate onto the filling, tilt the pan to coat the filling evenly, and chill to set, about 3 hours. Cut the bars while chilled, but they can be stored in an airtight container at room temperature for up to 3 days.

BASE:

1¾ cups (435 mL) chocolate
cookie crumbs
¼ cup (60 mL) icing sugar, sifted
2 Tbsp (30 mL) cocoa powder, sifted
2 Tbsp (30 mL) all-purpose flour
½ cup (125 mL) unsalted butter, melted

FILLING:

4 oz (125 g) bittersweet chocolate,
chopped
2 egg whites, at room temperature
¼ tsp (1 mL) salt
½ cup (125 mL) water
2 cups (500 mL) sugar
½ cup (125 mL) white corn syrup
1 tsp (5 mL) vanilla extract

TOPPING:

6 oz (175 g) milk chocolate, chopped

note from anna's kitchen
For insight into the delectable world of chocolate, check out Chocolate 101 on page 9.

D'Artagnan Bars (page 68) and *Peanut Butter Nanaimo Bars* (page 67)

BOUNTIFUL COCONUT ALMOND BARS
• Makes one 8-inch (20 cm) square pan | Cuts into 25 or 36 bars •

*T*HESE BARS HAVE a soft chocolate base that holds a macaroon-like coconut filling just like the candy bar of a similar name. Topped with a layer of chocolate, these truly earn candy-bar status.

1. Preheat the oven to 350°F (175°C). Grease and line an 8-inch (20 cm) square pan with parchment paper so that the paper comes up the sides.
2. Melt the butter and chocolate in a small saucepot over low heat, stirring until smooth, then remove from the heat. Stir in the sugar, then add the egg and vanilla, stirring until blended. Add the flour and stir. Spread this mixture into the bottom of the prepared pan (it will be a very thin layer) and bake for 10 minutes until it loses its shine. Cool while preparing the filling.
3. For the filling, stir the coconut, almonds, condensed milk, vanilla, and salt to combine, and spread this over the cooled base. Bake for about 25 minutes, until a light golden brown. Cool to room temperature before adding the topping.
4. For the topping, melt the chocolate and butter in a metal bowl placed over a saucepot of barely simmering water, stirring until melted. Pour this mixture over the cooled coconut filling and spread evenly.
5. Chill the pan for about 2 hours to set the chocolate. Cut the squares while chilled, but then store and enjoy the squares at room temperature. The squares will keep in an airtight container for up to 5 days.

BASE:

¼ cup (60 mL) unsalted butter

1 oz (30 g) unsweetened chocolate, chopped

½ cup (125 mL) sugar

1 egg

½ tsp (2 mL) vanilla extract

⅓ cup (80 mL) all-purpose flour

FILLING:

1⅓ cups (330 mL) sweetened, flaked coconut

1 cup (250 mL) sliced almonds

1 tin (300 mL) sweetened condensed milk

1 tsp (5 mL) vanilla extract

¼ tsp (1 mL) salt

TOPPING:

5 oz (150 g) semisweet chocolate, chopped

2 Tbsp (30 mL) unsalted butter

CHOCOLATE PEANUT PRETZEL SQUARES
• Makes one 8-inch (20 cm) square pan | Cuts into 25 squares •

*S*ALTY AND CRUNCHY, sweet and soft, these squares deliver for just about any craving. The base is quite similar to chocolate chip cookie dough, and the topping is reminiscent of chocolate haystacks.

1. Preheat the oven to 350°F (175°C). Lightly grease an 8-inch (20 cm) square pan and line the bottom and sides with parchment paper so that the paper hangs over the sides by a few inches.
2. Cream the butter with the sugars until smooth and fluffy. Beat in the egg yolks and vanilla.
3. In a separate bowl, stir the flour, oats, and salt to combine, then stir this into the butter mixture until blended. Spread the batter into the prepared pan.
4. Bake for about 30 minutes, until lightly browned. While the base is baking, prepare the topping.
5. For the topping, melt and stir the chocolate with the butter and corn syrup in a metal or glass bowl placed over a saucepot of barley simmering water. Remove the bowl from the heat and stir in the chopped pretzel pieces and the peanuts. Pierce the warm base with a paring knife (this allows the topping to grip on) and spread the chocolate mixture over the base. Chill until set, at least 2 hours. Slice the squares with a hot, dry knife. Serve at room temperature. The squares will keep in an airtight container or refrigerated for 5 days.

BASE:

1 cup (250 mL) unsalted butter, at room temperature
½ cup (125 mL) packed dark brown sugar or demerara sugar
½ cup (125 mL) sugar
2 egg yolks
1 tsp (5 mL) vanilla extract
1 cup (250 mL) all-purpose flour
1 cup (250 mL) regular oats
½ tsp (2 mL) salt

TOPPING:

8 oz (240 g) semisweet chocolate, chopped
3 Tbsp (45 mL) unsalted butter, at room temperature
2 Tbsp (30 mL) corn syrup
1 cup (250 mL) pretzel pieces, lightly crushed
¾ cup (185 mL) chopped peanuts (salted or unsalted)

RASPBERRY CRUMBLE BARS
• *Makes one 8-inch (20 cm) square pan | Cuts into 18 bars* •

egg-
FREE

CARDAMOM GIVES THESE squares an unexpected kick that complements the raspberry jam, but allspice is just as nice if you don't have cardamom in your pantry.

2½ cups (625 mL) all-purpose flour
½ cup (125 mL) sugar
2 Tbsp (30 mL) cornmeal
½ tsp (2 mL) baking powder
½ tsp (2 mL) salt
¼ tsp (1 mL) ground cardamom or ground allspice
1 cup (250 mL) cool unsalted butter, cut in pieces
1 cup (250 mL) raspberry jam

1. Preheat the oven to 350°F (175°C) and line an 8-inch (20 cm) square pan with parchment paper so the paper hangs over the sides a little.
2. Stir the flour, sugar, cornmeal, baking powder, salt, and cardamom or allspice to blend. Cut in the butter until the mixture is a rough, crumbly texture (this can be done in a food processor and pulsed until crumbly). Firmly press 3 cups of the crumble into the bottom of the prepared pan. Stir the raspberry jam to soften it and spread this evenly over the pressed crumble. Sprinkle the remaining crumble on top and press down gently.
3. Bake the bars for about 30 minutes, until they just begin to brown around the edges. Cool the bars to room temperature, then chill them for at least 2 hours before slicing into 18 bars. The bars will keep in the refrigerator for up to 5 days.

note from anna's kitchen
Most crumble squares follow a common technique for assembly. The trick to a crumble-style square that stays together when sliced is to firmly press down the base layer, top with the fruit, sprinkle the top layer overtop, then just gently press down on the top layer.

CINNAMON-APPLE ALMOND STREUSEL SQUARES
• *Makes one 8-inch (20 cm) square pan* •
Cuts into 25 squares

egg-
FREE

IF I DON'T have time to make an apple pie but crave the taste, I make these squares in its place.

BASE:
¾ cup (185 mL) ground almonds
⅔ cup (160 mL) all-purpose flour
¼ cup (60 mL) icing sugar, sifted
½ cup (125 mL) cool unsalted butter, cut in pieces

STREUSEL:
1½ cups (375 mL) all-purpose flour
⅓ cup (80 mL) packed light brown sugar
1 tsp (5 mL) ground cinnamon
¼ tsp (1 mL) ground nutmeg
¼ tsp (1 mL) baking powder
6 Tbsp (90 mL) cool unsalted butter, cut in pieces
1½ cups (375 mL) peeled and coarsely grated tart apple, such as Granny Smith or Mutsu
Icing sugar, for dusting

1. Preheat the oven to 350°F (175°C). Line an 8-inch (20 cm) square pan with parchment paper so that the paper hangs over the sides a little.
2. For the base, stir the ground almonds, flour, and icing sugar together. Cut in the butter (by hand, using beaters, or in a food processor) until the mixture is a rough and crumbly texture. Press this into the prepared pan and chill it while preparing the streusel.
3. For the streusel, stir the flour, brown sugar, cinnamon, nutmeg, and baking powder together. Cut in the butter by hand until the mixture is a rough and crumbly texture. Stir in the grated apple to coat it well. Gently press this onto the chilled base.
4. Bake for about 35 minutes, until it just begins to turn golden. Cool completely before slicing, and dust with icing sugar to garnish. The squares can be stored in an airtight container for 3 days.

OAT AND DRIED FRUIT SQUARES
• Makes one 8-inch (20 cm) square pan | Cuts into 25 squares •

egg-
FREE

*I*N THE SAME family as date squares, these squares offer a complexity of taste and texture because of the mixed dried fruit. But these are easier to make than traditional date squares since the dried fruit is simply sprinkled over the oat layer—no need to cook it down.

1. Preheat the oven to 375°F (190°C) and line an 8-inch (20 cm) square pan with parchment paper so that it hangs over the sides just a little.
2. Melt the butter in a small saucepot. Remove the pot from the heat and stir in the brown sugar and corn syrup until evenly blended. In a bowl, combine the oats and spices, pour the butter mixture overtop, and stir to blend.
3. Press half of this oat mixture into the prepared pan. Sprinkle the dried fruit evenly over the oat base, then top with the remaining oat mixture, pressing gently (it's all right if the fruit peeks through the top layer here and there).
4. Bake the squares for about 20 minutes, until they are an even golden brown. Cool the pan completely before using the parchment paper to pull out the square as a whole, then slice. The squares will keep in an airtight container for up to 4 days.

¾ cup (185 mL) unsalted butter

¼ cup (60 mL) packed light brown sugar

¼ cup (60 mL) golden corn syrup

2¾ cups (685 mL) rolled oats

½ tsp (2 mL) ground cinnamon

¼ tsp (1 mL) ground allspice

⅔ cup (160 mL) coarsely chopped pitted dates

½ cup (125 mL) coarsely chopped pitted prunes

⅓ cup (80 mL) dried cranberries

PEACHY KAMUT® CRUMBLE SQUARES
• Makes one 8-inch (20 cm) square pan | Cuts into 36 squares •

Kᴀᴍᴜᴛ® ɪs ᴀ specific brand of an ancient wheat grain, and is best suited to organic growing. It has an earthy, nutty taste similar to whole wheat flour, but yields a more delicate structure.

1. Preheat the oven to 350°ꜰ (175°ᴄ). Grease and line an 8-inch (20 cm) square pan with parchment paper so that the paper comes up the sides of the pan.
2. Mix the Kamut® flour, demerara sugar, cornstarch, flaxseed, cinnamon, and allspice to combine. Cut in the butter until the mixture is a rough and crumbly texture. Whisk the egg white with a fork, and stir it into the crumble (which will remain a crumbly texture). Press two-thirds of this mixture into the prepared pan. Stir the jam to soften it, and spread it over the surface of the base. Sprinkle the remaining crumble dough over the jam and gently press it down.
3. Bake for 20 to 25 minutes, until it browns just a little. Let it cool to room temperature before chilling to slice. The squares can be stored in the refrigerator for up to 5 days.

1½ cups (375 mL) Kamut® flour
⅓ cup (80 mL) packed demerara or dark brown sugar
¼ cup (60 mL) cornstarch
2 Tbsp (30 mL) ground flaxseed
½ tsp (2 mL) ground cinnamon
¼ tsp (1 mL) ground allspice
½ cup (125 mL) cool unsalted butter, cut in pieces
1 egg white
1 cup (250 mL) peach jam

egg-free
VARIATION

You can make this recipe egg-free by replacing the egg white with an additional 1 tablespoon (15 mL) of ground flaxseed stirred with 1 tablespoon (15 mL) of applesauce. Stir this into the crumble mixture before pressing the dough into the pan.

Oat and Dried Fruit Squares (page 73) and *Peachy Kamut® Crumble Squares* (page 74)

pies and tarts

Pie is a staple dessert in North America, and fruit and cream pies have not just been a staple at home and in diners, but in fine-dining restaurants, too. But this universally popular dessert is also one of the more time-consuming desserts to make, and it seems to have the most warnings in its process, making us a little fearful and too quick to second-guess ourselves, particularly in making the crust.

In North America, the recipe methods are often filled with negatives—don't let the butter get warm, don't overwork the dough, don't add too much water—to the point where we *don't* end up making the recipe at all!

In doing a little research, I found that the European technique, especially the French, for *pâte brisée* and *pâte à foncer* (the same as pie pastry) is a lot more relaxed and far more positive. They do not fuss over cold butter, and, in fact, many recipes call for room-temperature butter. They work the dough quite thoroughly, and they use a fair bit of liquid, making the dough easy to roll without cracking.

So with a positive and relaxed approach, and a good ratio of ingredients, anyone can make a tender, tasty, and flaky pie dough.

PIE DOUGH ESSENTIALS

Making pie dough can be broken down into four general areas for contemplation: the ingredients, mixing, resting, and rolling. Here are the basics behind each.

Ingredients

FATS: BUTTER, MARGARINE, SHORTENING, OR LARD Bakers debate fats as passionately as others debate politics. Over the years, I have created and used many pie pastry recipes with all of the above fats, alone and in combination.

» *Butter* Unlike shortening or lard, butter's consistency changes dramatically from chilled to room temperature, and because the butter softens as the dough is mixed, it can falsely create a sense that a dough could be ruined if overworked. Butter-based pie dough requires less liquid (egg and water) than the other three fat choices, and is actually quite easy to handle once the dough has had a chance (about 30 minutes) to sit out of the fridge. Plain and simple, for taste and workability, butter is my preferred choice.

» *Lard* Although some still swear by using this rendered pork fat in pie pastry (particularly for butter tarts), it can result in a sandy, albeit tender, texture to the pastry dough.

» *Margarine* Hydrogenated margarine handles better than unhydrogenated in pastry dough, but then you have the issue of trans fats, making butter the better option if you have to choose. Margarine can be an appropriate dairy-free option, but you will have to add 1 to 2 tablespoons (15 to 30 mL) more of cool water to bring the dough together to make it workable.

» *Shortening* Vegetable shortening is shelf-stable and hydrogenated. Because of this hydrogenation, it is easiest to work into pie dough, but the combination of trans fats plus a sometimes-greasy taste and texture makes this a less popular option these days. Shortening-based pie dough needs more water than a butter pastry to make it workable.

EGG Some pie pastry recipes call for egg, others do not. An egg offers moisture, reducing the amount of water needed to bring the dough together, and the yolk provides richness and tenderness, while the white gives the dough structure.

WATER The majority of pie pastry recipes list a range of water to add, like 2 to 5 tablespoons (30 to 75 mL), giving you, the baker, room to wonder how much is needed. With accurate measuring and extensive testing, the piedough recipe in this book (page 82) takes the guesswork out of the water content. Two tablespoons (30 mL) of water provide enough moisture to bring the dough together and roll without cracking, and it is little enough to keep a tender and flaky texture.

VINEGAR OR LEMON JUICE A little acidity is the key to a flaky and tender pastry. Protein development can cause pie dough to shrink back when you roll it, or to shrink in the pie plate. The acid shortens the gluten, or protein strands, in dough.

SUGAR Sugar is added for a similar effect as the acidity, to shorten the protein development and make for a tender pastry. It sweetens the dough, but only a touch, so that the same pastry dough can be used for savoury recipes like quiche.

Mixing

How can you tell when pie dough has been mixed to just the right texture? Regardless of the mixing tool, the dough should come together, but stray crumbs can be present if they can easily be pressed into the dough when shaping it into a disc (if the crumbs are dry and floury, then mix the dough a touch more). It's all right for a few thin streaks of butter to still be visible in the dough. The tool you use will impact how long it takes to reach this point.

BY HAND Mixing by hand using a pastry cutter or even two criss-crossing butter knives is the best way to keep in touch with your dough since you are directing the action. If you are blessed with cold hands (it is one of the few times I am grateful to have naturally cold hands), you can use your fingers to cut in the butter.

This process takes longer than using beaters, a stand mixer, or a food processor, but the results will be the same. It's best to actually cut the butter into small pieces while cold, then let it sit out for 30 minutes before working it into the dough. This may seem contrary to how you may have been taught, but the slightly softer butter cuts into the flour faster so you run a lower risk of overworking the dough. Additionally, slightly softened butter works in more evenly—cold butter can shatter and break into uneven pieces so you are left with some butter worked into the dough a little too much and other bits that are still chunky.

STAND MIXER Using the paddle attachment, it is easy to evenly incorporate first the butter and then the liquids into the flour. Always mix on the lowest or second lowest speed to avoid exercising and lengthening those glutens.

Butter that has been cut into pieces and left out for 30 minutes is also recommended here. It will take only a minute or so to work the butter into the flour compared to twice that time for ice-cold butter (which would be twice the time exercising that flour!).

FOOD PROCESSOR The quick action of the blade makes pie dough come together in a snap, but be sure to use only the pulse function to keep control. This is the one tool with which I recommend using cold butter directly from the fridge, since the friction of the fast-moving blade will warm up that butter just a touch.

ELECTRIC BEATERS This is not a favourable choice since the dough can get stuck in the beaters and the motor could even overheat once the liquid is added. Mix by hand instead.

Resting

Time is a pie pastry's good friend during the entire process, and most of that time is used for resting the dough, wrapped and, in most cases, refrigerated. It is critically important to let the dough rest for a minimum of an hour before rolling it. It is less about rechilling the butter as it is about letting those protein strands, the glutens, relax. Every time you work dough, whether mixing it or rolling it, you should give it time to rest. That little bit of time will save you much frustration down the road, since this simple step is a necessary contribution to a pie crust that is tender and flaky and does not shrink as it bakes.

Rolling

The same principle of making the dough with slightly softened butter applies to rolling the pie dough: pull the dough out of the refrigerator 30 minutes before you wish to roll it and you'll find it rolls easily, with little cracking. In fact, because it rolls so easily and quickly, you'll be exercising those glutens less, ensuring a tender pastry.

Think about it in the way you butter toast: If you try to spread cold butter on your toast, what happens? It cracks and breaks, it's hard to manage, and you tear your toast in the process. And if you spread slightly softened butter? It spreads easily and evenly, and your toast remains intact.

To test that your dough is soft enough to roll, press your thumb into it. You should be able to make an indentation with just a little pressure. If it doesn't yield, give the dough another 10 minutes to warm up.

ROLLING PIN BASICS

Materials

WOOD The most common and most practical choice. Wood holds an even temperature, which is why professional pastry kitchens are equipped with wooden tables used for most rolling tasks.

MARBLE More of a novelty. Marble does stay cool, so buttery pastry will stay chilled. The weight of the marble does provide good leverage when rolling firmly set dough.

PLASTIC A more affordable rolling pin option, but plastic

pins sometimes have a visible seam, and this line may show up or leave a mark in the pastry being rolled.

Styles

FRENCH-CURVED PIN The preferred choice. This pin has no handles, so you roll with your hands directly overtop the pastry, so you can feel it as you roll. The gentle curve allows you to shape the dough effortlessly, with very little spring-back because you are not forcing the dough in a back-and-forth direction. Perfect for all pastries, but best suited to delicate rolling tasks.

FRENCH-FLAT PIN Similar to the curved pin in that it has no handles, but it lacks the curve. You still have great control, and this style can sometimes be a little thicker than the curved pin, giving you more rolling leverage. A great all-purpose pin.

HANDLED ROLLING PIN The most familiar. This pin has handles separate from the base of the pin. You do get good leverage when rolling, but with your hands at the sides of the dough, you can lose a sense of the dough and risk getting cracks or rolling unevenly without realizing it.

Cleaning

After rolling your pastry, gently scrape off any flour or dough pieces, hand wash with very little soap, and dry immediately. Like a cast-iron pan, your wooden rolling pin becomes "seasoned" from the butter after repeated rolling. You'll find that after frequent use, you'll hardly have to dust your rolling pin with flour and pastry dough will rarely stick to it.

MIRACULOUS MERINGUES

Meringues seem simple enough, but getting comfortable with whipped egg whites can sometimes take a little practice. These guidelines will take a little guesswork out of the process for you.

Basic Types of Meringue

COMMON MERINGUE This is made of room-temperature egg whites whipped with a little sugar. This is typically the topping for Lemon Meringue Pie (pages 92–94), or it can be baked until crisp in a low-temperature oven to make bird's nests or simple cookies.

SWISS MERINGUE This is made when egg whites and sugar are whipped while placed over a pot of simmering water, which cooks the egg whites. Once the mixture is whipped after coming off of the heat, it becomes seven-minute frosting. This meringue suits desserts that aren't refrigerated, as it will melt or become sticky once chilled.

ITALIAN MERINGUE This is made when room-temperature egg whites are whipped, then sugar that has been cooked to 239°F (115°C) is poured into them while whipping. This is the most stable of the meringues and is the base for Italian buttercream frosting, a wedding-cake staple, and it is fantastic for Lemon Meringue Pie (pages 92–94). It's a little sweeter than a common meringue, and its very fine bubble structure and cooked sugar keeps the meringue in place and prevents weeping.

What Happened?

Here are some common pitfalls that happen to professional and home bakers alike, and how to avoid or fix them.

EGG WHITES WON'T WHIP This could be because of residual oil in the bowl or on the beaters, or because a little egg yolk slipped in when separating the eggs. Fat is the enemy of volume in egg whites, so to ensure that no oil effects your whites, slightly dampen a cloth with white vinegar and wipe your bowl and beaters with it before adding the whites. (If you have already begun beating, notice the whites aren't whipping, and believe oil is the culprit, it's best to start again with a clean bowl and new egg whites). Another reason whites won't whip is because they are cold. Room-temperature egg whites are flexible and stretch to a fuller volume than cold egg whites, so just wait for your egg whites to warm up a bit.

WEEPING MERINGUE If, after a few hours in the fridge, sugar droplets start forming on the outside of the meringue, you may have over-whipped your egg whites. When the bubbles in a common meringue are stretched to their maximum through over whipping, a temperature change can cause them to burst, and they'll release a little of the sugar they've been holding, resulting in a weeping meringue. Humidity can also be a culprit here. If it is a hot and humid summer day, and the fridge has been opened and closed repeatedly, this can also cause a bit of weeping. Unfortunately, once meringue weeps, there is no fix for it other than eating the evidence. The Italian meringue recipe for the Lemon Meringue Pie (pages 92–94) in this book typically doesn't weep.

SLIDING MERINGUE Does your meringue slide around on the top of your pie? This could be due to one or two things. First, an over-whipped meringue slides on the lemon filling for the same reason it weeps: the sugar is coming out of the meringue. Second, the shock of a drastic temperature change can cause sliding meringue. Putting room-temperature meringue onto an ice-cold filling and then cooking it in a hot oven can cause the meringue to sweat, and the filling might even get condensation on its surface; this moisture layer will cause the meringue to slide. To avoid this, bake the meringue on a pie filling that has fully cooled to room temperature, or, if the filling was made ahead of time and chilled, give the pie a chance to warm up a little before baking on the meringue.

Whipped into Action

Recipes call for three levels of whipping for egg whites, determined by the desired final result. To have full control over your meringue, and to give yourself a wider range of time from soft to stiff peak, try whipping your egg whites on one speed below high. This does not compromise the volume of the meringue at all, and you'll have a better opportunity to evaluate your whites. Your beaters or whisk are the best way to gauge the peak of your whites.

SOFT PEAK This is the first level past foamy, when the meringue takes on a white colour. When you lift your beaters from the whites and invert them, the whites should curl over easily.

MEDIUM PEAK This is the point not too long after soft peak, and when you lift the beaters and turn them upside down, the meringue should just bend at the tip, not fully curl over.

STIFF PEAK After you've crossed soft and medium peak, stiff peak soon follows. When you invert your beaters, the meringue should stand upright, with no bend at all.

If you fear that you may have over-whipped your egg whites at any level of peak, time is your cure. Over whipped whites will deflate after 5 to 10 minutes. Just let the whites sit in the bowl where they will settle and even separate slightly, then re-whip gently either by hand or on medium speed (not low or high) with beaters and hit that perfect peak you missed the first time around.

Soft peak

Medium peak

Stiff peak

DOUBLE-CRUST PIE DOUGH
• Makes enough pastry for one 2-crust pie •

foundation
RECIPE

THIS PIE PASTRY recipe has all the taste and texture elements it should. The butter makes it melt-in-your-mouth tasty, the egg gives it structure so that it won't become soggy, and the little bit of acidity promotes tenderness.

Although some recipes in this chapter call for a single pie crust, I recommend making this double-crust recipe and freezing half for later use. A double-crust recipe is easier to mix (and measuring half an egg for a single-crust recipe is possible but not always precise).

1 cup (250 mL) cold unsalted butter
2⅓ cups (580 mL) all-purpose flour
4 tsp (20 mL) sugar
1 tsp (5 mL) salt
1 egg, directly from the fridge
2 Tbsp (30 mL) cold water
2 tsp (10 mL) white vinegar
   or lemon juice

1. While it's cold, cut the butter into small pieces and then leave it out of the fridge for 30 minutes. Combine the flour, sugar, and salt. Add the butter to the flour, mixing it in until the dough is a rough, crumbly texture.
2. In a separate bowl, whisk the egg, water, and vinegar or lemon juice, and add it to the dough all at once, mixing until the dough comes together. Shape the dough into 2 logs or discs, wrap them each in plastic wrap, and chill them for at least 1 hour before rolling.
3. The pie dough can be frozen for up to 6 months and thawed in the refrigerator.

note from anna's kitchen
For the full scoop on pie dough, including using a mixer or food processor, please refer to Pie Dough Essentials (pages 78–79). And for notes on why unsalted butter is best, see pages 12–13.

Shaping dough for a pie shell

FRESH APPLE STREUSEL PIE
• *Makes one 9-inch (23 cm) pie* | *Serves 8* •

*A*LTHOUGH IN THIS book I have provided many classic fillings for fresh- and cooked-fruit pies in two simple charts (page 88 and page 90), apple pie seems to stand out on its own. Apple pie is the most popular fruit pie to make, and its filling, sweetness, and set are different from other fruit fillings.

1. Pull the chilled pie dough out of the fridge 30 minutes before rolling. Preheat the oven to 375°F (190°C). Lightly dust the bottom of a 9-inch (23 cm) pie plate with flour and place it on a parchment- or foil-lined baking tray.

2. On a lightly floured surface, roll out the pastry to just under $\frac{1}{4}$ inch (6 mm) thick. Lift the rolled dough and line the pie plate with it. Trim away any excess dough that hangs more than 1 inch (2.5 cm) over the edge of the pie plate. Tuck this outside bit of pastry under itself, and pinch this crust into a decorative pattern. Sprinkle the oats over the rolled pie pastry (this absorbs excess liquids and helps to keep the bottom crust crisp), and chill it while preparing the rest of the filling and the streusel.

3. To prepare the apples, first toss the slices with the lemon juice, then stir in the sugar, butter pieces, flour, and cinnamon. Set aside.

4. To prepare the streusel, stir the flour, $\frac{1}{3}$ cup (80 mL) oats, brown sugar, cinnamon, and salt to combine. Cut in the butter until the mixture is a rough crumbly texture.

5. Spoon the apples into the chilled pie shell and pat down. Sprinkle the streusel over the apples, then bake the pie on the prepared tray for 20 minutes. Reduce the oven temperature to 350°F (175°C) and continue to cook the pie on the tray for 40 to 45 minutes more, until the outside crust is evenly browned and the apple filling is bubbling at the edges. Cool the pie for at least 3 hours before slicing, or chill to serve cold. The pie will keep in the refrigerator for up to 4 days.

½ recipe Double-Crust Pie Dough (page 82), chilled

FILLING:

3 Tbsp (45 mL) rolled oats

6 cups (1.5 L) peeled and thinly sliced apples, such as Cortland, Spartan, Spy, Honey Crisp, Granny Smith, Mutsu, or any combination

2 Tbsp (30 mL) lemon juice

⅔ cup (160 mL) sugar

2 Tbsp (30 mL) cool unsalted butter, cut in pieces

2 Tbsp (30 mL) all-purpose flour

1 tsp (5 mL) ground cinnamon

STREUSEL:

1 cup (250 mL) all-purpose flour

⅓ cup (80 mL) rolled oats

¼ cup (60 mL) packed light brown sugar

1 tsp (5 mL) ground cinnamon

½ tsp (2 mL) salt

6 Tbsp (90 mL) cool unsalted butter, cut in pieces

note from anna's kitchen
The apple variety you select for your pie is a personal choice—it depends on your own tastes and the tastes of those you are serving—but this recipe suggests the most popular apples. Having judged many apple pie contests over the years, I have found that most prize-winning pies are made of a mix of at least two, but usually three, apple varieties.

TWO-CRUST CARAMEL APPLE PIE

• Makes one 9-inch (23 cm) pie | Serves 8 •

*T*HIS APPLE PIE is sort of a cross between *tarte tatin* (a French apple pie) and a traditional apple pie. By first caramelizing the sugar and then stirring in the apples so they soften just a bit, you get an evenly sweetened pie, with excess juices thickened by the caramel so that they stay in the pie as you slice it and don't run over the bottom of the pie plate.

1. Pull the chilled pie dough out of the fridge 30 minutes before rolling. Lightly dust the bottom of a 9-inch (23 cm) pie plate with flour, and place it on a parchment- or foil-lined baking tray.

2. On a lightly floured surface, roll out one disc of the pastry to just under ¼ inch (6 mm) thick. Lift the rolled dough, line the pie plate with it, and sprinkle the pastry with the oats. Roll out the second disc of pastry to ¼ inch (6 mm) thick. Cut a 1-inch (2.5 cm) hole in the centre of the pastry (so steam can escape as the pie bakes). Chill both the lined pie plate and rolled top crust while preparing the filling.

3. Preheat the oven to 400°F (200°C). In a large, heavy-bottomed saucepot, bring the water, sugar, and lemon juice up to a boil without stirring. Continue to boil the sugar without stirring, occasionally brushing the sides of the pot with water, until the sugar caramelizes, about 3 minutes. Add the apples all at once and stir to coat. Add the butter and cinnamon, and stir. Once the juices return to a simmer, remove the pot from the heat and cool for 5 minutes.

4. Pull the chilled pie shell from the fridge and pour the apples and all the juices into it (the juices will absorb into the apples as the pie bakes). Top the fruit with the second rolled piece of pie pastry. Trim excess dough and pinch the edges of the pastries into a decorative pattern. Whisk the egg with the 2 tablespoons (30 mL) of water, and brush the pie dough with the mixture. Sprinkle with sugar.

5. On the prepared baking tray, bake the pie for 15 minutes, then reduce the oven temperature to 375°F (190°C) and bake for another 30 to 40 minutes, until the crust is an even golden brown. Let the pie cool at least 3 hours before slicing, or chill to serve cold. The pie will keep in the refrigerator for up to 4 days.

1 recipe Double-Crust Pie Dough (page 82), chilled
3 Tbsp (45 mL) rolled oats
¼ cup (60 mL) water
1 cup (250 mL) sugar
2 Tbsp (30 mL) lemon juice
6 cups (1.5 L) peeled and sliced apples, such as Mutsu or Granny Smith
3 Tbsp (45 mL) unsalted butter
1 tsp (5 mL) ground cinnamon

FOR BRUSHING:

1 egg
2 Tbsp (30 mL) water
Turbinado or granulated sugar, for sprinkling

FRESH FRUIT PIE

• *Makes one 9-inch (23 cm) pie | Serves 8* •

*A*FRESH FRUIT PIE should be just that: fresh, and simple. The greatest effort goes into making the crust, so with that done, the filling is a simple tossing of ingredients.

Here is a chart of filling-ingredient ratios for a nicely set (not too runny, not too thick) and nicely sweetened (not too sweet, not too tart) fruit pie.

1 recipe Double-Crust Pie Dough (page 82), chilled
2 Tbsp (30 mL) rolled oats

FOR BRUSHING:

1 egg
1 Tbsp (15 mL) water
Turbinado sugar, for sprinkling

FRUIT	QUICK-COOK TAPIOCA	SUGAR	OTHER
3 cups (750 mL) quartered fresh strawberries 3 cups (750 mL) diced fresh rhubarb	2 Tbsp (30 mL)	1½ cups (375 mL)	1 tsp (5 mL) vanilla extract
6 cups (1.5 L) diced fresh rhubarb	2 Tbsp (30 mL)	1¾ cups (435 mL)	1 tsp (5 mL) vanilla extract
5 cups (1.25 L) fresh blueberries	2 Tbsp (30 mL)	1 cup (250 mL)	3 Tbsp (45 mL) lemon juice 2 tsp (10 mL) lemon zest
5 cups (1.25 L) fresh raspberries	2 Tbsp (30 mL)	1¼ cups (310 mL)	1 Tbsp (15 mL) lemon juice 1 tsp (5 mL) vanilla extract
6 cups (1.5 L) peeled and sliced peaches	2 Tbsp (30 mL)	1 cup (250 mL)	1 tsp (5 mL) vanilla extract ¼ tsp (1 mL) ground cinnamon

1. While the pie dough is chilling, prepare the fruit. Toss the fruit with the tapioca and let the mixture sit for 5 minutes so the tapioca can soften. Stir in the sugar and other ingredients to coat.
2. Pull the pastry out of the fridge 30 minutes before rolling. Preheat the oven to 400°F (200°C). Place a 9-inch (23 cm) pie plate onto a parchment-lined baking tray and dust the pie plate with flour (do not grease).

3. On a lightly floured work surface, roll out the first pastry disc to just under ¼ inch (6 mm) thick and line the prepared pie plate. Sprinkle the oats over the pastry. Spoon the filling into the shell. Roll out the remaining pastry disc and cut out a small hole in the centre of the pastry. Place the rolled pastry overtop the fruit and press the edges together. Trim away any excess dough, and pinch the edges to create a pattern (or use a fork to pinch the pastry edges together).

4. Whisk the egg and water, brush the surface of the pastry with the egg mixture, and sprinkle the pie with turbinado sugar.

5. On the prepared baking tray, bake the pie for 12 minutes at 400°F (200°C), then reduce the heat to 375°F (190°C) and bake for about 40 more minutes, until the crust is a rich golden brown and the filling is bubbling. Cool the pie for at least 2 hours before slicing. The pie can be made a day ahead and served chilled.

notes from anna's kitchen

1. You can use other fresh fruits and berries, and in any combination. Use the table to gauge the volume of fruit and sugar. For example, use the rhubarb proportions for a blackberry pie, and the blueberry proportions for bumbleberry, a mixed-berry pie. What remains constant is the tapioca for thickening.

2. Quick-cook tapioca is the ideal choice to thicken the juices that cook out of the fruit. Tapioca softens quickly, imparts no flavour, thickens without being stodgy, and, unlike cornstarch, doesn't need to hit 212°F (100°C) to thicken. You could use tapioca starch instead, but quick-cook tapioca can be found in the baking aisle of all grocery stories, whereas tapioca starch is a little more specialized and can be purchased at health and bulk stores.

3. Fresh fruit works better than frozen in a pie recipe. Some fruits have tougher skins after being frozen, and some fruits, like raspberries, are far too watery to use for pie after they've been frozen.

4. If using a convection oven, bake the pie at 375°F (190°C) with the fan on for the first 12 minutes, then simply turn the fan off but leave the temperature at 375°F (190°C) for the remaining 40 minutes.

COOKED FRUIT PIE
• Makes one 9-inch (23 cm) pie | Serves 8 •

*T*HE FRUIT PIE on pages 88–89 suits uncooked, fresh fruit; these cooked fillings can be made using frozen fruit, since the simmering process softens the skins and allows excess liquids to be controllably thickened. Cornstarch, as opposed to tapioca, is used here since the fruit filling is fully simmered.

1 recipe Double-Crust Pie Dough (page 82), chilled
2 Tbsp (30 mL) rolled oats

FOR BRUSHING:
1 egg
1 Tbsp (15 mL) water
Turbinado sugar, for sprinkling

FRUIT	SUGAR	CORNSTARCH	OTHER
6 cups (1.5 L) blueberries (fresh or frozen)	1½ cups (375 mL)	3½ Tbsp (52.5 mL)	3 Tbsp (45 mL) lemon juice 2 tsp (10 mL) lemon zest
6 cups (1.5 L) raspberries (fresh or frozen)	1½ cups (375 mL)	3½ Tbsp (52.5 mL)	1 Tbsp (15 mL) lemon juice 1 tsp (5 mL) vanilla extract
6 cups (1.5 L) pitted tart cherries (fresh or frozen)	1⅓ cups (330 mL)	4 Tbsp (60 mL)	¼ tsp (1 mL) ground cinnamon 1 tsp (5 mL) vanilla extract
5 cups (1.25 L) blackberries (fresh or frozen)	1¼ cups (310 mL)	2 Tbsp (30 mL)	1 Tbsp (15 mL) lemon juice 1 tsp (5 mL) vanilla extract
6 cups (1.5 L) peeled and sliced peaches (fresh or frozen)	1 cup (250 mL)	2 Tbsp (30 mL)	1 tsp (5 mL) vanilla extract ¼ tsp (1 mL) ground cinnamon

1. While the pie dough is chilling, prepare the fruit. In a saucepot, bring the fruit up to a simmer. In a bowl, stir the sugar and cornstarch together, and stir this into the simmering fruit. Add the remaining ingredients and simmer just until the fruit has thickened, stirring gently so as not to break down the fruit too much. Scrape the fruit into a bowl and cool the filling to room temperature. The filling can be made ahead and chilled until ready to assemble.

2. Pull the pastry from the fridge 30 minutes before rolling. Preheat the oven to 400°F (200°C). Place a 9-inch (23 cm) pie plate onto a parchment-lined baking tray and dust the pie plate with flour.

3. On a lightly floured work surface, roll out the first pastry disc to just under ¼ inch (6 mm) thick and line the prepared pie plate. Sprinkle the oats on the bottom of the pastry shell. Spoon the filling into the shell. Roll out the remaining pastry disc and cut out a small hole in the centre of the pastry (so steam can escape as the pie bakes). Place the rolled pastry overtop the fruit and press the edges together. Trim away any excess dough, and pinch the edges to create a pattern (or use a fork to pinch the pastry edges together).

4. Whisk the egg and water, brush the surface of the pastry with the egg mixture, and sprinkle the pie with turbinado sugar.

5. On the prepared baking tray, bake the pie for 12 minutes at 400°F (200°C), then reduce the heat to 375°F (190°C) and bake for about 40 more minutes, until the crust is a rich golden brown and the filling is bubbling. Cool the pie for at least 2 hours before slicing. The pie can be made a day ahead and served chilled.

note from anna's kitchen

If using a convection oven, bake the pie at 375°F (190°C) with the fan on for the first 12 minutes, then simply turn the fan off but leave the temperature at 375°F (190°C) for the remaining 40 minutes. For more tips on convection baking, refer to page 8.

LEMON MERINGUE PIE
• *Makes one 9-inch (23 cm) pie | Serves 8* •

LEMON MERINGUE PIE is well worth the effort. Give yourself ample time to make the crust, the filling, and the meringue. The meringue for this recipe is quite different from the style you typically see on a lemon meringue pie. It requires using a candy thermometer, but the result is a stable and fluffy meringue that has a very fine bubble structure, and it does not weep or slide off the filling.

1. Pull the chilled dough from the fridge 30 minutes before rolling. On a lightly floured surface, roll out the dough to ⅛ inch (3 mm) thick. Line a 9-inch (23 cm) pie shell with the dough, and trim and cinch the edges. Chill for 20 minutes.

2. Preheat the oven to 375°F (190°C). Overtop of the dough, line the pie shell with aluminum foil and weigh it down with pie weights, rice, or dried beans.

3. Bake for 20 minutes, then remove the foil and weights and bake for 10 to 12 more minutes, until the centre of the pie shell is dry and the edges are lightly browned. While the pie is hot from the oven, whisk the one egg white to loosen it, then brush this over the surface of the pie shell (this creates a barrier to prevent the crust from going soggy). Allow the shell to cool.

4. For the filling, bring the water, 1 cup (250 mL) of the sugar, and the lemon zest up to a full simmer in a saucepot. In a bowl, whisk the remaining ¼ cup (60 mL) of the sugar with the cornstarch, then whisk in the lemon juice and egg yolks. Pour the boiling water over the lemon mixture, then pour the entire liquid mixture back into the pot and whisk over medium heat until it thickens and just begins to bubble, about 4 minutes. Put the butter in a large bowl, and strain the mixture into the bowl and stir until the butter melts. Place a piece of plastic wrap over the filling and let it cool to room temperature. Then scrape the filling into the pie shell and chill just to set, about 2 hours.

5. For the meringue, preheat the oven to 375°F (190°C). Pull the chilled and filled pie out of the fridge to warm it up a little (30 to 40 minutes). If preparing and chilling the filling further ahead, let it warm up for about 75 minutes before topping with meringue.

½ recipe Double-Crust Pie Dough (page 82), chilled
1 egg white

FILLING:

1¾ cups (435 mL) water
1¼ cups (310 mL) sugar
1 Tbsp (15 mL) finely grated lemon zest
6½ Tbsp (97.5 mL) cornstarch
⅔ cup (160 mL) fresh lemon juice
5 egg yolks (reserve the whites for the meringue)
2 Tbsp (30 mL) unsalted butter

ITALIAN MERINGUE:

5 egg whites, at room temperature
1 cup (250 mL) sugar
1 tsp (5 mL) cream of tartar
¼ cup (60 mL) water

CONTINUED . . .

CONTINUED . . .

6. Whip the egg whites with ¼ cup (60 mL) of sugar and the cream of tartar until the mixture holds a medium peak when the beaters are lifted.

7. Place the remaining ¾ cup (185 mL) of sugar plus the ¼ cup (60 mL) of water in a saucepot and bring it to a boil. Without stirring, boil the sugar, occasionally brushing the sides of the pot with water, until it reaches 239°F (115°C) (this takes only about 3 minutes).

8. *Carefully* pour the hot sugar down the side of the bowl of whipped egg whites while whipping at medium-high speed (do not pour the sugar directly onto the beaters). Whip the meringue at high speed until cooled, about 3 minutes.

9. Scrape the meringue onto the centre of the lemon filling, and gently spread and swirl. Place the pie shell onto a baking sheet and bake for about 4 minutes, just until lightly browned. Let the meringue cool to room temperature before chilling. The pie can be prepared up to a day in advance and stored in the refrigerator for 2 days.

note from anna's kitchen

For more tips on making a successful meringue, check out Miraculous Meringues on pages 80–81.

GINGERBREAD CREAM PIE
• *Makes one 9-inch (23 cm) pie | Serves 8* •

*R*ICH, RICH, RICH! This pie has all the flavour elements of gingerbread, but in a butterscotch-inspired creamy filling.

1. Pull the chilled dough from the fridge 30 minutes before rolling. On a lightly floured surface, roll out the dough to ⅛ inch (3 mm) thick. Line a 9-inch (23 cm) pie shell with the dough, trim, and pinch the edges. Chill for 20 minutes.

2. Preheat the oven to 375°F (190°C). Line the pie shell with aluminum foil and weight with pie weights, rice, or dried beans. Bake for 20 minutes, then remove the foil and weights and bake for 10 to 12 more minutes, until the centre of the pie shell is dry and the edges are lightly browned. Allow to cool.

3. For the filling, heat the butter and brown sugar in a saucepot over medium heat, stirring until bubbling. Whisk in the cream and molasses, and stir until just below a simmer. In a bowl, whisk the egg yolks, cornstarch, ginger, spices, salt, and milk. Slowly pour the hot cream mixture into the egg mixture, whisking constantly until blended. Return the mixture to the pot and whisk over medium heat until thickened and just beginning to bubble, about 4 minutes.

4. Strain and pour into the cooled pie shell. Place a piece of plastic wrap directly on the surface of the filling and chill it until set, at least 6 hours.

5. For the topping, whip cream to soft peaks and fold in the sugar, skim milk powder, vanilla, and cinnamon. Dollop and spread over the gingerbread filling, and chill until ready to serve. The pie will keep, refrigerated, for up to 2 days.

½ recipe Double-Crust Pie Dough (page 82), chilled

FILLING:

1 cup (250 mL) unsalted butter
1¼ cups (310 mL) packed dark brown sugar
1 cup (250 mL) whipping cream
½ cup (125 mL) fancy molasses
4 egg yolks
⅓ cup (80 mL) cornstarch
2 tsp (10 mL) finely grated fresh ginger
¾ tsp (4 mL) ground cinnamon
¼ tsp (1 mL) ground nutmeg
¼ tsp (1 mL) ground cloves
¾ tsp (4 mL) salt
1¾ cups (435 mL) milk

TOPPING:

1½ cups (375 mL) whipping cream
2 Tbsp (30 mL) sugar
1½ Tbsp (22.5 mL) instant skim milk powder
1 tsp (5 mL) vanilla extract
¼ tsp (1 mL) ground cinnamon

CHOCOLATE BANANA CREAM PIE WITH PEANUT BUTTER WHIP

• *Makes one 9-inch (23 cm) pie | Serves 8* •

*T*HIS IS A very thick and rich chocolate cream pie, thicker than a traditional pudding filling. Topped with a peanut butter whipped cream, and with sliced bananas hidden under the filling, this will bring out the kid in anyone.

1. Pull the pie dough out of the fridge 30 minutes before rolling. On a lightly floured surface, roll out the dough to ⅛ inch (3 mm) thick. Line a 9-inch (23 cm) pie shell with dough, trim, and cinch the edges. Chill for 20 minutes.

2. Preheat the oven to 375°F (190°C). Line the pie shell with aluminum foil and weight with pie weights, rice, or dried beans. Bake for 20 minutes, then remove the foil and weights and bake for 10 to 12 more minutes, until the centre of the pie shell is dry and the edges are lightly browned. While still hot, brush the surface of the pie shell with the egg white (it will create a barrier to prevent the crust from going soggy). Allow the pie shell to cool.

3. Arrange the sliced bananas over the bottom of the cooled pie shell, overlapping if needed. Heat the milk and cream in a saucepot over medium heat to just below a simmer. In a bowl, whisk the egg yolks, sugar, cornstarch, vanilla, and salt and, while whisking, slowly add the hot milk mixture. Return the mixture to the pot and cook over medium heat while whisking constantly (switch to a spatula now and again to ensure you are stirring into the corners) until the mixture just begins to reach a simmer (a few bubbles will break the surface). Place the chopped chocolate in a bowl, and pour the custard through a strainer placed over the bowl and let sit for one minute. Whisk until the chocolate has melted, then pour the custard over the bananas in the pie shell. Place a piece of plastic wrap over the custard so that it touches the entire surface and chill until set, about 4 hours.

4. To prepare the peanut butter whip, whip the cream with the skim milk powder until the cream holds a soft peak when the beaters are lifted. Whip in the icing sugar and vanilla. In a bowl, stir the peanut butter to soften it and add about half of the whipped cream, stirring until blended. Fold this peanut butter mixture into the other half of the whipped cream and spread overtop the chilled pie. Garnish the pie with chocolate shavings and chill until ready to serve. The pie will keep in the refrigerator for up to 2 days.

½ recipe Double-Crust Pie Dough (page 82), chilled
1 egg white

FILLING:

2 to 3 bananas, sliced
1¼ cups (310 mL) milk
½ cup (125 mL) whipping cream
4 egg yolks
¼ cup (60 mL) sugar
2½ Tbsp (37.5 mL) cornstarch
1 tsp (5 mL) vanilla extract
⅛ tsp (0.5 mL) salt
6 oz (175 g) semisweet or bittersweet chocolate, chopped

PEANUT BUTTER WHIP:

1½ cups (375 mL) whipping cream
1½ Tbsp (22.5 mL) skim milk powder
⅓ cup (80 mL) icing sugar, sifted
1 tsp (5 mL) vanilla extract
⅓ cup (80 mL) peanut butter, any kind you prefer
Chocolate Shavings (dark) (page 321), for garnish

PUMPKIN PIE
• Makes one 9-inch (23 cm) pie | Serves 8 •

MAKING A PUMPKIN pie is like baking a custard in a pie shell. Most sinfully delicious pumpkin pie recipes are loaded with whipping cream. The use of sweetened condensed milk in this recipe achieves just the right sweetness and silky texture, and it cuts down on the need for excessive whipping cream.

1. Pull the chilled pie dough from the fridge 30 minutes before rolling. Preheat the oven to 375°F (190°C).
2. On a lightly floured surface, knead the pie dough slightly to soften, then roll out the dough to a circle just under ¼ inch (6 mm) thick. Dust a 9-inch (23 cm) pie plate with flour and place the rolled pastry into the shell, crimping the edges to create a pretty design. Chill the pie shell while preparing the filling.
3. For the filling, whisk the pumpkin purée, condensed milk, spices, cream, and eggs until evenly blended. Place the chilled pie plate onto a baking tray and pour in the pumpkin filling.
4. Bake the pie for 20 minutes, then reduce the oven temperature to 350°F (175°C) and bake the pie for about 40 more minutes, until the crust is nicely browned and the filling is set but still has a jiggle in the centre. Cool the pie to room temperature, then chill for at least 3 hours before serving. The pie can be served chilled, or warm it in a 300°F (150°C) oven for 15 minutes before serving.

½ recipe Double-Crust Pie Dough (page 82), chilled

FILLING:

2 cups (500 mL) plain pumpkin purée
1 tin (300 mL) sweetened condensed milk
1 tsp (5 mL) ground cinnamon
½ tsp (2 mL) ground ginger
¼ tsp (1 mL) ground allspice
¼ tsp (1 mL) ground cloves
⅛ tsp (0.5 mL) ground nutmeg
½ cup (125 mL) whipping cream
3 eggs

note from anna's kitchen

For a wet filling like this one, try replacing half of the all-purpose flour in the pie dough recipe with whole wheat flour. The whole wheat flour adds a pleasant nutty taste, stays nice and tender, and fully bakes on the bottom—no soggy crusts here!

CHOCOLATE PECAN PIE
• *Makes one 9-inch (23 cm) pie | Serves 8 to 10* •

THINK OF A gooey butter tart. Now imagine loads of tender pecans stirred in. Now imagine this with chocolate richness. Ta-dah.

1. Pull the chilled pie dough from the fridge 30 minutes before rolling. Preheat the oven to 375°F (190°C).
2. On a lightly floured surface, knead the pie dough slightly to soften, then roll out the dough to a circle just under ¼ inch (6 mm) thick. Dust a 9-inch (23 cm) pie plate with flour and place the rolled pastry into the shell, crimping the edges to create a pretty design. Chill the pie shell while preparing the filling.
3. In a medium saucepot over medium heat, melt the butter, then stir in the brown sugar and corn syrup. Bring this to a full simmer while stirring, then continue to simmer and stir for 1 minute. Stir in the cream and simmer and stir for 1 more minute. Remove the pan from the heat and stir in the salt, vanilla, and chocolate, stirring until the chocolate has melted. Add the pecans and stir to coat. In a little dish, beat the eggs, then add them to the pecan mixture, stirring until incorporated. Scrape the filling into the chilled pie shell.
4. Bake the pie on a baking tray for 40 to 45 minutes, until the crust is golden brown and the filling has set. Cool the pie to room temperature. Store the pie in the refrigerator for up to 4 days.

½ recipe Double-Crust Pie Dough (page 82), chilled

FILLING:
¾ cup (185 mL) unsalted butter
¾ cup (185 mL) packed light brown sugar
½ cup (125 mL) golden corn syrup
¼ cup (60 mL) whipping cream
½ tsp (2 mL) salt
1 tsp (5 mL) vanilla extract
4 oz (125 g) bittersweet chocolate, chopped
2½ cups (625 mL) pecan halves
2 eggs

note from anna's kitchen
This pie is best served at room temperature or just a little chilled, so pull the pie from the fridge an hour before serving.

MINCEMEAT PIE
• *Makes one 9-inch (23 cm) pie | Serves 8* •

A GOOD MINCEMEAT PIE is a wonderful thing, and I think we've become too accustomed to the store-bought versions that are more syrup than substance. This mincemeat pie has a good balance of everything autumn: dried fruit, nuts, spices and honey, and maple syrup, too. If you are a fan of raisin pie, this takes it to the next level.

1. Pull the chilled pie dough from the fridge 30 minutes before rolling. Preheat the oven to 375°F (190°C).
2. On a lightly floured surface, knead one disc of the pie dough slightly to soften, then roll out the dough to a circle just under ¼ inch (6 mm) thick. Dust a 9-inch (23 cm) pie plate with flour and place the rolled pastry into the shell. Roll the second disc out into a circle of the same thickness, place it onto a plate or tray, and chill both while preparing the filling.
3. In a medium saucepot over medium heat, stir the apples, raisins, dates, prunes, walnuts, apple juice (or cider), lemon juice, orange zest, cocoa, tapioca, cinnamon, ginger, allspice, and cloves until the mixture just begins to bubble. Add the honey and maple syrup, and stir until the fruit simmers. Then remove from the heat and cool to room temperature.
4. Spoon the filling into the chilled pie shell and spread to level. Cut a hole in the centre of the second pastry sheet and place it over the mincemeat. Trim and pinch the edges, creating a pretty design. Whisk the egg with the water, brush the top of the pie pastry with the egg wash, and place the pie on a parchment-lined baking tray.
5. Bake the pie for 15 minutes, then reduce the oven temperature to 350°F (175°C) and bake the pie for about 45 more minutes, until the crust is an even golden brown. Cool the pie for at least 3 hours before slicing to serve. The pie can be served warm or chilled, and can keep in the refrigerator for up to 4 days.

1 recipe Double-Crust Pie Dough (page 82), chilled

MINCEMEAT:

2 cups (500 mL) peeled and diced apples, such as Mutsu or Granny Smith, cut in ½-inch (1 cm) pieces
1 cup (250 mL) Thompson raisins
½ cup (125 mL) chopped pitted dates
½ cup (125 mL) chopped pitted prunes
1 cup (250 mL) walnut pieces
⅓ cup (80 mL) apple juice or cider
3 Tbsp (45 mL) lemon juice
1 Tbsp (15 mL) finely grated orange zest
1 Tbsp (15 mL) cocoa powder
2 tsp (10 mL) quick-cook tapioca
1 tsp (5 mL) ground cinnamon
1 tsp (5 mL) ground ginger
¼ tsp (1 mL) ground allspice
¼ tsp (1 mL) ground cloves
½ cup (125 mL) honey
½ cup (125 mL) maple syrup

FOR BRUSHING:

1 egg
2 Tbsp (30 mL) water

RAISIN BUTTER TARTS
• Makes 12 butter tarts •

T HESE BUTTER TARTS have that just-right filling—a little gooey but not too drippy. I like to use golden raisins because they are not as sweet as Thompson raisins.

1. Pull the pie dough from the refrigerator 30 minutes before rolling. Preheat the oven to 400°F (200°C) and lightly grease a 12-cup muffin tin.
2. Lightly dust a work surface with flour and unwrap the pastry logs. Slice each log into six pieces. Roll each piece to about $\frac{1}{4}$ inch (6 mm) in thickness, trim with a 5-inch (12 cm) round cutter and line each muffin cup with a piece of dough (the tart shells should come up about $\frac{1}{2}$ inch/1 cm higher than the edge of the muffin cup). Chill the lined muffin tin while preparing the filling.
3. By hand, whisk the sugar, corn syrup, and butter in a bowl until combined. Whisk in the eggs, then the vinegar and vanilla. Sprinkle a few raisins in the bottom of each muffin cup and pour the mixture over the raisins.
4. Bake the tarts for 5 minutes, then reduce the oven temperature to 375°F (190°C) and continue baking until the butter tart filling starts to dome, about 20 more minutes. Cool the tarts to room temperature in the tin, then gently rotate them to loosen them. Chill the tarts in the tin before removing them onto a serving plate. The tarts will keep in the refrigerator for up to 5 days.

1 recipe Double-Crust Pie Dough (page 82), shaped in 2 logs and chilled

FILLING:

¾ cup (185 mL) packed dark brown sugar
¾ cup (185 mL) corn syrup
½ cup (125 mL) unsalted butter, melted
2 eggs, at room temperature
1 tsp (5 mL) white vinegar
1 tsp (5 mL) vanilla extract
½ cup (125 mL) golden raisins

note from anna's kitchen
Most pie pastry is rolled to less than ¼ inch (6 mm) thick, but in the case of butter tarts, we've become accustomed to a slightly thicker crust, possibly to make it easier to negotiate that gooey filling.

PORTUGUESE CUSTARD TARTS
• Makes 12 tarts •

*T*HESE EGGY CUSTARD tarts are a personal favourite. They have a distinctively flaky pastry, and while many custard tart recipes out there call for frozen puff pastry, you can easily keep these a from-scratch product by simply layering in a little extra butter to the pie dough.

1. Pull the pie dough from the fridge 30 minutes before rolling.

2. On a lightly floured surface, roll out the entire piece of pie dough into a rectangular shape that is 20 inches (50 cm) by 12 inches (30 cm) and $\frac{1}{4}$ inch (6 mm) thick. Evenly spread 5 Tbsp (75 mL) of butter over the surface of the pastry, and roll it up from the short end (to create a spiral). Wrap and chill the dough while preparing the filling.

3. Heat the cream and milk in a heavy-bottomed saucepot over medium heat to just below a simmer. In a bowl, whisk the eggs yolks, sugar, cornstarch, and vanilla. While whisking, slowly pour the hot cream into the egg mixture, then pour this back into the pot. Whisk the custard constantly over medium heat until it thickens and just begins to bubble, about 4 minutes. Strain the custard into a bowl, stir in the remaining 1 Tbsp (15 mL) of butter, and place a sheet of plastic wrap directly on the surface of the custard to prevent a skin from forming. Cool the custard on the counter to room temperature, then chill for $1\frac{1}{2}$ hours.

4. Preheat the oven to 375°F (190°C) and lightly grease a 12-cup muffin tin. Remove the pastry dough from the fridge and cut 12 discs from the log. Roll out each portion on a lightly floured surface to just shy of $\frac{1}{4}$ inch (6 mm) thick and trim with a 5-inch (12 cm) round cutter. Press each portion into the muffin tin so that the edges of each tart shell are about $\frac{1}{2}$ inch (1 cm) above the edge of each muffin cup. Spoon the chilled custard into the pastry.

5. Bake the tarts for 35 to 45 minutes, until the pastry is golden brown and the custard has browned on top somewhat. Cool the tarts in the tin before removing to serve at room temperature or chilled. The tarts can be stored in the refrigerator for up to 3 days.

1 recipe Double-Crust Pie Dough (page 82), wrapped in one piece, chilled

5 Tbsp (75 mL) + 1 Tbsp (15 mL) unsalted butter, at room temperature

1 cup (250 mL) half-and-half cream

¾ cup (185 mL) milk

5 egg yolks

½ cup (125 mL) sugar

2 Tbsp (30 mL) + 1 tsp (5 mL) cornstarch

1 Tbsp (15 mL) vanilla extract

note from anna's kitchen
For tips on baking in a convection oven compared to a conventional oven, refer to page 8.

SWEET-CRUST TART SHELL
Makes one 9-inch (23 cm) baked tart shell

foundation
RECIPE

THE METHOD FOR making this tart dough is very much like making cookie dough and it's just as simple. There is no need to roll the dough cold; in fact, you can feel comfortable kneading the dough to soften it just enough so that it's easy to roll—no need to wrestle with an ice-cold pastry that cracks because of the cold butter!

The tarts in this book that are made using this tender, sweet dough are designed for this pastry. They are delicate in nature, and the fillings are not so wet or so heavy that they weigh down or shatter the crust.

½ cup (125 mL) unsalted butter, at room temperature

¼ cup (60 mL) sugar

2 egg yolks

½ tsp (2 mL) vanilla extract

1 cup (250 mL) all-purpose flour

¼ tsp (1 mL) salt

1. Beat the butter and sugar together until fluffy. Stir in the egg yolks and vanilla. Stir in the flour and salt until the dough comes together. Shape the dough into a disc, wrap it in plastic wrap, and chill for at least 2 hours, until firm.

2. Preheat the oven to 350°F (175°C). Knead the pastry dough on a lightly floured surface to soften it enough so that it can be easily rolled. Dust the pastry with a little flour, and roll it out to just over 11 inches (28 cm) in diameter and about $\frac{1}{4}$ inch (6 mm) thick. Line a 9-inch (23 cm), removable-bottom, fluted tart pan with the dough and trim the edges. Chill the pastry for 20 minutes in the fridge, or 10 minutes in the freezer.

3. Place the chilled tart pan on a baking tray. Dock the bottom of the pastry shell with a fork and bake the pastry for 16 to 20 minutes, until just the edges are golden brown and the centre of the shell looks dry. Cool completely before filling.

notes from anna's kitchen

1. Some pastry dough needs to be blind-baked (baked while weighted down with pie weights or dried beans) to prevent it from bubbling or doming as it bakes. Because this dough and the Sable Tart Shell (page 108) are similar to cookie dough, they bake up without any bubbles at all. Docking the pastry with a fork is key, though, to preventing a crust that domes in the middle. As the tart shell bakes, the holes allow any air to escape while the dough is still soft and pliable, and as it bakes, the pastry expands and the holes fill in a bit so you won't have a filling that leaks through the bottom.

2. Fill the pie shell soon after baking it, as it is fragile when not filled. However, the dough can be chilled for up to 3 days and then baked, or it can be frozen for up to 3 months and then thawed in the fridge before baking.

STRAWBERRY LAVENDER CHEESECAKE TART
Makes one 9-inch (23 cm) tart | Serves 8 to 10

A SUBTLE ADDITION OF fresh lavender complements fresh strawberries. The filling of this tart is a New York–style cheesecake filling, which suits the tender pastry crust and the fresh berries on top.

1. Preheat the oven to 325°F (160°C). Put the baked and cooled tart shell on a baking tray.

2. Beat the cream cheese with ½ cup (125 mL) of the sour cream until smooth. While beating and scraping down the sides of the bowl, gradually add ½ cup (125 mL) of the sugar. Beat in the egg, egg yolk, and 1 teaspoon (5 mL) of the vanilla until smooth, and scrape the first layer of filling into the tart shell.

3. Bake for 20 minutes on the baking tray. While baking, prepare the second layer of filling. Stir the remaining ½ cup (125 mL) sour cream with the remaining 2 tablespoons (30 mL) of sugar and 1 teaspoon (5 mL) of vanilla. Once the first layer has baked for 20 minutes, gently spread the second layer overtop and bake for 10 more minutes. Cool the tart to room temperature, then chill in the pan for at least 3 hours before removing the outer ring of the pan to serve.

4. For the strawberries, heat the jam with the lavender in a small saucepot over low heat for 10 minutes, stirring often, then cool to room temperature. Place the strawberries in a bowl and stir the jam into the strawberries.

5. To serve, slice the cheesecake tart into wedges and spoon the strawberries overtop.

6. The tart will keep in the refrigerator for a day with the strawberries on top, and for up to 3 days if you add the strawberries right before serving.

1 recipe Sweet-Crust Tart Shell (page 104), baked and cooled

FILLING:

2 pkg (8 oz/250 g each) cream cheese, at room temperature
1 cup (250 mL) full-fat sour cream
½ cup (125 mL) + 2 Tbsp (30 mL) sugar
1 egg
1 egg yolk
2 tsp (10 mL) vanilla extract

STRAWBERRIES:

½ cup (125 mL) strawberry jam (homemade, if you have it!)
2 tsp (10 mL) finely chopped fresh lavender leaves or flowers, or 1 tsp (5 mL) dried
2 cups (500 mL) hulled and quartered fresh strawberries

note from anna's kitchen
For an explanation behind using full-fat sour cream in baking, refer to page 13.

CLASSIC FRUIT FLAN
• Makes one 9-inch (23 cm) tart | Serves 8 to 10 •

*T*AKING THE TIME to arrange the fruits nicely is key to a beautiful tart. Choose fruits that are tender and will slice easily, and try to arrange the fruits in a circular pattern so that when you slice the tart, every slice will yield a similar portion. The apple jelly in this recipe protects the fruits so that they stay fresh-looking and do not brown, but the list below names the fruits that are most likely to turn brown once sliced.

1. Keep the baked tart shell in its pan. Melt the white chocolate in a metal or glass bowl placed over a pot of barely simmering water, stirring until melted. Brush to coat the bottom and sides of the cooled tart shell with the chocolate, and chill the shell while preparing the pastry cream.

2. Heat the milk in a heavy-bottomed saucepot until just below a simmer. In a small bowl, whisk the eggs, sugar, and cornstarch. Whisk half of the hot milk into the egg mixture, then pour this entire mixture back into the pot with the remaining milk. Whisk the custard constantly over medium heat until it thickens and just begins to bubble, about 3 to 4 minutes. Strain the custard into a bowl, stir in the vanilla and butter until melted, then cover the bowl with plastic wrap so that the wrap directly covers the surface of the custard. Cool the custard to room temperature, then chill it in the pan for at least 2 hours.

3. To assemble the tart, spoon the custard into the tart shell and spread it evenly. Top the custard with the fresh fruit, creating an appealing design. Melt the apple jelly over low heat, then brush it over the fruit. Chill the tart in the pan until you are ready to serve. The tart can be stored in the refrigerator for up to a day.

1 recipe Sweet-Crust Tart Shell (page 104), baked and cooled

2 oz (60 g) white chocolate, chopped

PASTRY CREAM:

1 cup (250 mL) milk

2 eggs

¼ cup (60 mL) sugar

2½ Tbsp (37.5 mL) cornstarch

2 tsp (10 mL) vanilla extract

2 Tbsp (30 mL) unsalted butter

FRUITS:

4 cups (1 L) assorted fresh, tender fruits, such as raspberries, blueberries, or strawberries, and peeled and sliced kiwi, pineapple, mango, or even dragon fruit

¼ cup (60 mL) apple jelly

FRUITS PRONE TO OXIDIZATION
Apples
Apricots
Bananas (but not suited to this tart)
Peaches
Pears
Plums

note from anna's kitchen

The fruits listed in the ingredient list are just a starting point. You can use any tender and delicate fruits you wish, but keep in mind that some fruits turn brown (oxidize) once sliced and exposed to the air. If you would really like to use these fruits, it's best to toss them in a little lemon juice before arranging them on the tart, or consider that poaching or gently roasting the fruits will avoid this altogether.

APPLE CANNOLI TART
• *Makes one 9-inch (23 cm) tart | Serves 8 to 10* •

SABLE TART SHELL
• *Makes one 9-inch (23 cm) baked tart shell* •

foundation
RECIPE

*T*HIS APPLE TART has a ricotta filling that tastes exactly like a cannoli—a nice combination that suits fall, winter, or spring.

1 recipe Sweet-Crust Tart Shell (page 104),
   baked and cooled

FILLING:

2½ cups (625 mL) sliced apples, such as Cortland,
   Granny Smith, or Honey Crisp
3 Tbsp (45 mL) sweet Marsala wine
1⅓ cups (330 mL) ricotta cheese
¼ cup (60 mL) + 1 Tbsp (15 mL) sugar
2 Tbsp (30 mL) finely grated bittersweet chocolate
1 egg
1 egg yolk
1 tsp (5 mL) finely grated lemon zest
⅛ tsp (0.5 mL) ground nutmeg
2 Tbsp (30 mL) unsalted butter, melted

1. Preheat the oven to 350°F (175°C). Put the pan containing the cooled, baked tart shell on a baking tray.
2. Toss the apple with the Marsala and set aside, stirring occasionally.
3. In a separate bowl, whisk the ricotta, ¼ cup (60 mL) of the sugar, the grated chocolate, egg, egg yolk, lemon zest, and nutmeg together. Strain the Marsala from the apples into this ricotta mixture and blend. Pour the ricotta filling into the baked tart shell and arrange the apples overtop. Brush the apples with the melted butter, and sprinkle with the remaining 1 tablespoon (15 mL) of sugar.
4. Bake the tart on the baking tray for about 25 minutes, until the apples are tender when pierced with a fork. Cool the tart to room temperature, then chill in the pan until ready to serve. The tart will keep in the refrigerator for up to 2 days.

*T*HIS SWEET DOUGH is designed for wetter fillings. The icing sugar and pastry flour give it a delicate, tender texture (a sandiness, in fact, hence the name *sable*, which means *sand* in French); the whole egg makes it water-resistant enough for wet fillings.

⅓ cup (80 mL) unsalted butter, at room temperature
¼ cup (60 mL) icing sugar
1 egg, at room temperature
2 Tbsp (30 mL) milk
1 tsp (5 mL) vanilla extract
1 cup (250 mL) cake and pastry flour
¼ tsp (1 mL) salt

1. Beat the butter and the icing sugar together until fluffy. Stir in the egg, then add the milk and vanilla. Stir in the flour and salt until the dough comes together (the dough will be sticky). Shape the dough into a disc, wrap it in plastic wrap, and chill it for at least 2 hours, until firm.
2. Preheat the oven to 350°F (175°C). Knead the pastry dough on a lightly floured surface to soften it just slightly. Dust the pastry with a little flour, and roll it out to just over 11 inches (28 cm) in diameter and just under ¼ inch (6 mm) thick. Line a 9-inch (23 cm), removable-bottom, fluted tart pan, and trim the dough that hangs over the edges. Chill the pastry for 20 minutes in the fridge, or 10 minutes in the freezer.
3. Place the chilled tart pan on a baking tray. Dock the bottom of the pastry shell with a fork, and bake the dough for 20 to 24 minutes, until just the edges are golden brown and the centre of the shell looks dry. Cool completely before filling.

note from anna's kitchen
Fill the pie shell soon after baking it, as it is fragile when not filled. However, the dough can be chilled for up to 3 days and then baked, or it can be frozen for up to 3 months and then thawed in the fridge before baking.

VANILLA CRÈME BRÛLÉE TART
• Makes one 9-inch (23 cm) tart | Serves 8 to 10 •

 CLASSIC CRÈME BRÛLÉE filling is baked into this tart shell and topped with the requisite caramelized-sugar top—simple but divine.

1. Preheat the oven to 300°F (150°C). Place the pan containing the baked, cooled tart shell on a parchment- or foil-lined baking tray.
2. Whisk the egg yolks, whole egg, and 1/3 cup (80 mL) of the sugar together. Scrape the seeds of the vanilla bean into the egg mixture and whisk them in. Pour in the whipping cream while whisking the eggs. Pour this carefully into the pastry shell and use a paper towel to dab away any air bubbles that are on the surface of the custard.
3. Carefully carry the tray to the oven and place it on the centre shelf. Place a dish filled with 1 1/2 cups (375 mL) of boiling water near the tart pan (it can be on the rack above or below the tart pan, or beside it), and bake the tart for about 40 minutes, until the tart is set but about 3 inches (8 cm) in the centre still have a little jiggle. Cool the tart to room temperature before chilling it in the pan for at least 2 hours.
4. When you are ready to serve the tart, sprinkle the remaining 1/4 cup (60 mL) of sugar evenly over the top of the tart. Use a butane kitchen torch to carefully melt and then caramelize this sugar. Once it cools for 1 minute, it will be crunchy. You can caramelize the top of the tart up to 3 hours in advance. The tart can be stored in the refrigerator for up to 2 days (after a day, the sugar loses a bit of its crunch, but it's just as tasty).

1 recipe Sable Tart Shell (page 108), baked and cooled

FILLING:
5 egg yolks
1 egg
1/3 cup (80 mL) + 1/4 cup (60 mL) sugar
1 vanilla bean, or 1 Tbsp (15 mL) vanilla extract
2 cups (500 mL) whipping cream

note from anna's kitchen
To make 8 individual tarts, simply double the ingredients in the Sable Tart Shell recipe and roll, line, and bake eight 4-inch (10 cm), fluted tart shells for about 15 minutes. Prepare the filling as above and bake the filled tarts for about 20 minutes.

LEMON TART (TARTE AU CITRON)
• Makes one 9-inch (23 cm) tart | Serves 8 to 10 •

*T*HIS IS A true classic, and a must-have in every pastry chef's repertoire.

1. Preheat the oven to 325°F (160°C). Place the pan containing the baked, cooled tart shell on a parchment-lined baking tray.
2. Whisk the eggs, egg yolk, and sugar until smooth. Whisk in the cream, sour cream, zest, and juice until evenly combined. Pour this carefully into the tart shell.
3. Bake the tart on the tray for about 25 minutes, until the tart is set except for the middle 3 inches (8 cm), which should have a little jiggle. Cool the tart to room temperature, then chill in the pan for at least 2 hours before removing the outer ring of the pan to serve.
4. The tart can be stored in the refrigerator for up to 2 days.

1 recipe Sable Tart Shell (page 108), baked and cooled
3 eggs
1 egg yolk
½ cup (125 mL) sugar
⅔ cup (160 mL) whipping cream
⅓ cup (80 mL) sour cream
1 Tbsp (15 mL) finely grated lemon zest
⅓ cup (80 mL) fresh lemon juice

notes from anna's kitchen

The simplicity of this tart makes it the perfect ending to a meal, but you can get inventive and make any number of variations. For example:

1. Arrange the whole tart with fresh berries, or serve berries on the side.
2. Make a crunchy crème brûlée top for the tart by following the finishing technique in step 4 of the Vanilla Crème Brûlée Tart (page 109).
3. For a different citrus version, replace the lemon zest and juice with lime zest and juice.

PIÑA COLADA TART
• *Makes one 9-inch (23 cm) tart | Serves 8 to 10* •

*T*HIS CHEESECAKE-STYLE TART is not made like a traditional cheesecake but more in the style of tiramisu, resulting in filling that is fluffy but decadently rich at the same time.

1. Beat the cream cheese to soften it, then set it aside.
2. Whisk the egg yolks, sugar, lime zest, lime juice, rum, and vanilla in a metal bowl. Place the bowl over a pot of gently simmering water, and whisk the mixture by hand, or with electric beaters, until it leaves a "ribbon" when the whisk is lifted, about 5 minutes.
3. Add half of this warm egg mixture to the cream cheese and beat until smooth. Fold the remaining half of the mixture into the cream cheese by hand. Fold in the pineapple and coconut. Spoon the filling into the cooled tart shell (still in the pan) and spread evenly. Chill the tart for at least 3 hours in the pan before removing the outer ring of the pan to serve. Sprinkle with toasted coconut before serving. The tart will keep in the refrigerator for up to 2 days.

1 recipe Sable Tart Shell (page 108), baked and cooled

FILLING:

1 pkg (8 oz/250 g) cream cheese, at room temperature

3 egg yolks

½ cup (125 mL) sugar

2 tsp (10 mL) finely grated lime zest

3 Tbsp (45 mL) lime juice

2 Tbsp (30 mL) rum

2 tsp (10 mL) vanilla extract

14 oz (398 mL) tin crushed pineapple, well drained

⅔ cup (160 mL) sweetened, flaked coconut

Toasted coconut, for garnish

notes from anna's kitchen

1. If you do not wish to use rum, replace the 2 tablespoons (30 mL) of rum with 2 tablespoons (30 mL) of pineapple juice from the drained, crushed pineapple.
2. Tinned pineapple is best for this recipe since, once drained, it won't let out any more liquid as the tart sets. If you wish to use fresh pineapple, it's best to crush it, stir it with 1 tablespoon (15 mL) of sugar, let it sit for an hour, then squeeze out excess juice.

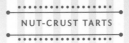
NUT-CRUST TART SHELL
• *Makes one 9-inch (23 cm) baked tart shell* •

foundation
RECIPE

egg-
FREE

THIS CRUST RECIPE can be made using any of four types of nuts, and it works consistently. The natural oils in nuts add fat and moisture to the pastry, so less butter is required than in other styles of pastry crusts.

1. In a food processor, pulse the nuts and 2 tablespoons (30 mL) of the flour until the nuts are finely ground. Add the remaining ¾ cup (185 mL) of flour and the sugar and salt, and pulse to blend. Add the butter and pulse the mixture until it has a sandy texture. Add the cold water, then pulse until the dough comes together in a ball. Shape the dough into a disc, wrap it in plastic wrap, then chill the dough until it is firm, at least an hour. Alternatively, the dough can be prepared and then frozen (thaw it in the fridge before rolling).

2. Preheat the oven to 350°F (175°C). On a lightly floured surface, break the chilled dough into 4 pieces and then push them together, kneading them to soften them slightly (this will make it easier to roll the dough without cracking it). Roll out the dough until it is just under ¼ inch (6 mm) thick and carefully lift it to line a 9-inch (23 cm), removable-bottom tart pan. Press the crust into the corners and trim away any excess dough. Chill the dough for 10 minutes.

3. Pierce the bottom of the dough with a fork, place the tart pan on a baking tray, and bake it for 25 to 30 minutes, until the crust is golden brown around the edges and the pastry is dry in the centre. Let the tart shell cool and fill it soon after.

⅓ cup (80 mL) coarsely chopped nuts (walnuts, pecans, almonds, or hazelnuts)

¾ cup (185 mL) + 2 Tbsp (30 mL) all-purpose flour

1 Tbsp (15 mL) sugar

¼ tsp (1 mL) salt

6 Tbsp (90 mL) cold unsalted butter, cut in pieces

1 Tbsp (15 mL) cold water

note from anna's kitchen
A food processor is the ideal tool for this recipe, but if you do not have one, then use ½ cup (125 mL) of finely ground nuts and mix the dough by hand or with beaters using the same method.

CRANBERRY FRANGIPANE TART
• *Makes one 9-inch (23 cm) tart | Serves 8 to 10* •

FRANGIPANE IS A sweet and moist combination of ground almonds, butter, sugar, and eggs, and it contrasts nicely with tart cranberries in this variation on a traditional dessert.

1. Preheat the oven to 350°F (175°C). Place the pan containing the crust onto a baking tray.
2. Pulse the almonds with the sugar in a food processor until the almonds are finely ground. Add the butter, egg, egg yolk, extracts, and cinnamon, and pulse until the mixture is evenly blended.
3. Transfer the almond filling to a bowl. If using thawed frozen cranberries, toss them with 1 tablespoon (15 mL) of flour. Stir the cranberries into the almond filling and scrape the filling into the cooled crust.
4. Bake on the tray for 40 to 45 minutes, until the filling is set and evenly browned. Cool to room temperature in the pan before removing the outer ring of the pan to slice. Dust with icing sugar before serving. The tart can be served at room temperature or chilled. The tart will keep in the refrigerator for up to 4 days.

1 recipe almond Nut-Crust Tart Shell (page 113), baked and cooled

FILLING:

⅔ cup (160 mL) whole unpeeled almonds
⅔ cup (160 mL) sugar
¾ cup (185 mL) unsalted butter, at room temperature
1 egg
1 egg yolk
1 tsp (5 mL) vanilla extract
¼ tsp (1 mL) almond extract
⅛ tsp (0.5 mL) ground cinnamon
1½ cups (375 mL) fresh or thawed frozen cranberries
1 Tbsp (15 mL) flour, if using frozen cranberries
Icing sugar, for dusting

note from anna's kitchen
If using frozen cranberries, it is important to thaw them before stirring them into the filling to keep the filling smooth and to make sure the tart bakes evenly. I find this rule applies to using frozen fruit in most recipes. If you bake with frozen fruit, it can tighten or even seize the batter, and the batter around the frozen berry can remain soggy, even once baked. As a general rule, if using frozen fruit in a muffin, coffee cake, or tart, thaw the fruit and, before stirring it into your batter, toss it with a little flour to absorb the excess moisture and prevent juices from bleeding out.

ROCKY ROAD TART

• *Makes one 9-inch (23 cm) tart | Serves 8 to 10* •

CHOCOLATE, WALNUTS, AND marshmallows make up the winning combination of Rocky Road. This tart has a soft, brownie-like filling that is topped with walnuts and marshmallows bathed in chocolate.

1. Preheat the oven to 350°F (175°C). Place the pan containing the crust onto a baking tray.
2. Place the butter and unsweetened and semisweet chocolates in a metal or glass bowl, and stir the mixture over a pot of barely simmering water until the chocolate has melted. Remove the bowl from the heat and set aside.
3. Using electric beaters or a standup mixer fitted with the whisk attachment, whip the eggs, sugar, and vanilla on high speed until they hold a ribbon when the beaters are lifted, about 5 minutes. Reduce the speed to medium-low and pour in the chocolate. Sift the flour and salt over the chocolate mixture and blend just until it is incorporated.
4. Pour the filling into the baked tart shell and bake it on the tray for about 30 minutes, until the top of the tart cracks a little. Prepare the topping while the tart is baking.
5. For the topping, place the milk chocolate, butter, and oil in a bowl, and set the bowl over a pot of barely simmering water, stirring until the chocolate is melted. Remove the bowl from the heat and let the chocolate cool for 10 minutes. Stir in the walnut pieces and marshmallows until they are fully coated. While the baked tart filling is still warm from the oven, pierce it with a fork, then evenly spread the chocolate topping over it. Chill the tart for an hour in the pan, just to set the chocolate topping, then store and serve it at room temperature. The tart will keep, covered, for up to 3 days.

1 recipe walnut Nut-Crust Tart Shell (page 113), baked and cooled

FILLING:

¼ cup (60 mL) unsalted butter

2 oz (60 g) unsweetened chocolate, chopped

2 oz (60 g) semisweet chocolate, chopped

2 eggs, at room temperature

¾ cup (185 mL) sugar

1 tsp (5 mL) vanilla extract

½ cup (125 mL) all-purpose flour

¼ tsp (1 mL) salt

TOPPING:

3 oz (90 g) milk chocolate, chopped

3 Tbsp (45 mL) unsalted butter

1 tsp (5 mL) vegetable oil

1 cup (250 mL) walnut pieces, lightly toasted

1 cup (250 mL) mini marshmallows

note from anna's kitchen

This is one of the few instances in baking where, if you cannot find couverture milk chocolate (please see pages 9–10 for more details on chocolate), you *can* use a chopped up chocolate bar or milk chocolate chips. Remember that quality counts, so go for a good name.

RASPBERRY PECAN TART
• *Makes one 9-inch (23 cm) fluted tart* | *Serves 8 to 10* •

THIS FILLING IS gooey and sweet, but it still slices cleanly and easily. The fresh raspberries offer refreshing little bursts of juice and make this quite an elegant dessert.

1. Preheat the oven to 325°F (160°C). Place the pan containing the crust onto a baking tray.
2. Whisk the brown sugar with the eggs, egg yolk, and vanilla until blended. Stir in the pecans, coconut, flour, baking powder, and salt. Gently fold in the raspberries.
3. Pour the mixture into the cooled crust and bake on the tray for about 45 minutes, until evenly browned and set. Cool the tart to room temperature in the pan before removing the outer ring of the pan to slice. The tart can be served at room temperature or chilled. The tart will keep in the refrigerator for up to 4 days.

note from anna's kitchen
This tart would be lovely served with Vanilla Crème Anglaise (page 319).

1 recipe pecan Nut-Crust Tart Shell (page 113), baked and cooled

FILLING:

1 cup (250 mL) packed light brown sugar

2 eggs

1 egg yolk

1 tsp (5 mL) vanilla extract

1½ cups (375 mL) coarsely chopped pecans

1 cup (250 mL) sweetened, shredded coconut

½ cup (125 mL) all-purpose flour

½ tsp (2 mL) baking powder

¼ tsp (1 mL) salt

1 cup (250 mL) fresh raspberries

CHOCOLATE-CRUST TART SHELL

• *Makes one 9-inch (23 cm) baked tart shell* •

foundation
RECIChE

THIS CRUST HAS a rich, balanced chocolate character, but it is not so intense that it overwhelms the fillings you bake in it.

1. Using a food processor or standup mixer fitted with the paddle attachment, blend the flour, cocoa, brown sugar, and salt. Add the butter and blend until the mixture is an even, crumbly texture. In a small dish, whisk the egg yolk, milk, and vanilla, and pour it into the flour mixture, blending until the dough fully comes together. Shape the dough into a disc, wrap it in plastic wrap, and chill it until firm, at least 1 hour.

2. On a lightly floured work surface, gently knead the chilled chocolate dough to soften it slightly. Roll out the dough into a circle about 12 inches (30 cm) across and about $\frac{1}{4}$ inch (6 mm) thick. Line an ungreased 9-inch (23 cm), removable-bottom tart pan with the pastry and trim away any excess dough. Chill the tart shell for 30 minutes.

3. Preheat the oven to 350°F (175°C). Place the chilled tart shell on a baking tray and dock the bottom of the pastry with a fork. Bake the tart shell for about 25 minutes, until the pastry has an even, dull appearance. Cool the shell while preparing the filling.

1 cup (250 mL) all-purpose flour
¼ cup (60 mL) regular or Dutch process cocoa powder
¼ cup (60 mL) packed light brown sugar
¼ tsp (1 mL) salt
6 Tbsp (90 mL) cool unsalted butter, cut in pieces
1 egg yolk
2 Tbsp (30 mL) milk
1 tsp (5 mL) vanilla extract

MOCHA LATTE MOUSSE TART

• Makes one 9-inch (23 cm) tart | Serves 8 to 10 •

---

*I*N THIS TART, a sinfully rich coffee mousse hides a ganache layer underneath it, giving this tart that layered look we appreciate so much in a well-made latte.

1. For the ganache layer, place the chocolate in a bowl. Heat the cream to just below a simmer, then pour it over the chocolate. Let it sit for a minute, then gently stir the mixture until the chocolate has melted. Pour this into the cooled crust and spread it evenly across the bottom. Chill while preparing the latte mousse.

2. For the latte mousse, stir the hot coffee with the instant coffee until it is melted. In a small dish, stir the gelatin powder and cold water, and let it sit for 1 minute. Add the gelatin to the hot coffee and stir until dissolved, re-heating the coffee over low heat if needed. Stir in the condensed milk and vanilla, and cool to room temperature.

3. Whip the cream to soft peak and fold this into the cooled coffee mixture (this mousse will be very fluid). Pour this into the prepared crust and chill in the pan for at least 3 hours. Sprinkle the top of the tart with cinnamon before removing the outer ring of the pan and serving. The tart will keep in the refrigerator for up to 3 days.

1 recipe Chocolate-Crust Tart Shell (page 118), baked and cooled

GANACHE LAYER:

2 oz (60 g) bittersweet chocolate, chopped
¼ cup (60 mL) whipping cream

LATTE MOUSSE:

3 Tbsp (45 mL) hot, strong coffee
1½ Tbsp (22.5 mL) instant coffee granules
2 tsp (10 mL) gelatin powder
2 Tbsp (30 mL) cold water
1 tin (300 mL) sweetened condensed milk
1 tsp (5 mL) vanilla extract
¾ cup (185 mL) whipping cream
Ground cinnamon, for garnish

MILK CHOCOLATE SILK TART
• *Makes one 9-inch (23 cm) tart | Serves 8 to 10* •

*T*HIS IS NOT a ganache-style tart, like a *tarte au chocolat*, but it is a lighter, airier version. It's not quite as fluffy as a chocolate mousse, and the addition of butter gives it a silky, melt-in-your mouth texture that can't be resisted.

1. Place a medium pot filled with 1 inch (2.5 cm) of water on the stove and bring it to a gentle simmer. In a metal or glass bowl that fits over the pot but without touching the water, whisk the eggs, sugar, water, and salt. Whisk the egg mixture over the simmering water until it doubles in volume and holds a ribbon when the whisk is lifted, about 8 minutes.

2. Remove the bowl from the heat and stir in the chopped milk chocolate. Switch to a spatula and stir gently until the chocolate is melted. Allow this chocolate mixture to cool to room temperature, about 20 minutes.

3. Using electric beaters or a stand mixer fitted with the paddle attachment, or by hand, beat in the butter until evenly incorporated. In a separate bowl and with clean beaters, whip the cream and vanilla until it holds a soft peak. Fold the whipped cream into the chocolate mixture in 2 additions, and spread this into the cooled tart shell. Chill the tart in the pan for at least 2 hours before topping with the chocolate shavings and removing the outer ring of the pan to serve. The tart will keep in the refrigerator for up to 4 days.

1 recipe Chocolate-Crust Tart Shell (page 118), baked and cooled

FILLING:

3 eggs
½ cup (125 mL) sugar
2 Tbsp (30 mL) water
½ tsp (2 mL) salt
12 oz (360 g) milk chocolate, chopped
½ cup (125 mL) unsalted butter, at room temperature
1 cup (250 mL) whipping cream
2 tsp (10 mL) vanilla extract
Chocolate Shavings (dark) (page 321), for garnish

note from anna's kitchen

All of the tarts and pies in this chapter that have a creamy filling are most easily cut using a hot, dry knife. Dip a chef's knife into a pitcher of hot tap water for 20 seconds, wipe off the blade with a towel, then make a clean slice. Dip and wipe the knife after each slice.

PUMPKIN CHEESECAKE AND CHOCOLATE TART
• *Makes one 9-inch (23 cm) tart | Serves 8 to 10* •

*I*N THIS TART, a chocolate ganache layer hides a silky pumpkin cheesecake filling within. The combination of pumpkin and chocolate may seem unexpected, but it is a divine and well-matched duo, especially when traditional pumpkin pie spices are mixed in.

1. Preheat the oven to 350°F (175°C).
2. Using electric beaters or a food processor, or even by hand, combine the cream cheese and brown sugar until the brown sugar dissolves. Stir in the pumpkin, cornstarch, cinnamon, cardamom, and ginger, then add the whole egg and egg yolks.
3. Pour this mixture into the cooked, cooled chocolate crust, and bake the tart on a baking tray for about 20 minutes until, like a cheesecake, it is set around the outside with just a bit of a jiggle in the centre. Cool the tart to room temperature.
4. For the ganache, melt the chocolate, butter, and corn syrup in a metal or glass bowl set over a pot of barely simmering water, stirring with a spatula until smooth. Pour this gently on the centre of the pumpkin cheesecake, and carefully spread it toward the outside, leaving 1 inch (2.5 cm) of the pumpkin visible at the edge. Chill the tart for at least 2 hours in the pan before removing the outer ring of the pan and slicing the tart to serve. The tart can be stored in the refrigerator for up to 3 days.

1 recipe Chocolate-Crust Tart Shell (page 118), baked and cooled

FILLING:

1 pkg (8 oz/250 g) cream cheese, at room temperature

½ cup (125 mL) packed dark brown sugar

1 cup (250 mL) plain pumpkin purée

1 Tbsp (15 mL) cornstarch

½ tsp (2 mL) ground cinnamon

½ tsp (2 mL) ground cardamom

½ tsp (2 mL) ground ginger

1 egg

2 egg yolks

GANACHE TOPPING:

2 oz (60 g) bittersweet chocolate, chopped

3 Tbsp (45 mL) unsalted butter

1 Tbsp (15 mL) corn syrup

CLASSIC FRUIT CRISP
• *Serves 6 to 8* •

egg-
FREE

ONE OF THE easier desserts to make, a crisp is also easy to personalize by using your favourite fruits, or use what is in peak season or available to you.

1. Preheat the oven to 350°F (175°C).
2. Toss the prepared fruit with ¼ cup (60 mL) of the brown sugar and the vanilla, and spread it into an 8-cup (2 L) baking dish.
3. Stir the oats, the remaining ½ cup (125 mL) of brown sugar, flour, and the cinnamon in a bowl. Pour in the melted butter and stir until evenly combined. Sprinkle this over the fruit and bake for 35 to 40 minutes, until the fruit is bubbling at the edges and the crisp is evenly browned. Cool for 15 minutes before serving with ice cream. The crisp will keep in the refrigerator for up to 2 days.

6 cups (1.5 L) mixed fruit, diced if needed
¾ cup (185 mL) packed light brown sugar
½ tsp (2 mL) vanilla extract
1¼ cups (310 mL) regular rolled oats
⅓ cup (80 mL) all-purpose flour
½ tsp (2 mL) ground cinnamon
½ cup (125 mL) unsalted butter, melted

notes from anna's kitchen

Fruit for crisp can be any combination of your favourites. Follow these basic tips to customize your own crisps:

1. Use fresh fruits that are in season for the best results.
2. A crisp is a great way to use up slightly overripe fruits, but cut away any bruising or scarring to avoid a bitter or flat taste.
3. Any fruit that you like in a pie will work in a crisp, and remember that a low-acid fruit benefits from a more acidic companion, such as pear with cranberry, strawberry with rhubarb, and apricot with peach. Apple can also work with these other fruit to make them sparkle.
4. Any fruit that you would not enjoy cooked will not work here, such as melon, citrus, or diced bananas.
5. Delicate fruits such as raspberries and blueberries cook down to a much smaller volume. For a berry crisp, use 2 to 3 cups (500 to 750 mL) of diced apples or peaches with the remaining measure in berries to give your crisp structure without losing any berry taste.

APPLE COOKIE CRUMBLE
• Serves 6 to 8 •

A CRISP EARNS ITS name, a cobbler is cake-like with a crunchy top, and a crumble is typically quite sweet with a good crumble to it (earning its name honestly). I've discovered that Basic Brown Sugar Cookie Dough (page 17) bakes beautifully into an apple crumble topping. Now that's a recipe with multi-tasking power.

1. Preheat the oven to 350°F (175°C).
2. Toss the apples with the brown sugar and ½ teaspoon (2 mL) of the cinnamon, and spread them in an 8-cup (2 L) baking dish.
3. Prepare the cookie dough recipe and stir the remaining ½ tsp (2 mL) of ground cinnamon into the dough. Crumble pieces of the cookie dough over the apples, leaving gaps here and there to allow for the dough to expand.
4. Bake the crumble for 35 to 40 minutes, until the top of the crumble has browned and the crumble has cooked through (you can tell by lifting a piece of the dough). Let the crumble cool for 15 minutes before serving it with ice cream. The crumble will keep in the refrigerator for up to 2 days.

6 cups (1.5 L) peeled and sliced apples, such as Granny Smith, Mutsu, Cortland, McIntosh, Spartan, or Honey Crisp
3 Tbsp (45 mL) packed light brown sugar
1 tsp (5 mL) ground cinnamon
1 recipe Basic Brown Sugar Cookie Dough (page 17)

PEACH BERRY COBBLER
· Serves 6 to 8 ·

COBBLER TOPPING IS like scone meeting cake—the heat of the oven creates a lovely crunchy top to the cobbler and the steam from the baking fruits creates a moist, cake-like interior.

1. Preheat oven to 375°F (190°C).
2. Toss the peaches, raspberries, and blueberries with 3 Tbsp (45 mL) of the sugar and ¼ tsp (1 mL) of the cinnamon, and spread the mixture on the bottom of an 8-cup (2 L) baking dish (preferably ceramic—see pages 6–7 for more on pan choice).
3. Whisk the eggs, the remaining ½ cup (125 mL) of sugar, and the melted butter together in a large bowl. Whisk in the milk. Sift in the flour, cornmeal, baking powder, and salt, and stir until combined (the batter will be wet).
4. Spoon the batter over the fruit, leaving a little space between spoonfuls to allow for expansion as the cobbler bakes. Stir a little sugar and cinnamon together, and sprinkle this overtop the cobbler.
5. Bake for 35 to 45 minutes, until the peach juices are bubbling and the topping is cooked through (you can lift a piece up to check that it is cooked through). Serve the cobbler warm with ice cream. The cobbler will keep in the refrigerator for up to 2 days.

6 cups (1.5 L) peeled and sliced
    fresh peaches
1 cup (250 mL) fresh raspberries
½ cup (125 mL) fresh blueberries
3 Tbsp (45 mL) + ½ cup (125 mL) sugar,
    plus extra for cinnamon sugar
¼ tsp (1 mL) ground cinnamon,
    plus extra for cinnamon sugar
2 eggs
6 Tbsp (90 mL) unsalted butter, melted
⅔ cup (160 mL) milk
2 cups (500 mL) all-purpose flour
2 Tbsp (30 mL) cornmeal
4 tsp (20 mL) baking powder
½ tsp (2 mL) salt

note from anna's kitchen
You can easily dress up a rustic dessert such as this with the simple addition of Vanilla Crème Anglaise (page 319).

Simple Cakes

These cake recipes are intended to be simple not just in name and in method, but in presentation as well. These cakes are not meant for frosting or filling with mousse, but they are meant to be simply served as a slice on their own, or with a little fresh fruit or a dollop of whipped cream on the side.

Cupcakes

Cupcakes have had a resurgence in popularity that has lasted long enough to surpass the label of a "trend." Cupcakes that endure the test of time go beyond mere cake and frosting. While you can turn many of the layer-cake and frosting recipes in this book into cupcakes, the cupcake recipes offer a little more depth and character, making them a real treat to make and to eat.

Classic Cakes

Although the layer cakes in this section are each matched with a frosting, feel free to change the cake and frosting combinations to suit your friends' and family's tastes (especially if you're making a birthday cake for someone special).

Whipped Cakes

Whipped cakes are light and airy, with whipped eggs acting as the main component behind that desired fluffy result.

Pound and Bundt Cakes

This style of cake, while dense and a bit heavier than other styles, makes for easy-to-slice cakes that present well without frosting and can stay fresh and moist for days. Unlike the original pound cake recipes, the pound cake recipes in this chapter do not follow the formula of a pound of butter, pound of sugar, pound of eggs, pound of flour. Having put that to the test just once, I can attest that the cakes in this chapter are far more palatable (the "pound" test resulted in a greasy, doughy, flavourless mass).

Cheesecakes

A real crowd-pleaser, a cheesecake just takes a little forethought—it is best served the day after you bake it.

To prepare a cheesecake successfully, without any cracks, here are a few tips.

Special Occasion and Wedding Cakes

Cakes for special occasions and weddings often feature a specific method, flavour combination, or assembly.

SEMOLINA ORANGE SYRUP CAKE
• *Makes one 9- × 13-inch (23 × 33 cm) cake | Serves 16* •

THIS IS A simple cake that feeds a large group. It needs to stay in the pan to soak up the orange syrup as it cools, so it is best portioned and plated in the kitchen.

1. Preheat the oven to 350°F (175°C) and grease a 9- × 13-inch (23 × 33 cm) cake pan.

2. Beat the butter, ¾ cup (185 mL) of the sugar, and the orange zest until fluffy, then add the egg yolks and beat them in. Beat in the vanilla. In a separate bowl, sift the flour, semolina, baking powder, salt, and cinnamon, and add this to the butter mixture, alternating with the milk, starting and ending with the flour, and blending well after each addition.

3. Whip the egg whites until foamy, then slowly pour in the remaining ¼ cup (60 mL) of sugar and whip until the whites hold a soft peak. Fold the whites into the cake batter and scrape the batter into the prepared pan.

4. Bake for about 30 minutes, until a tester inserted in the centre of the cake comes out clean. While the cake is baking, prepare the syrup.

5. In a saucepot, bring the sugar, orange juice, lemon juice, water, and orange zest up to a simmer, and cook just until the sugar fully dissolves. Set aside to cool to just above room temperature. Ten minutes after the cake is pulled from the oven, slowly pour the cooled syrup over the entire surface of the cake and let it soak in. Cool the cake completely before cutting into squares and serving. The cake can be stored in the refrigerator for up to 3 days.

CAKE:

½ cup (125 mL) unsalted butter, at room temperature

1 cup (250 mL) sugar

2 tsp (10 mL) finely grated orange zest

3 eggs, at room temperature, separated

1 tsp (5 mL) vanilla extract

1 cup (250 mL) all-purpose flour

1 cup (250 mL) durum semolina

1 Tbsp (15 mL) baking powder

¼ tsp (1 mL) salt

¼ tsp (1 mL) ground cinnamon

1 cup (250 mL) milk, at room temperature

SYRUP:

¾ cup (185 mL) sugar

⅓ cup (80 mL) orange juice

⅓ cup (80 mL) lemon juice

3 Tbsp (45 mL) water

2 tsp (10 mL) finely grated orange zest

note from anna's kitchen

An easy way to fold delicate ingredients together, like folding the whites into the base of this cake batter, is to use a whisk. Folding with a whisk will gently incorporate the whites into the batter without deflating them.

HAZELNUT RICOTTA CAKE
• *Makes one 8-inch (20 cm) round cake* | *Serves 8* •

THIS IS A simple cake because it doesn't require frosting or filling, and it can be fully prepared in the bowl of a food processor. Serve this cake with fresh berries, or a dollop of lightly sweetened whipped cream, or ricotta with a pinch of cinnamon.

1 cup (250 mL) whole dry-roasted hazelnuts
⅔ cup (160 mL) sugar
⅓ cup (80 mL) vegetable oil
½ cup (125 mL) ricotta cheese
2 eggs
1 tsp (5 mL) vanilla extract
2 tsp (10 mL) finely grated orange zest
¾ cup (180 mL) all-purpose flour
1 tsp (5 mL) baking powder
¼ tsp (1 mL) salt

1. Preheat the oven to 350°F (175°C) and grease an 8-inch (20 cm) cake pan.
2. Using a food processor, pulse the hazelnuts and sugar until the hazelnuts are finely ground. Add the oil, ricotta, eggs, vanilla, and orange zest, and pulse to blend. Add the flour, baking powder, and salt, and pulse just until combined. Gently scrape the batter into the prepared pan.
3. Bake the cake for about 35 minutes, until a tester inserted in the centre of the cake comes out clean. Allow the cake to cool for 30 minutes before turning out to cool completely. The cake can be stored, well-wrapped, at room temperature for up to 3 days.

note from anna's kitchen
Ricotta cheese is one of the few dairy products where the light, or lower-fat, version can be used in place of the regular if you wish.

CLASSIC GINGERBREAD CAKE
• *Makes one 8-inch (20 cm) square cake* •
Cuts into 16 squares

THIS RECIPE FEATURES a classic proportion of spices. You can take this ratio of cinnamon, ginger, nutmeg, allspice, and cloves, and make a larger batch. Then you have it on hand for pumpkin pie or spiced muffins, or even to add a pinch to coffee grounds when brewing a pot.

GINGERBREAD:
6 Tbsp (90 mL) unsalted butter, at room temperature
½ cup (125 mL) packed dark brown sugar
2 eggs, at room temperature
½ cup (125 mL) fancy molasses
1 tsp (5 mL) finely grated lemon zest
1⅔ cups (410 mL) all-purpose flour
1½ tsp (7.5 mL) ground cinnamon
1½ tsp (7.5 mL) ground ginger
½ tsp (2 mL) ground nutmeg
½ tsp (2 mL) ground allspice
¼ tsp (1 mL) ground cloves
¾ tsp (4 mL) baking powder
¼ tsp (1 mL) baking soda
½ cup (125 mL) hot water
½ cup (125 mL) dark chocolate chips

1. Preheat the oven to 350°F (175°C) and line the bottom and sides of an 8-inch (20 cm) square pan with parchment paper, so that the paper comes up the sides of the pan.
2. Beat the butter and brown sugar together in a large mixing bowl. Add the eggs one at a time, mixing well after each addition. Stir in the molasses and lemon zest.
3. In a separate bowl, stir to blend the flour, cinnamon, ginger, nutmeg, allspice, cloves, baking powder, and baking soda. Add the flour mixture to the butter mixture and stir until blended. Stir in the hot water then add in the chocolate chips. Scrape the batter into the prepared pan.
4. Bake for about 35 minutes, until a tester inserted in the centre of the cake comes out clean. Cool the cake to room temperature, then slice and serve. The gingerbread will keep in an airtight container for up to 5 days or in the freezer for 2 months.

Hazelnut Ricotta Cake

FLOURLESS CHOCOLATE TORTE
• Makes one 9-inch (23 cm) round cake | Serves 10 to 12 •

gluten-
FREE

*T*HIS SIMPLE FRENCH-STYLE chocolate torte is super decadent. It melts away on the tip of your tongue.

1. Preheat the oven to 300°F (150°C). Grease a 9-inch (23 cm) springform pan, line the bottom with parchment, then grease and dust the entire pan with sugar, tapping out any excess.
2. Melt the chocolate and butter in a metal or glass bowl placed over a pot of barely simmering water, stirring constantly. Once the chocolate has melted, remove the bowl from the heat and let the mixture cool slightly.
3. Whip the egg whites with 2 tablespoons (30 mL) of the sugar until the whites hold a soft peak (the whites will curl when the beaters are lifted). Set aside.
4. In another bowl, whip the egg yolks with the remaining $\frac{1}{4}$ cup (60 mL) of sugar, salt, and the vanilla until the mixture doubles in volume, about 4 minutes. Fold the melted chocolate mixture into the whipped yolks, then fold the whites into the mixture in 2 additions. Spread the batter into the prepared pan.
5. Bake the torte for 35 minutes, until it barely jiggles when moved. As soon as you remove the cake from the oven it will begin to fall, but it is supposed to. Cool the cake to room temperature then chill for at least 2 hours before slicing and serving.
6. The cake should be stored in the refrigerator and sliced while cold, but, if you can, allow the cake slices to sit out at room temperature for 10 to 20 minutes before serving to really build that melt-in-your-mouth warmth. The cake will keep in the refrigerator for up to 4 days.

10 oz (300 g) bittersweet chocolate, chopped
¾ cup (185 mL) unsalted butter, cut in pieces
3 egg whites
2 Tbsp (30 mL) + ¼ cup (60 mL) sugar
5 egg yolks
Pinch salt
1 tsp (5 mL) vanilla extract

note from anna's kitchen
For tips on melting chocolate, refer to pages 9–10.

LEMON MERINGUE CUPCAKES
• *Makes 16 cupcakes* •

*I*N THIS RECIPE, a tasty lemon cake is topped with a spoonful of lemon marmalade, which then has meringue piped around it to hide the surprise.

1. Preheat the oven to 350°F (175°C) and line 16 muffin cups with large paper liners.
2. Cream the butter, sugar, and lemon zest until smooth. Beat in the egg and vanilla. In a separate bowl, sift the pastry flour, baking powder, and salt. In a small bowl, stir the buttermilk and lemon juice together, and add this to the butter mixture, alternating with the flour, starting and ending with the flour, and blending well after each addition. Spoon the batter into the paper liners.
3. Bake the cupcakes for 20 to 25 minutes, until the tops of the cupcakes spring back when gently pressed. Cool the cupcakes in the tins for 10 minutes, then remove them from the tins to cool completely.
4. For the topping, preheat the oven to 375°F (190°C) and place the cooled cupcakes on a baking tray. Spoon about a teaspoon of marmalade or lemon curd on top of each cupcake, keeping the filling as close in the centre as possible. Whip the egg whites with the cream of tartar until foamy, then slowly add the sugar while whipping. Whip the whites until they hold a stiff peak (the whites stand upright when the beaters are lifted).
5. Spoon the meringue into a piping bag and pipe swirls on top of each cupcake, being sure to completely cover the marmalade or curd. Bake the cupcakes for 6 to 8 minutes, until the meringue browns slightly, and cool to room temperature. The cupcakes can be stored in the refrigerator for up to 2 days but are best enjoyed at room temperature.

CUPCAKES:

½ cup (125 mL) unsalted butter,
  at room temperature
1¼ cups (310 mL) sugar
2 tsp (10 mL) finely grated lemon zest
1 egg, at room temperature
1 tsp (5 mL) vanilla extract
2 cups (500 mL) cake and pastry flour
2½ tsp (12 mL) baking powder
½ tsp (2 mL) salt
¾ cup (185 mL) buttermilk,
  at room temperature
2 Tbsp (30 mL) lemon juice
5 to 6 Tbsp (75 to 90 mL) lemon
  marmalade, or Lemon Curd (page 147)

MERINGUE:

4 egg whites, at room temperature
½ tsp (2 mL) cream of tartar
⅔ cup (160 mL) sugar

notes from anna's kitchen

1. To make room for even more marmalade, you can spoon a little cake out of the centre of the cooled cupcakes.
2. This meringue recipe is quick and simple, like the traditional topping on lemon meringue pie. For a new take on meringue that avoids any weeping or slipping, take a peek at the Lemon Meringue Pie recipe on page 92.

RED VELVET CUPCAKES
• *Makes 15 cupcakes* •

USING RAW BEETS is a natural way to add a gentle pink tone to cupcakes, but don't expect a vivid red colour. For that brilliant red you see in photos and from commercial bakeries, you have to use food colouring. The choice is yours.

1. Preheat the oven to 350°F (175°C) and line 15 muffin cups with large paper liners.

2. Beat the butter, brown sugar, and white sugar together at high speed for 1 minute. Add the egg and vanilla, and beat until smooth.

3. In a separate bowl, sift the flour, cocoa, baking powder, baking soda, and salt.

4. In another bowl, stir the buttermilk, grated beets, and vinegar together. Add the flour mixture to the butter mixture, alternating with the buttermilk mixture and blending well after each addition. Spoon an even amount of the batter into each cupcake liner.

5. Bake for 18 to 20 minutes, until the top of the cupcakes spring back when gently pressed. Cool the cupcakes for 10 minutes in the tins, then take them out to cool completely on a cooling rack.

6. For the frosting, beat the butter and cream cheese until fluffy, about 3 minutes. Add the icing sugar and vanilla, and beat gently until the sugar is incorporated, then beat more vigorously until the icing is fluffy. Pipe or spread the frosting onto each cupcake. The cupcakes should be stored chilled but served at room temperature. They will keep in the refrigerator for up to 3 days.

CUPCAKES:

6 Tbsp (90 mL) unsalted butter, at room temperature
6 Tbsp (90 mL) packed dark brown sugar
6 Tbsp (90 mL) white sugar
1 egg, at room temperature
½ tsp (2 mL) vanilla extract
1¼ cups (310 mL) all-purpose flour
2 Tbsp (30 mL) regular cocoa powder
½ tsp (2 mL) baking powder
½ tsp (2 mL) baking soda
¼ tsp (1 mL) salt
¾ cup (185 mL) buttermilk
3 Tbsp (45 mL) finely grated raw beets
2 tsp (10 mL) white vinegar

CREAM CHEESE FROSTING:

½ cup (125 mL) unsalted butter, at room temperature
¾ pkg (6 oz/175 g) cream cheese, at room temperature
2 cups (500 mL) icing sugar, sifted
1 tsp (5 mL) vanilla extract

note from anna's kitchen
For a more intensely red colour, you can replace the grated beets with 2 teaspoons (10 mL) of red food colouring, then add another ½ cup (125 mL) of buttermilk to the recipe.

STRAWBERRY SHORTCAKE CUPCAKES
• *Makes 12 cupcakes* •

*T*HESE PRETTY CUPCAKES have that classic strawberries-and-cream character. The whipped cream frosting is strengthened by a little cream cheese, making it hold slices of strawberries easily. Keep them chilled until right before you wish to serve them.

1. Preheat the oven to 350°F (175°C) and line a 12-cup muffin tin with large paper liners.

2. Using electric beaters or a stand mixer fitted with the paddle attachment, beat the butter and sugar together on high speed for 1 minute. Add the eggs one at a time, beating well and scraping the bowl after each addition, then beat in the vanilla.

3. In a separate bowl, sift the flour, cornstarch, baking powder, and salt. Add this, alternating with the sour cream, in 3 additions, starting and ending with the flour. Spoon this batter into the prepared muffin tin.

4. Bake the cupcakes for about 18 minutes, until a tester inserted in the centre of a cupcake comes out clean. Let the cupcakes cool for 15 minutes before removing and cooling completely before frosting.

5. To prepare the frosting, whip the cream until it holds a soft peak, then set it aside. Beat the cream cheese and butter together until light and fluffy. Beat in the icing sugar and vanilla, then fold in the whipped cream in 2 additions. Using a piping bag fitted with a large star tip, pipe the frosting onto each cupcake. Insert the strawberry slices into the cream, arranged to look like flower petals—once the frosting chills, it holds the slices securely. Chill until ready to serve.

6. The cupcakes are best eaten the day they are assembled, but you can make the cupcakes a day ahead and store them at room temperature.

CUPCAKES:

½ cup (125 mL) unsalted butter, at room temperature

⅔ cup (160 mL) sugar

3 eggs, at room temperature

1½ tsp (7.5 mL) vanilla extract

1½ cups (375 mL) all-purpose flour

1 Tbsp (15 mL) cornstarch

1½ tsp (7.5 mL) baking powder

¼ tsp (1 mL) salt

⅓ cup (80 mL) sour cream

CREAM FROSTING:

1 cup (250 mL) whipping cream

½ pkg (4 oz/120 g) cream cheese, at room temperature

¼ cup (60 mL) unsalted butter, at room temperature

⅔ cup (160 mL) icing sugar, sifted

1 tsp (5 mL) vanilla extract

2 cups (500 mL) sliced fresh strawberries

Spiced Cupcakes with Coconut Icing, top left (page 140), *Strawberry Shortcake Cupcakes*, top centre (page 138), and *Truffle-Centred Chocolate Cupcakes*, bottom right (page 141)

SPICED CUPCAKES WITH COCONUT ICING
• *Makes 18 cupcakes* •

*T*HESE CUPCAKES ARE delicate and tender, and the spice blend is more like chai flavours than gingerbread.

1. Preheat the oven to 375°F (190°C) and line 18 muffin cups with paper liners.
2. Sift the flour, ½ cup (125 mL) of sugar, the brown sugar, baking powder, salt, and spices into a large mixing bowl.
3. Make a well in the centre of the flour mixture and add the oil, buttermilk, molasses, and vanilla. Beat for one minute with electric beaters. Add the egg yolks and beat for another minute.
4. In a separate bowl and using cleaned beaters, whip the egg whites until foamy. Gradually pour in the remaining ½ cup (125 mL) of sugar, and whip until the whites hold a stiff peak. Fold the whites gently into the batter and spoon into the muffin cups.
5. Bake for 15 to 18 minutes, until the cupcakes spring back when pressed. Allow them to cool in the tin.
6. For the icing, beat the butter until fluffy. On low speed, beat in 1¾ cups (435 mL) of the icing sugar, then add the coconut milk. Beat in the vanilla and coconut extract (if using), then beat in the remaining 1¾ cups (435 mL) of the icing sugar. If the icing is too thin, add a touch more icing sugar, and if it's too thick, add a touch more coconut milk. Spread the icing onto the cupcakes and garnish with shredded coconut. The cupcakes can be stored in an airtight container for up to 2 days.

CUPCAKES:

2 cups + 2 Tbsp (530 mL) cake
   and pastry flour
1 cup (250 mL) sugar
½ cup (125 mL) packed light brown sugar
1 Tbsp (15 mL) baking powder
1 tsp (5 mL) salt
½ tsp (2 mL) ground cinnamon
½ tsp (2 mL) ground cardamom
¼ tsp (1 mL) ground allspice
¼ tsp (1 mL) ground black pepper
⅓ cup (80 mL) vegetable oil
¾ cup (185 mL) buttermilk
1 Tbsp (15 mL) fancy molasses
1½ tsp (7.5 mL) vanilla extract
2 eggs, separated

COCONUT ICING:

¼ cup (60 mL) unsalted butter,
   at room temperature
3½ cups (875 mL) icing sugar, sifted
½ cup (125 mL) coconut milk
1 tsp (5 mL) vanilla extract
½ tsp (2 mL) coconut extract (optional)
Sweetened, flaked coconut, for garnish

notes from anna's kitchen

1. For an attractive alternate garnish, use a vegetable peeler to peel large coconut curls from the meat of a fresh, shelled coconut. Place the curls on a parchment-lined baking tray, dust them generously with icing sugar, and bake in a 350°F (175°C) oven for 10 minutes. Cool before putting them on the cupcakes.

2. The use of extracts like coconut or rum flavouring is purely a matter of taste. Since these are flavourings and not natural extracts, they can sometimes overwhelm a dessert (in the case of coconut extract, too much can make a dish smell like suntan lotion).

TRUFFLE-CENTRED CHOCOLATE CUPCAKES
• Makes 20 cupcakes •

A FROSTING RECIPE HAS been included here (for a cupcake to be a cupcake, it really needs frosting), but, honestly, the truffle centre makes these a completely decadent delight even without the frosting.

1. To prepare the truffles, heat the cream to a simmer and pour it over the chopped chocolate. Let it sit for a minute, then gently whisk to blend. Chill this mixture until set, about 2 hours. Spoon this ganache into 20 truffles, shaping them between your hands into ¾-inch (2 cm) balls. Chill the truffles until ready to use.

2. Preheat the oven to 375°F (190°C) and line 20 muffin cups with paper liners.

3. For the cupcakes, melt the chocolate and butter together in a saucepot, stirring over low heat, then stir in ⅔ cup (160 mL) of the brown sugar and ⅓ cup (80 mL) of the milk. Stir over medium heat until the sugar has dissolved (don't worry if the mixture does not look smooth—it will even out later). Pour this mixture into a bowl, whisk in the remaining ⅔ cup (160 mL) of brown sugar, and cool to room temperature. Whisk in the eggs one at a time, blending well after each addition. Whisk in the vanilla.

4. In a separate bowl, sift the flour, baking soda, and salt. Add this to the chocolate mixture in 3 additions, alternating with the remaining ½ cup (125 mL) of milk, starting and ending with the flour, and whisking well after each addition (the batter will be quite fluid). Pour the batter into the prepared muffin cups, filling to halfway.

5. Gently place a truffle in the centre of each cupcake—do not press it in, as it will settle and become completely enveloped by the batter as it bakes. Bake the cupcakes for about 20 minutes, until the cake springs back when gently pressed. Cool the cupcakes completely before frosting.

6. For the frosting, stir the chocolate and butter in a saucepot over low heat until melted. Transfer this to a bowl and whisk in the sour cream and vanilla. Beat in the icing sugar until the mixture is smooth and spreadable, adding a touch more icing sugar if needed. Spread or pipe the frosting onto each cupcake. The cupcakes should be stored at room temperature in an airtight container and will keep for up to 2 days. Do not refrigerate.

TRUFFLES:

6 Tbsp (90 mL) whipping cream
3 oz (90 g) bittersweet chocolate, chopped

CUPCAKES:

2 oz (60 g) unsweetened chocolate, chopped
½ cup (125 mL) unsalted butter
1⅓ cups (330 mL) packed light brown sugar
⅓ cup (80 mL) + ½ cup (125 mL) milk
2 eggs, at room temperature
1 tsp (5 mL) vanilla extract
1⅓ cups (330 mL) all-purpose flour
1 tsp (5 mL) baking soda
½ tsp (2 mL) salt

FROSTING:

3 oz (90 g) unsweetened chocolate, chopped
3 Tbsp (45 mL) unsalted butter
½ cup (125 mL) sour cream
1 tsp (5 mL) vanilla extract
2 cups (500 mL) icing sugar, sifted, plus extra to adjust consistency

notes from anna's kitchen

1. If consumed within 24 hours of baking, the truffle filling will be soft and almost fluid. After a day, the truffle sets further, but it is still satisfyingly delicate.

2. If you do not wish to make the frosting for these cupcakes, simply dust them with a little icing sugar.

RICH VANILLA CAKE WITH FUDGE FROSTING
• *Makes one 8-inch (20 cm), 2-layer cake | Serves 12* •

*T*ENDER, MOIST, AND tasty, this vanilla cake, with a light buttery hue, suits a rich fudge frosting.

1. Preheat the oven to 350°F (175°C). Grease two 8-inch (20 cm) cake pans, and line the bottom of the pans with parchment paper. Grease the parchment and dust it lightly with flour.
2. Using a mixer or electric beaters, beat the butter and sugar until it is light and fluffy. Add the eggs one at a time, mixing well after each addition. Add the vanilla.
3. In a separate bowl, sift both the flours with the baking powder and salt. Add this alternately with the buttermilk on low speed, starting and ending with the flour, and scraping the bowl after each addition. Divide the batter between the 2 prepared pans and spread evenly.
4. Bake the cakes for about 30 minutes, until a tester inserted in the centre of the cake comes out clean. Allow the cake to cool for 30 minutes before turning each out onto a rack to cool completely before frosting.
5. Place the first cake layer onto a serving platter and spread about ½ cup (125 mL) of the frosting over the top of the cake. Place the second cake layer on top of the first and spread a thick layer of frosting on top of the cake, then spread the remaining frosting onto the sides, using an offset spatula to swirl the frosting. Allow the frosting to set at room temperature, and store and serve the cake at room temperature.

⅔ cup (160 mL) unsalted butter,
    at room temperature
1⅓ cups (330 mL) sugar
3 eggs, at room temperature
1 Tbsp (15 mL) vanilla extract
1 cup (250 mL) all-purpose flour
1 cup (250 mL) cake and pastry flour
2 tsp (10 mL) baking powder
¼ tsp (1 mL) salt
1 cup (250 mL) buttermilk,
    at room temperature
1 recipe Fudge Frosting (recipe follows)

note from anna's kitchen
Any extra frosting can be scraped into a piping bag so that you can pipe garnishes on the sides and top.

FUDGE FROSTING
• *Makes about 2½ cups (625 mL)* •

THIS IS A textbook fudge frosting, for when you crave that classic chocolate frosting taste, texture, and appearance.

1. Melt the butter and chocolate in a metal or glass bowl placed over a pot of barely simmering water, stirring gently until melted. Remove the bowl from the heat and cool the mixture to room temperature.
2. Using electric beaters or in a stand mixer fitted with the paddle attachment, add the cocoa, vanilla, and 1 cup (250 mL) of the icing sugar, beating first on low speed and then increasing the speed and beating until smooth. Beat in the sour cream, then add the remaining 1 cup (250 mL) of icing sugar and beat until smooth.

½ cup (125 mL) unsalted butter,
    at room temperature
4 oz (120 g) bittersweet chocolate,
    chopped
⅓ cup (80 mL) cocoa powder, sifted
2 tsp (10 mL) vanilla extract
2 cups (500 mL) icing sugar, sifted
⅔ cup (160 mL) sour cream

note from anna's kitchen
This frosting is enough to cover the 3-layer chocolate cake on page 144.

CHOCOLATE LAYER CAKE WITH CARAMEL FROSTING
• Makes one 8-inch (20 cm), 3-layer cake | Serves 12 to 14 •

THIS CHOCOLATE CAKE is dark, rich, and moist—everything a chocolate cake for a crowd should be.

1. Preheat the oven to 350°F (175°C). Grease three 8-inch (20 cm) round cake pans and dust them with flour, tapping out the excess. Line the bottom of each pan with parchment paper.

2. Using electric beaters or a mixer fitted with the paddle attachment, beat the butter and brown sugar on medium-high speed for 3 minutes, scraping the sides of the bowl often, until the mixture is fluffy. Add the eggs one at a time, beating well after each addition. Mix in the vanilla.

3. In a separate bowl, sift the flour, cocoa, baking powder, baking soda, and salt. Add this to the butter mixture, alternating with the buttermilk, starting and ending with the flour mixture and mixing well after each addition. Scrape the batter into the prepared pans and spread it to level.

4. Bake the cake for 25 to 30 minutes, until a tester inserted in the centre of the cake comes out clean. Allow the cake to cool for 20 minutes in the pans, then turn each out on a rack to cool completely before frosting.

5. Peel away the parchment paper, place 1 cake layer on a plate, and spread a generous dollop of caramel frosting to cover the top. Repeat with the other 2 layers. Frost the sides of the cake. Let the cake set, uncovered, for 2 hours. The cake will keep at room temperature, covered, for up to 2 days.

¾ cup (185 mL) unsalted butter, at room temperature
2 cups (500 mL) packed light brown sugar
4 eggs, at room temperature
2 tsp (10 mL) vanilla extract
2⅓ cups (580 mL) all-purpose flour
1 cup (250 mL) regular cocoa powder (not Dutch process)
1½ tsp (7.5 mL) baking powder
½ tsp (2 mL) baking soda
½ tsp (2 mL) salt
1½ cups (375 mL) buttermilk, at room temperature
1 recipe Caramel Frosting (recipe follows)

CARAMEL FROSTING
• Makes about 2½ cups (625 mL) •

egg-
FREE

THIS CARAMEL FROSTING is more the consistency of butter fudge—you can sense the sugar at the first bite, but then it melts away into caramel goodness.

1. Heat ½ cup (125 mL) of the butter, the brown sugar, and the salt in a heavy-bottomed saucepot over medium heat, stirring occasionally. Bring to a full boil and boil for 4 minutes, just stirring once or twice. Whisk in the cream and boil until it reaches 245°F (118°C) on a candy thermometer. Remove from the heat and cool for 30 minutes, stirring once or twice.

2. Using electric beaters or a mixer fitted with the paddle attachment, beat the frosting mixture (it should still feel warm) and add the icing sugar. Continue beating until it is a little above room temperature (don't worry if it's a bit grainy—it will smooth out), then add the remaining ½ cup (125 mL) of butter and the vanilla, beating until the frosting is smooth and of a spreadable consistency.

1 cup (250 mL) unsalted butter, at room temperature
2 cups (500 mL) packed dark brown sugar
½ tsp (2 mL) salt
½ cup (125 mL) whipping cream
2½ cups (625 mL) icing sugar, sifted
1 tsp (5 mL) vanilla extract

note from anna's kitchen
If the caramel frosting starts to set while you are still frosting the cake, you can heat it just slightly and beat it to soften it up again.

LEMON LAYER CAKE WITH LEMON CURD AND BUTTERCREAM FROSTING
• *Makes one 8-inch (20 cm), 3-layer cake | Serves 10 to 12* •

LIGHT AND TENDER, this cake is subtly lemon-flavoured, with the zest adding the lemon flavour and the buttermilk enhancing the gentle tartness.

1. Preheat the oven to 350°F (175°C). Grease three 8-inch (20 cm) cake pans, line the bottom of each pan with parchment paper, and sprinkle the sides of the pans with sugar, tapping out any excess.

2. Beat the butter, sugar, and zest at high speed until light and fluffy. In a separate bowl, sift the flour, baking powder, and salt. In another bowl, whisk the buttermilk, egg whites, and vanilla. Alternately add the flour and buttermilk to the butter mixture in small additions, starting and ending with the flour, and mixing well after each addition. Divide the batter evenly between the 3 pans and spread to level. Bake the cake for 30 to 35 minutes, until a tester inserted in the centre of the cake comes out clean. Cool the cakes for 20 minutes in the pans, then turn them out to cool completely.

3. Peel away the parchment paper and place the first layer on a platter. Spoon a cupful of buttercream into a piping bag fitted with a plain tip and pipe a ring around the top edge. Spoon a generous ½ cup (125 mL) of the lemon curd into the ring and spread it evenly. Repeat with the second layer. Top with the third layer, spread the top and outsides of the cake with the buttercream, then pipe any details you wish (or garnish with fresh berries). Chill the cake for at least 2 hours to set the buttercream.

4. The cake should be stored in the refrigerator for up to 2 days, but it is best enjoyed after being pulled from the fridge an hour before serving.

½ cup (125 mL) unsalted butter, at room temperature
1½ cups (375 mL) sugar
1 Tbsp (15 mL) finely grated lemon zest
2 cups (500 mL) + 2 Tbsp (30 mL) cake and pastry flour
1 Tbsp (15 mL) baking powder
½ tsp (2 mL) salt
1¼ cups (310 mL) buttermilk, at room temperature
4 egg whites, at room temperature (save the yolks for the lemon curd)
1 tsp (5 mL) vanilla extract
1 recipe Lemon Buttercream (page 147)
1 recipe Lemon Curd (page 147)

note from anna's kitchen
Just like meringue (pages 80–81), buttercream frosting has similar styles:

BASIC BUTTERCREAM
This style of buttercream is simply a blend of butter and icing sugar with a little milk. This can result in a frosting that is quite sweet and has a little gritty texture, but it is a favourite choice for cupcakes.

SWISS BUTTERCREAM
The recipe on the facing page is a Swiss buttercream. The sugar dissolves into the egg whites when heated and gives the meringue a nice volume and a great stability, making it ideal for grand cakes including wedding cakes, provided they remain indoors (it's not suited to an outdoor summer wedding).

ITALIAN BUTTERCREAM
Making this buttercream involves cooking the sugar to 239°F (115°C) before pouring it into egg whites and adding the butter. The pastry chef's top choice for wedding cakes, it is incredibly stable and can endure a long time out of the fridge.

FRENCH BUTTERCREAM
This buttercream relies on rich egg yolks instead of whites to lend flavour and a smooth texture. French buttercream can be used for a filling as much as a frosting, which is why it serves so well in the Dobos Torte on page 168.

LEMON BUTTERCREAM

• Makes about 3 cups (750 mL) •

gluten-
FREE

THIS STYLE OF buttercream is smooth and silky, and it holds its shape well, making it ideal for piping or decorating. Although a cake made with this buttercream should be kept in the refrigerator, the buttercream is best enjoyed after it has sat out for 30 minutes to an hour—the frosting softens nicely, making it easy to slice and serve, and it melts easily when you take a bite.

1. Whisk the sugar and egg whites together in a metal bowl. Place the bowl over a pot of simmering water, and whisk by hand until the sugar has dissolved and the mixture is hot, about 3 minutes. Remove from the heat.
2. Switch to electric beaters (or a stand mixer) and whip the whites until they have cooled to room temperature (they will more than double in volume), about 6 minutes. While beating, add the butter a little at a time, then mix in the lemon juice and vanilla and beat until the frosting is smooth and fluffy.
3. Use the frosting at room temperature. If you wish to make the frosting ahead of time, chill it to store, but then bring it to room temperature and beat it to make it smooth and spreadable. The frosting will keep in the refrigerator for up to a week.

1 cup (250 mL) sugar

4 egg whites

1½ cups (375 mL) unsalted butter,
  at room temperature

¼ cup (60 mL) lemon juice

1 tsp (5 mL) vanilla extract

LEMON CURD

• Makes about 1¼ cups (310 mL) •

gluten-
FREE

THIS CURD CAN also double as a rich filling for a lemon tart (it is a little too rich and delicate for a lemon meringue pie, though), or it can be served alongside fresh berries, or as part of a shortcake with White Chocolate Black Pepper Scones (page 225).

1. Whisk the sugar, lemon juice, lemon zest, egg yolks, and whole egg together in a metal bowl. Place the bowl over a pot of simmering water and gently whisk the mixture by hand (you do not need to whisk quickly, and can even step away now and again), until thickened to the point that the curd leaves a ribbon on top of itself when the whisk is lifted, about 15 minutes.
2. Remove the curd from the heat and strain it into a bowl. Whisk in the butter until it melts in completely, then chill the curd until it has set, about 2 hours. The curd will keep in the refrigerator for up to a week.

⅔ cup (160 mL) sugar

½ cup (125 mL) fresh lemon juice

2 tsp (10 mL) finely grated lemon zest

2 egg yolks

1 egg

½ cup (125 mL) unsalted butter,
  at room temperature

COCONUT CAKE
WITH SEVEN-MINUTE FROSTING
• *Makes one 8-inch (20 cm), 2-layer cake | Serves 10 to 12* •

THIS MOIST CAKE is sort of like vanilla cake with attitude. The use of coconut milk adds a nice and natural coconut richness, without being too overwhelmingly tropical.

1. Preheat the oven to 350°F (175°C). Grease and flour two 8-inch (20 cm) cake pans, tapping out any excess flour, then line the bottom of each pan with parchment paper.
2. Using electric beaters or a stand mixer fitted with the paddle attachment, beat the butter and ¾ cup (185 mL) of the sugar until light and fluffy. Add the egg yolks, beating well and scraping the bowl. Beat in the vanilla and lemon zest.
3. In a separate bowl, sift the flour, baking powder, and salt. Add to the butter mixture in 3 additions, blending on low speed and alternating with the coconut milk. Stir in the toasted coconut. The batter will be quite dense.
4. In a separate or cleaned bowl, whip the egg whites with the cream of tartar until they are foamy, then slowly pour in the remaining ¼ cup (60 mL) of sugar while whipping the whites to a soft peak. Fold half of the whites into the cake batter until not quite fully incorporated, then fold in the remaining whites until evenly incorporated.
5. Scrape the batter into the prepared pans and spread evenly. Bake the cakes for 25 to 30 minutes, until a tester inserted in the centre of the cake comes out clean.
6. Cool the cakes in the pans for 20 minutes, then turn the cakes out to cool completely before frosting with the Seven-Minute Frosting. Frost the cake layers with an offset spatula, making swirls as you go. Press the coconut onto the sides of the cake and let the cake set, uncovered, for 1 hour. The cake will keep, well covered, at room temperature for up to 3 days.

½ cup (125 mL) unsalted butter, at room temperature

1 cup (250 mL) sugar

4 eggs, at room temperature, separated

2 tsp (10 mL) vanilla extract

1 tsp (5 mL) finely grated lemon zest

2 cups (500 mL) all-purpose flour

1 Tbsp (15 mL) baking powder

½ tsp (2 mL) salt

⅔ cup (160 mL) coconut milk

⅔ cup (160 mL) sweetened, flaked coconut, lightly toasted

½ tsp (2 mL) cream of tartar

1 recipe Seven-Minute Frosting (page 150)

1 cup (250 mL) flaked, sweetened coconut, for garnish

CONTINUED . . .

CONTINUED . . .

SEVEN-MINUTE FROSTING
• Makes about 2½ cups (625 mL) •

dairy-FREE   gluten-FREE

LIGHT AND MARSHMALLOW-LIKE, this frosting is for cakes that do not need refrigeration. This frosting and the Maple Meringue Frosting (page 152) are of a similar style.

1. Fill a saucepot with 2 inches (5 cm) of water and bring to a simmer.
2. In a metal bowl, whisk the sugar, egg whites, cream of tartar, and water. Place the bowl over the pot of simmering water and whisk either by hand or with electric beaters at medium-high speed for 7 minutes. The frosting will turn white and double in volume, but it will still be a bit fluid by the end of the 7 minutes.
3. With the bowl off the heat, add the vanilla and whip the frosting on high speed until it becomes thicker and a spreadable consistency but is still warm, about 5 minutes. Use the frosting immediately, while still warm.

1½ cups (375 mL) sugar
2 egg whites, at room temperature
¼ tsp (1 mL) cream of tartar
¼ cup (60 mL) ice water
1 tsp (5 mL) vanilla

notes from anna's kitchen

1. Using ice water helps the mixture to heat up gradually while whisking—this allows the sugar to melt evenly before the frosting starts gaining volume.
2. If, after you've cooked your meringue for 7 minutes and are whipping it, you notice that it is grainy looking, don't panic. Simply add hot water, ½ teaspoon (2 mL) at a time, and whip it in until the icing looks smooth (this could take up to 2 tablespoons/30 mL of water). This should melt any sugar granules and return your frosting to its fluffy, marshmallowy state.

EARL GREY CHIFFON CAKE
WITH MAPLE MERINGUE FROSTING
• *Makes one 10-inch (25 cm) tube cake | Serves 16 to 20* •

*T*HIS IS A personal favourite. Infused Earl Grey tea lends a subtly fragrant citrus note to the chiffon, and the meringue frosting sweetened with maple syrup really adds something special.

1. Preheat the oven to 325°F (160°C).
2. Steep the tea bags in the boiling water until the water cools to room temperature. Without squeezing out excess liquid, remove the bags, then top up the water to its original ¾ cup (185 mL) measure.
3. Whip the egg whites with the cream of tartar until foamy, then add ¼ cup (60 mL) of the sugar and continue whipping until the whites hold a medium peak. Set aside.
4. Sift the flour, the remaining 1¼ cups (310 mL) of the sugar, the baking powder, and salt into a large bowl or into the bowl of a stand mixer fitted with the whip attachment. Add the cooled tea, oil, egg yolks, vanilla, and lemon zest. Whip this mixture on high until it is thick, about 4 minutes. Add the melted milk chocolate and whip it on low speed until blended. Fold in half of the whipped egg whites by hand until they are incorporated, then fold in the remaining whites (the batter will be quite fluid). Pour this into a 10-inch (25 cm), ungreased tube pan.
5. Bake the cake for 50 to 55 minutes, until the top of the cake springs back when gently pressed. Invert the cake pan onto a cooling rack and cool the cake upside down in its pan. To extract the cake, run a spatula or knife around the outside edge of the cake, then tap the cake out onto a plate.
6. Use a spatula to spread the maple meringue over the entire surface of the cake (use a small spatula or butter knife to frost the cake inside the centre hole). Store the cake at room temperature until ready to serve and cover the interior cake with plastic wrap only once cut. The cake will keep for up to 3 days.

CONTINUED . . .

CAKE:

2 tea bags Earl Grey
¾ cup (185 mL) boiling water
8 egg whites, at room temperature
½ tsp (2 mL) cream of tartar
1½ cups (375 mL) sugar
2¼ cups (560 mL) cake and pastry flour
2½ tsp (12 mL) baking powder
¼ tsp (1 mL) salt
½ cup (125 mL) vegetable oil
5 egg yolks
1 tsp (5 mL) vanilla extract
1 tsp (5 mL) finely grated lemon zest
3 oz (90 g) milk chocolate, chopped and melted
1 recipe Maple Meringue Frosting (page 152)

CONTINUED . . .

MAPLE MERINGUE FROSTING
• *Makes about 2½ cups (625 mL)* •

dairy-
FREE

gluten-
FREE

THIS FROSTING RECIPE can be interchanged with Seven-Minute Frosting (page 150), wherever you wish to add a hint of caramel from the maple syrup. Even though this recipe uses maple syrup, the frosting comes up a bright white colour.

2 egg whites, at room temperature

½ tsp (2 mL) cream of tartar

2 Tbsp (30 mL) sugar

¾ cup (185 mL) pure maple syrup

1 tsp (5 mL) vanilla extract

1. Whip the egg whites with the cream of tartar until foamy, then add the sugar and whip the whites just to a soft peak.

2. Bring the maple syrup to a boil and cook uncovered and without stirring until it reaches a temperature of 242°F (117°C) on a candy thermometer. While beating on medium speed, carefully pour the maple syrup into the meringue by pouring it down the side of the bowl (this will help prevent splashing of hot syrup) and continue whipping until the mixture has cooled but is not quite room temperature, about 3 minutes. Stir in the vanilla. This frosting should be used immediately after making.

Earl Grey Chiffon Cake with Maple Meringue Frosting (pages 151–152)

ANGEL FOOD CAKE
• *Makes one 10-inch (25 cm) angel food cake | Serves 12* •

dairy-
FREE

low-
FAT

*L*IGHT AS AIR, this cake earns its halo because it has no added fat.

1¼ cups (310 mL) egg whites (about 9 whites),
   at room temperature
1 tsp (5 mL) cream of tartar
Pinch salt
1 cup (250 mL) fruit sugar (also known as
   quick-dissolve or castor sugar)
2 tsp (10 mL) vanilla extract
1 cup (250 mL) cake and pastry flour
½ tsp (2 mL) baking powder

1. Preheat the oven to 325°F (160°C).
2. Using electric beaters or in a mixer fitted with the whip attachment, whip the egg whites with the cream of tartar and salt, until they are foamy. While whipping, slowly add ½ cup (125 mL) of the sugar and whip until the whites hold a stiff peak (the whipped whites stand upright when the beaters are lifted). Stir in the vanilla.
3. In a separate bowl, sift the flour, the remaining ½ cup (125 mL) of sugar, and the baking powder twice. Fold the flour mixture into the whites in 3 equal additions, folding gently but quickly. Scrape the batter into a 10-inch (25 cm) *ungreased* angel food pan and bake the cake for 35 to 45 minutes, until the cake springs back when gently pressed. Immediately upon removing the cake from the oven, turn the pan upside down, until the cake has cooled completely. The cake will keep, well covered, at room temperature for up to 4 days.

notes from anna's kitchen
1. Using fruit sugar is important in this recipe since it is a finer grind than regular granulated sugar and dissolves more readily into the egg whites as they whip, resulting in a delicate and tender crumb structure.
2. For tips on meringues and whipping egg whites, please refer to pages 80–81.

CHOCOLATE CHIFFON CAKE
• *Makes one 10-inch (25 cm) tube cake | Serves 16* •

dairy-
FREE

*C*HIFFON CAKE DIFFERS from Angel Food Cake (also on this page) in that it uses whole (but separated) eggs and oil, giving the cake a very moist texture and taste.

1¾ cups (435 mL) cake and pastry flour
1 cup (250 mL) icing sugar
5 Tbsp (75 mL) Dutch process (alkalized) cocoa powder
1½ tsp (7.5 mL) baking powder
¼ tsp (1 mL) salt
1 cup (250 mL) coffee, at room temperature
½ cup (125 mL) vegetable oil
5 eggs, at room temperature, separated
½ tsp (2 mL) cream of tartar
¼ cup (60 mL) sugar

1. Preheat the oven to 325°F (160°C).
2. In a large mixer or in the bowl of a stand mixer fitted with the whip attachment, sift the flour, icing sugar, cocoa, baking powder, and salt. Add the coffee, oil, and egg yolks, and whip on high speed until the mixture is thick and glossy (it will look almost like chocolate mousse).
3. In a separate bowl, whip the egg whites and cream of tartar until they are foamy, then slowly pour in the sugar and continue whipping until the whites hold a stiff peak when the beaters are lifted. Fold a third of the whites into the chocolate batter, then fold in the remaining two-thirds.
4. Pour the batter (it will be fluid) into an *ungreased* 10-inch (25 cm) angel food cake or tube pan.
5. Bake for 45 to 50 minutes, until a tester inserted in the centre of the cake comes out clean. Cool the cake upside down. To remove the cake from the pan, run a palette or butter knife around the inside edge of the pan and tap the cake onto a plate. Serve the cake on its own, or with fresh berries, Raspberry Compote (page 320), and Chantilly Cream (page 320). The cake will keep, well wrapped, at room temperature for up to 4 days.

CHOCOLATE-GLAZED ZUCCHINI WALNUT BUNDT CAKE
• *Makes one 6-cup (1.5 L) Bundt cake | Serves 12 to 16* •

*L*IKE MANY OTHER fruit or vegetable cake styles (carrot, banana, etc.), the zucchini lends moisture to this recipe.

CAKE:

½ cup (125 mL) sugar
½ cup (125 mL) vegetable oil
½ cup (125 mL) maple syrup
2 eggs
1⅓ cups (330 mL) all-purpose flour
⅔ cup (160 mL) walnut pieces
1 tsp (5 mL) baking powder
1 tsp (5 mL) baking soda
1 tsp (5 mL) ground cinnamon
½ tsp (2 mL) salt
2 cups (500 mL) coarsely grated, loosely packed zucchini
1 cup (250 mL) chocolate chips

CHOCOLATE GLAZE:

6 oz (180 g) bittersweet or semisweet chocolate, chopped
6 Tbsp (90 mL) unsalted butter
¼ cup (60 mL) maple syrup

1. Preheat the oven to 350°F (175°C). Grease and flour a 6-cup (1.5 L) Bundt pan, tapping out the excess flour.
2. In a food processor, pulse the sugar, oil, maple syrup, and eggs until blended. Add the flour, walnut pieces, baking powder, baking soda, cinnamon, and salt, and pulse until blended. Add the grated zucchini and chocolate chips, and pulse gently until just combined. Pour the batter into the prepared pan.
3. Bake the cake for 50 to 55 minutes, until a tester inserted in the centre comes out clean. Cool the cake completely before turning out onto a plate.
4. For the glaze, stir the chocolate, butter, and maple syrup in a metal or glass bowl over a pot of barely simmering water until melted. Place the cooled cake on a rack over a parchment-lined baking tray. Pour the warm glaze over the entire surface of the cake, spreading to ensure it is fully covered. Let the cake set for an hour, then chill until ready to serve. The cake will keep in the fridge for up to 3 days.

GLAZED LEMON POPPY SEED POUND CAKE
• *Makes one 6-cup (1.5 L) Bundt cake* •
or one 9- × 5-inch (1.5 L) loaf

A POUND CAKE STAPLE, this recipe freezes well, as do the other pound cakes in this chapter.

CAKE:

1 cup (250 mL) unsalted butter, at room temperature
1 cup (250 mL) sugar
1 Tbsp (15 mL) finely grated lemon zest
4 eggs, at room temperature
2 tsp (10 mL) vanilla extract
2 cups (500 mL) all-purpose flour
1 tsp (5 mL) baking powder
¼ tsp (1 mL) salt
1½ Tbsp (22.5 mL) poppy seeds

GLAZE:

2 Tbsp (30 mL) lemon juice
¾ cup (185 mL) icing sugar, sifted

1. Preheat the oven to 275°F (140°C) and grease and flour a 6-cup (1.5 L) Bundt pan or a loaf pan.
2. Using electric beaters or a tabletop mixer, beat the butter, sugar, and zest until fluffy. Add the eggs one at a time, beating well after each addition. Beat in the vanilla.
3. In a bowl, sift the flour, baking powder, and salt together, and add it to the butter mixture in 2 additions, mixing on low speed. Stir in the poppy seeds. Scrape the batter into the prepared pan.
4. Bake the cake for 20 minutes, then increase the oven temperature to 325°F (160°C) and bake for another 50 to 60 minutes, until a skewer inserted in the centre of the cake comes out clean. Cool for 30 minutes in the pan, then turn the cake out to cool completely.
5. For the glaze, whisk the lemon juice and icing sugar together until smooth and pour over the cake. Let the glaze set, then wrap and store the cake at room temperature until ready to serve. The cake will keep, well wrapped, at room temperature for up to 5 days.

MARBLE POUND CAKE
• *Makes one 9- × 5-inch (2 L) loaf | Cuts into 12 to 16 slices* •

THE BATTERS THAT make up the vanilla and chocolate swirls in this recipe have an even consistency, making them easy to swirl before baking. The cake is tender, with very few crumbs upon slicing.

1. Preheat the oven to 325°F (160°C). Grease a 9- × 5-inch (2 L) loaf pan and dust it with flour, tapping out any excess.
2. Using electric beaters or in a stand mixer fitted with the paddle attachment, beat the butter and sugar until fluffy, about 2 minutes. Add the eggs one at a time, beating well after each addition. Stir in the vanilla.
3. In a separate bowl, sift the flour, baking powder, and salt. Add this to the butter mixture, alternating with the sour cream and blending well after each addition, starting and finishing with the flour. Scrape half of this batter into another bowl.
4. Melt the chocolate by stirring it in a metal or glass bowl placed over a pot of barely simmering water. Add the warm chocolate to one of the bowls of batter and stir until blended. Dollop vanilla batter and chocolate batter in alternate spoonfuls into the pan. Use a paring knife to swirl the batter. Bake the cake for 60 to 70 minutes, until a tester inserted in the centre of the cake comes out clean. Cool the cake for 30 minutes in the pan, then turn it out to cool completely.
5. The cake will keep up to 5 days stored at room temperature in an airtight container.

¾ cup (185 mL) unsalted butter, at room temperature

1 cup (250 mL) sugar

4 eggs, at room temperature

2 tsp (10 mL) vanilla extract

2 cups (500 mL) all-purpose flour

1¼ tsp (6 mL) baking powder

¼ tsp (1 mL) salt

⅔ cup (160 mL) sour cream

4 oz (120 g) bittersweet chocolate, chopped

note from anna's kitchen

Loaf pans seem to have the greatest variation in size. While an 8-inch (20 cm) square pan is 8 inches (20 cm), and a 9-inch (23 cm) pie plate is 9 inches (23 cm), loaf pans can be 8¾ × 5¼ inches or 9⅛ × 4¾ inches, or many other combinations. The recipes in this book have been tested using a 9- × 5-inch pan. You can use pans slightly larger or smaller, but the bake time may have to be adjusted slightly—a loaf in a shorter but deeper pan could take more time to bake than one in a wider, longer pan. Unless your pan is more than ½ inch (1 cm) less in width and length, you shouldn't run into an issue with the batter spilling over as it rises. Ultimately, you can test that your loaf pan will hold your cake by measuring its volume. If the pan can hold 6 cups (1.5 L), then you should be fine.

CARROT APPLE CAKE
• *Makes one 10-inch (25 cm) tube cake* | *Serves 10 to 12* •

dairy-
FREE

THIS CAKE BEST suits the flat sides of an angel food cake tube pan as opposed to a patterned Bundt pan.

1. Preheat the oven to 375°F (190°C) and grease an angel food cake pan.
2. Whisk the oil, brown sugar, apple cider or juice, and eggs until smooth. In a separate bowl, sift together the flour, baking powder, salt, cinnamon, and allspice. Whisk this into the oil mixture, then stir in the grated carrots and apple. Pour this mixture into the prepared pan (it will fill only about half) and bake the cake for about 45 minutes, until a tester inserted in the centre of the cake comes out clean. Cool the cake for 40 minutes before turning it out onto a plate to cool completely. The cake can be stored, well wrapped, at room temperature for up to 4 days.

1 cup (250 mL) vegetable oil

1 cup (250 mL) packed light brown sugar

¼ cup (60 mL) apple cider or apple juice

4 eggs

2¼ cups (560 mL) all-purpose flour

2 tsp (10 mL) baking powder

½ tsp (2 mL) salt

1 tsp (5 mL) ground cinnamon

¼ tsp (1 mL) ground allspice

3½ cups (875 mL) coarsely grated, loosely packed carrots

1 cup (250 mL) peeled, coarsely grated, loosely packed tart apple, such as Granny Smith

note from anna's kitchen
To play on the classic carrot cake flavour combination, you can top the cake with a cream cheese frosting (see Red Velvet Cupcakes, page 132) and store the cake chilled.

HONEY DATE BUNDT CAKE
• Makes one 8-cup (2 L) Bundt cake | Serves 16 to 20 •

*T*HIS IS A buttery and rich Bundt cake. The chopped dates in the cake plump up as it bakes, giving this cake a taste and texture similar to a sticky toffee pudding.

1. Preheat the oven to 325°F (160°C). Grease and flour an 8-cup (2 L) Bundt pan or angel food cake pan.
2. Melt the butter and honey together in a medium saucepot over medium heat, stirring occasionally. Remove the pan from the heat and cool for 15 minutes. Whisk the brown sugar, sour cream, egg, fresh ginger, and vanilla into the butter mixture.
3. In a separate bowl, sift the flour, baking powder, baking soda, cinnamon, and salt. Pour the butter mixture into the flour and stir until evenly blended. Stir in the chopped dates and pour the batter into the prepared pan. Bake the cake for 55 to 65 minutes, until a tester inserted in the centre of the cake comes out clean. Cool the cake for 30 minutes in the pan, then turn the cake out to cool completely. Dust with icing sugar before serving. The cake can be stored, covered, at room temperature for up to 5 days.

1¾ cups (435 mL) unsalted butter
1 cup (250 mL) honey
1 cup (250 mL) packed light brown sugar
¾ cup (185 mL) sour cream
1 egg
1 Tbsp (15 mL) finely grated fresh ginger
2 tsp (10 mL) vanilla extract
3 cups (750 mL) all-purpose flour
1 tsp (5 mL) baking powder
1 tsp (5 mL) baking soda
1 tsp (5 mL) ground cinnamon
½ tsp (2 mL) salt
2 cups (500 mL) chopped pitted dates
Icing sugar, for dusting

LUSCIOUS VANILLA CHEESECAKE
• *Makes one 9-inch (23 cm) cheesecake | Serves 12 to 16* •

*F*ANTASTICALLY RICH, DENSE, yet not too heavy, this basic, fundamental recipe is delicious on its own, and with fresh fruit or a sauce, like Raspberry Compote or Mango Coulis on page 320.

1. Preheat the oven to 350°F (175°C). Lightly grease a 9-inch (23 cm) springform pan and place it on a baking tray.

2. Stir the graham crumbs and sugar together, then pour in the melted butter and stir until the graham crumbs are coated (the mixture will still be crumbly). Press the crumbs into the prepared pan, coming an extra inch up the sides (using a ramekin or sturdy glass will help you get the crumbs evenly into the corners). Bake the crust for 12 minutes, then cool while preparing the filling.

3. Reduce the oven temperature to 300°F (150°C). Using electric beaters or a stand mixer fitted with the paddle attachment, beat the cream cheese and cornstarch until fluffy. While beating, slowly add the sugar, scraping the sides and bottom of the bowl often. Beat in the sour cream and vanilla, again scraping the sides and bottom of the bowl well.

4. Add the eggs one at a time, beating and scraping the bowl well after each addition. Pour the filling into the cooled crust (the filling will come up higher than the crust).

5. Bake for 55 minutes. Turn the oven off and leave the cheesecake in the oven for another 10 minutes, cracking the oven door slightly. Remove the cake from the oven.

6. After the cake cools for 30 minutes, run a palette knife around the outside edge of the cheesecake to loosen it from the pan. Cool the cheesecake completely to room temperature before chilling it for a minimum of 6 hours. To serve, remove the springform ring from the pan and slice using a hot, dry knife. The cake will keep in the refrigerator for up to 3 days.

CRUST:

1½ cups (375 mL) graham cracker crumbs

3 Tbsp (45 mL) sugar

¼ cup (60 mL) unsalted butter, melted

FILLING:

4 pkg (8 oz/250 g each) cream cheese, at room temperature

2 Tbsp (30 mL) cornstarch

1¼ cups (310 mL) sugar

½ cup (125 mL) sour cream

1 Tbsp (15 mL) vanilla extract or vanilla bean paste

3 eggs, at room temperature

notes from anna's kitchen

1. For the inside scoop behind eggs, refer to the notes on page 10.

2. Allowing the cheesecake to cool completely to room temperature before chilling is an easy and important step. Accelerating the cooling can cause the cheesecake to contract, causing a crack.

RICH CHOCOLATE CHEESECAKE

• *Makes one 9-inch (23 cm) cheesecake* | *Serves 12 to 16* •

gluten-
FREE

THIS IS A dense cheesecake for true chocolate-lovers. Ground almonds give the crust structure and a little variety from a traditional graham crust.

1. Preheat the oven to 350°F (175°C). Lightly grease a 9-inch (23 cm) springform pan and place it on a baking tray.

2. For the crust, pulse the almonds with the sugar, cocoa, cornstarch, and cinnamon until the almonds are finely ground. Add the egg white and oil, and pulse until evenly blended. Press the crust into the bottom of the prepared pan and bake for 15 minutes. Cool the crust while preparing the filling and reduce the oven temperature to 300°F (150°C).

3. Melt the bittersweet and unsweetened chocolates in a metal or glass bowl set over a pot of barely simmering water, stirring constantly until melted. Remove the bowl from the heat and cool.

4. Beat the cream cheese until fluffy, then add the sugar ½ cup (125 mL) at a time, beating well and scraping the sides of the bowl after each addition. Beat in the sour cream and vanilla. Beat in the melted chocolate, then add the eggs one at a time, beating well and scraping the sides after each addition. Scrape the cheesecake filling into the cooled crust.

5. Bake the cheesecake for about 60 minutes, until the outside is set but the centre still has a little jiggle to it. Allow the cheesecake to cool for 20 minutes, then run a palette knife around the outside edge of the cheesecake to loosen the sides from the pan. Cool the cheesecake to room temperature before chilling overnight (or a minimum of 6 hours), removing the outside ring, and slicing. Garnish with chocolate curls. The cheesecake slices best using a hot, dry knife, and can keep in the refrigerator for up to 4 days.

CRUST:

1 cup (250 mL) whole, unblanched almonds
¼ cup (60 mL) sugar
3 Tbsp (45 mL) cocoa powder
3 Tbsp (45 mL) cornstarch
¼ tsp (1 mL) ground cinnamon
1 egg white
2 Tbsp (30 mL) vegetable oil

FILLING:

6 oz (180 g) bittersweet chocolate, chopped
3 oz (90 g) unsweetened chocolate, chopped
3 pkg (8 oz/250 g each) cream cheese, at room temperature
2 cups (500 mL) sugar
1 cup (250 mL) sour cream, at room temperature
2 tsp (10 mL) vanilla extract
4 eggs, at room temperature
Dark chocolate shavings, for garnish (page 320)

note from anna's kitchen

When beating your cream cheese and adding the sugar, you can beat at a high speed. Once you start adding the eggs, reduce the speed to low so as not to add too much air. Whipped eggs will soufflé in the oven, which is not the issue; once the cheesecake starts cooling those souffléd eggs will fall and that's when a crack can develop, even hours after the cheesecake is out of the oven.

EUROPEAN LEMON CHEESECAKE
• *Makes one 9-inch (23 cm) cheesecake | Serves 8 to 10* •

*P*RESSED COTTAGE CHEESE is the key ingredient to this recipe, making this more in the style of Eastern European cheesecakes. If you cannot find pressed cottage cheese, use the same weight of dry ricotta cheese.

1 pkg (8 oz/250 g) pressed cottage cheese (10% milk fat)

¾ cup (185 mL) sugar

¼ cup (60 mL) all-purpose flour

2 Tbsp (30 mL) cornstarch

1 Tbsp (15 mL) finely grated lemon zest

2 Tbsp (30 mL) lemon juice

2 tsp (10 mL) vanilla extract

4 eggs, at room temperature, separated

½ tsp (2 mL) cream of tartar

1. Preheat the oven to 350°F (175°C). Grease a 9-inch (23 cm) springform pan and coat it with sugar, tapping out any excess.

2. Using a food processor or electric beaters, blend the cottage cheese with ½ cup (125 mL) of the sugar. Add the flour, cornstarch, lemon zest, lemon juice, and vanilla, and blend well. Beat in the egg yolks.

3. In a clean bowl and with clean beaters, whip the egg whites with the cream of tartar until frothy, then pour in the remaining ¼ cup (60 mL) of sugar, continuing to whip the whites until they hold a medium peak (when the whites curl just slightly when the beaters are lifted). Fold the whites into the cheese mixture in 2 additions, then spread the cheesecake evenly in the prepared pan.

4. Bake the cheesecake for 10 minutes, then reduce the oven temperature to 325°F (160°C) and bake for about 25 more minutes, until the top just begins to colour. Let the cheesecake cool completely to room temperature, then chill for at least 2 hours before slicing. The cheesecake will keep in the refrigerator for up to 3 days.

note from anna's kitchen
Since the recipe uses whipped egg whites, this cake can develop a small crack 1 inch (2.5 cm) from the outside edge of the dessert and may deflate a little as it cools. This is to be expected in this recipe and not feared like with a typical North American–style cheesecake, which can develop a gaping crevice through the middle if improperly baked. Please check out the Notes on pages 160, 161, and 164 for tips on how to avoid unplanned cracks in a cheesecake.

WHITE CHOCOLATE RASPBERRY LIME CHEESECAKE
• Makes one 9-inch (23 cm) cheesecake | Serves 12 to 16 •

A CRUST MADE FROM the crumbs of Snickerdoodles (page 23) helps to make this cheesecake special, but you could use the crumbs from virtually any crunchy sugar cookie. The citrus and berries keep this cheesecake from being too sweet or heavy tasting.

1. Preheat the oven to 350°F (175°C) and grease a 9-inch (23 cm) springform pan.
2. Stir the cookie crumbs with the melted butter, and press them into the bottom and halfway up the side of the prepared pan. Bake for 10 minutes and cool while preparing the filling.
3. Reduce the oven temperature to 300°F (150°C). Beat the cream cheese and flour until light and fluffy. Slowly pour in the sugar while beating, and scrape the sides of the bowl a few times while adding. Beat in the sour cream, lime juice, zest, and vanilla until blended, and scrape the sides and bottom of the bowl. One at a time, add the whole eggs and egg yolk, beating well at low speed and scraping the bowl after each addition. By hand, fold in the white chocolate chunks and raspberries, and pour this into the cooled crust.
4. Place the pan on a baking tray and bake for about 40 minutes, until the outside edges of the cheesecake are set but the centre still has a little jiggle to it. Cool the cheesecake to room temperature, then chill until set, at least 6 hours. To serve, garnish to the top of the cheesecake with fresh raspberries and cut the cheesecake with a hot, dry knife. The cheesecake will keep in the refrigerator for up to 3 days.

CRUST:

½ recipe Snickerdoodles (page 23), processed into crumbs, or 2½ cups (625 mL) crumbs from other buttery sugar cookies
¼ cup (60 mL) unsalted butter, melted

FILLING:

2 pkg (8 oz/250 g each) cream cheese, at room temperature
2 Tbsp (30 mL) all-purpose flour
¾ cup (185 mL) sugar
½ cup (125 mL) sour cream
3 Tbsp (45 mL) lime juice
2 tsp (10 mL) finely grated lime zest
1 tsp (5 mL) vanilla extract
2 eggs, at room temperature
1 egg yolk, at room temperature
4 oz (125 g) white chocolate, chopped
1 cup (250 mL) fresh raspberries, plus extra for garnish

note from anna's kitchen

By running a palette knife around the inside edge of the springform pan, you separate the cake from the pan. This way, if the cheesecake does contract, it will pull away from the sides of the pan, making it less likely to crack in the middle.

VIENNESE SACHER TORTE
• Makes one 9-inch (23 cm) torte | Serves 10 to 12 •

low-
SUGAR

*N*EED A SHOWSTOPPER dessert for a special occasion? This is the one. It is a rich, moist chocolate cake slathered with apricot jam and decorated with a chocolate glaze. This torte is named after the Hotel Sacher in Vienna, Austria, and I learned this recipe from a talented pastry chef, Burgi Riegler, who actually worked there for a time. I dream of visiting Vienna at Christmastime and enjoying a cup of Viennese coffee while eating a slice of this torte at the hotel.

1. For the cake, preheat the oven to 350°F (175°C) and grease and sugar a 9-inch (23 cm) springform pan.

2. Melt the chocolate in a metal bowl over a pot of barely simmering water, stirring constantly. Remove this from the heat. With electric beaters or in a stand mixer fitted with a whip attachment, whip the melted chocolate with the butter and icing sugar, until smooth. Add the egg yolks one at a time, beating well after each addition. Gently fold in the sifted flour and salt.

3. In a separate bowl, whip the egg whites until foamy, then add the sugar. Continue whipping the whites until they hold a medium peak when the beaters are lifted. Fold a third of the whites into the chocolate mixture, then fold in the remaining two-thirds. Scrape the mixture into the prepared pan and level with a knife or spatula.

4. Bake for 50 to 60 minutes, until a tester inserted in the centre of the cake comes out clean. Allow the cake to cool completely.

5. Heat the apricot jam in a small pot on medium heat or in the microwave, and strain it, then cool the jam until it's spreadable. Slice the cake in half horizontally and spread a thin layer of jam over the bottom half. Top with the other cake layer and spread the apricot jam over the top and the sides to coat evenly. Chill the cake while preparing the chocolate glaze.

6. For the glaze, stir the chocolate, butter, and corn syrup in a metal or glass bowl over a pot of gently simmering water until melted. Allow the glaze to cool to room temperature, stirring occasionally (it will thicken just slightly).

7. Place the cake on a cooling rack set over a baking sheet lined with parchment paper. Pour the glaze onto the centre of the cake in one stream. With an offset spatula, gently coax the fluid glaze to the edges of the cake and let it drip over the sides. Spread the glaze over any gaps and chill until set.

8. Once chilled, gently move the cake to a serving platter and garnish as desired. The traditional garnish is to write "Sacher" on the cake with the remaining glaze, but you can draw on a pattern of your choosing or simply leave it plain. The torte will keep in the refrigerator for up to 3 days.

CAKE:

4 oz (120 g) bittersweet chocolate, chopped

½ cup (125 mL) unsalted butter, at room temperature

¼ cup + 2 tsp (70 mL) icing sugar

6 eggs, separated

1 cup (250 mL) all-purpose flour, sifted

¼ tsp (1 mL) salt

½ cup + 2 Tbsp (155 mL) sugar

1 cup (250 mL) apricot jam

GLAZE:

12 oz (360 g) bittersweet chocolate, chopped

¾ cup (185 mL) unsalted butter, cut in pieces

1 Tbsp (15 mL) corn syrup

DOBOS TORTE
• *Makes one 8-inch (20 cm) torte | Serves 8* •

THIS HUNGARIAN TORTE is made of nine wafer-thin cake layers—the torte needs to have a minimum of five layers, a chocolate buttercream, and a layer of caramelized sugar on top to qualify as a Dobos torte. Instead of making a traditional sponge cake and trying to slice it into nine even layers (impossible!), the sponge cake is spread onto the underside of greased and floured cake pans.

Give yourself ample time and room for this torte. As is the tradition with European tortes, they are as elaborate to make as they look.

1. Preheat the oven to 350°F (175°C). Grease and flour the *underside* of three 8-inch (20 cm) cake pans, tapping off any excess flour.

2. Whip the egg yolks with ½ cup (125 mL) of the sugar at high speed until they have doubled in volume and are thick and pale, about 5 minutes. Beat in the vanilla. Sift in the flour and salt, and fold in. The batter will be thick.

3. In a clean bowl, whip the egg whites and cream of tartar until foamy, then slowly pour in the remaining 5 tablespoons (75 mL) of sugar and continue whipping until the whites hold a medium peak when the beaters are lifted. Fold the whites into the yolk batter in 2 additions.

4. Spoon about ½ cup (125 mL) of batter onto the bottom of each cake pan and spread it to the edges. Bake these cake layers for 7 to 9 minutes, until they turn a light golden brown. Let the cakes cool for about 5 minutes, then remove them from the pan by carefully running a palette knife under the entire surface of the cake, working from the outside in. It's all right if they have a few rough edges or a slight tear or crack, or if they seem firm in one place and soft in another—they will all be masked by the frosting and the cake will soften up.

5. Grease and re-flour the cake pans (no need to wash them), and repeat the process 2 more times for a total of 9 cake layers. Store the cake layers on a parchment-lined baking tray, only barely touching and between layers of parchment.

6. To prepare the caramel garnish, place all but 8 of the hazelnuts onto a parchment-lined baking tray. Lightly grease a 6- or 8-inch (15 or 20 cm) cookie cutter (or you can use the outside ring of an 8-inch/20 cm fluted pan) and a second parchment-lined baking tray, and place the cutter on the tray. Bring the sugar, lemon juice, and water up to a boil, and boil, uncovered and occasionally brushing down the sides of the pot, until the mixture caramelizes, about 7 minutes. Carefully pour about half of the hot sugar into the centre of the cookie cutter, then pour the remaining sugar over the hazelnuts and stir them to coat. Let the cookie-cutter ring set until almost cool, about 8 minutes, then remove the ring and with a greased chef's knife,

CAKE:

6 eggs, at room temperature, separated
½ cup (125 mL) + 5 Tbsp (75 mL) sugar
1 tsp (5 mL) vanilla extract
1 cup (250 mL) cake and pastry flour
¼ tsp (1 mL) salt
½ tsp (2 mL) cream of tartar

CARMEL GARNISH:

1½ cups (375 mL) whole toasted
   and peeled hazelnuts
1 cup (250 mL) sugar
1 Tbsp (15 mL) lemon juice
3 Tbsp (45 mL) water

ASSEMBLY:

1 recipe Chocolate Hazelnut Buttercream
   (page 170)

CONTINUED . . .

CONTINUED . . .

score the disc of sugar into 8 wedges. Cool completely. After the caramelized hazelnuts have cooled, pulse them in a food processor into a coarse crumble.

7. To assemble the cake, place one cake layer on a platter and cover it with a thin layer of buttercream, then top it with a second cake layer. Repeat this process until all 9 cake layers are used. Frost the top and sides of the cake. Press the caramelized hazelnut crumble onto the side of the cake. Arrange the 8 hazelnuts in a circle around the outside edge of the top of the cake, equally spaced apart. Rest each caramelized sugar wedge so that each wedge rests on a hazelnut, and angle them in the same direction, creating a fan pattern. Chill the cake completely before slicing to serve. The cake will keep in the refrigerator for up to 4 days.

CHOCOLATE HAZELNUT BUTTERCREAM
• *Makes about 2½ cups (625 mL)* •

THIS FRENCH-STYLE BUTTERCREAM is rich and dense and melts very easily on the tip of the tongue, so it suits a cake like a Dobos torte that sandwiches it between all those thin cake layers.

1. Melt the semisweet and bittersweet chocolate together in a metal or glass bowl placed over a pot of barely simmering water, stirring until melted. Set aside.
2. Place the egg yolks in a large bowl and whip with ¼ cup (60 mL) of the sugar until they are pale and have doubled in volume, about 3 minutes.
3. Bring the remaining ¼ cup (60 mL) of sugar, the water, and lemon juice to a boil over high heat and cook uncovered and without stirring, but occasionally brushing down the sides of the pot with water, until it reaches a temperature of 238°F (114°C). Carefully pour the hot sugar down the side of the bowl with the yolks in it while beating at slow speed. Once all of the sugar has been added, increase the speed to high and beat until cool, about 6 minutes. Beat in the melted chocolate, then beat in the butter a few pieces at a time. Beat in the Frangelico or brandy, the vanilla, and the salt.
4. Use the buttercream at room temperature. It can be prepared ahead of time and refrigerated. Then pull it out to warm it up to room temperature and beat until it is smooth and spreadable.

3 oz (90 g) semisweet chocolate, chopped

2 oz (60 g) bittersweet chocolate, chopped

5 egg yolks

½ cup (125 mL) sugar

1 Tbsp (15 mL) water

1 tsp (5 mL) lemon juice

1 cup (250 mL) unsalted butter, at room temperature

2 Tbsp (30 mL) Frangelico or brandy

1 tsp (5 mL) vanilla extract

½ tsp (2 mL) salt

LADY BALTIMORE CAKE
• *Makes one 9-inch (23 cm) cake | Serves 12* •

WITH THIS CAKE, a meringue frosting wraps a fluffy orange sponge cake, and dates, figs, pecans, and dried cherries are nestled in the centre. The retro version of the cake calls for candied fruit, but I prefer the more natural dried-fruit choices.

1. Preheat oven to 350°F (175°C), and grease and line two 9-inch (23 cm) cake pans with parchment paper.
2. Sift the flour, baking powder, and salt together, and set aside.
3. With electric beaters or in a tabletop mixer fitted with the paddle attachment, beat the butter and sugar until smooth. Beat in the vanilla and orange zest.
4. Combine the milk and water, and add, alternating with the flour, to the butter mixture, starting and ending with flour and beating well after each addition. With clean beaters, whip the egg whites and cream of tartar until they hold a medium peak (curl slightly when beaters are lifted). Fold the whites into the cake batter in 2 equal additions. Spread the batter into the prepared pans and level.
5. Bake for 35 to 40 minutes, until the top of the cake is only slightly browned and the cake springs back when gently pressed. Cool the cakes for 30 minutes, then turn out to cool completely.
6. Prepare the Seven-Minute Frosting recipe. In a separate bowl, stir together the dried fruit and pecans, and stir in one-third of the frosting while it's still slightly warm.
7. Place one cake layer on a serving plate and spread with the warm fruit/nut frosting. Top with the remaining cake layer and frost the entire cake. Feel free to swoosh and swirl while covering—the pattern will set. The cake should be stored at room temperature until ready to serve and then refrigerated once sliced. It will keep for up to 3 days.

CAKE:

2½ cups (625 mL) cake and pastry flour

1 Tbsp (15 mL) baking powder

¾ tsp (4 mL) salt

¾ cup (185 mL) unsalted butter,
   at room temperature

2 cups (500 mL) sugar

1 tsp (5 mL) vanilla extract

1 tsp (5 mL) finely grated orange zest

½ cup (125 mL) 2% milk,
   at room temperature

½ cup (125 mL) water, at room
   temperature

6 egg whites, at room temperature

¼ tsp (1 mL) cream of tartar

FROSTING:

1 recipe Seven-Minute Frosting (page 150)

FILLING:

½ cup (125 mL) chopped pitted
   Medjool dates

½ cup (125 mL) chopped dried
   Mission figs

½ cup (125 mL) dried cherries

½ cup (125 mL) chopped pecans

TIRAMISU TORTE
• Makes one 9-inch (23 cm) torte | Serves 12 to 16 •

*T*HIS IS A fantastic special-occasion cake, perfect for a birthday, anniversary, or other noteworthy date. Whereas traditional tiramisu is assembled in a pan and served directly from it, this torte is surrounded by ladyfingers and can be sliced just like a cake.

1. For the filling, whip the cream to soft peaks and set aside. Beat the mascarpone gently to soften and fold it into the whipped cream in 2 additions. You may have to use a whisk to fold this in a little more vigorously than with traditional folding in order to smooth out any lumps—if the whipped cream deflates a little, that is all right. Chill the mixture.

2. Whisk the egg yolks, sugar, and brandy in a metal or glass bowl placed over a pot of gently simmering water, whisking until the mixture has doubled in volume and the mixture makes and holds a ribbon when the whisk is lifted. Stir in the vanilla and remove the bowl from the heat to let the mixture cool for 10 minutes.

3. Whisk the chilled mascarpone mixture into the egg mixture in 2 additions (the filling will be quite fluid). Chill this while preparing the other components for assembly.

4. For the syrup, stir the sugar and hot coffee together, heating further if needed to ensure that the sugar has melted. Stir in the rum or brandy, and set aside.

5. To assemble the torte, slice the vanilla cake layer horizontally (as if to fill it with frosting) and place one 8-inch (20 cm) cake layer in the bottom of a 9-inch (23 cm) springform pan. Arrange the ladyfingers around the outside of this cake layer (the cake will help to keep them in place). Brush the cake layer with half of the coffee syrup and spread half of the mascarpone filling over the cake. Sprinkle a layer of grated chocolate over the filling and top with the remaining cake layer. Brush this with the remaining syrup, top with the remaining mascarpone cream, and sprinkle this with more grated chocolate. Cover the torte loosely and chill until set, about 4 hours.

6. For the topping, whip the cream with the skim milk powder until the cream holds a soft peak. Stir in the sugar, rum or brandy, and the vanilla, and spread this over the chilled filling. Top with a little more grated chocolate and chill until ready to serve.

7. To serve, remove the outer ring of the pan and slide the torte carefully onto a serving platter. The torte can be prepared up to a day in advance and will keep in the refrigerator for up to 3 days.

FILLING:

1 cup (250 mL) whipping cream

1 tub (500 g) mascarpone cheese

5 egg yolks

½ cup (125 mL) sugar

¼ cup (60 mL) brandy

2 tsp (10 mL) vanilla extract

SYRUP:

½ cup (125 mL) sugar

½ cup (125 mL) hot brewed coffee

2 Tbsp (30 mL) amber rum or brandy

ASSEMBLY:

1 cake layer from the Rich Vanilla Cake recipe (page 142)

16 to 24 ladyfinger biscuits, depending on the size of the biscuits

Chocolate Shavings (dark) (page 321), for garnish

TOPPING:

1 cup (250 mL) whipping cream

1 Tbsp (15 mL) instant skim milk powder

1 Tbsp (15 mL) sugar

1 Tbsp (15 mL) amber rum or brandy

1 tsp (5 mL) vanilla extract

CARAMEL APPLE UPSIDE DOWN CAKE
• *Makes one 9-inch (23 cm) cake | Serves 12* •

APPLES MAKE AN ideal ingredient in an upside down cake since they caramelize so nicely and the juice melds with the sugar syrup, making for a shiny, saucy glaze when the cake is inverted.

1. Preheat the oven to 350°F (175°C). Grease a 9-inch (23 cm) cake pan and place it on a parchment-lined baking tray.

2. For the caramel apple layer, arrange the apples tightly together in the bottom of the prepared pan. Pour the water and lemon juice into a small saucepot, then add the sugar and butter. Bring this mixture to a boil without stirring and continue to boil, occasionally brushing down the sides of the pot with water, until it is a rich caramel colour, 4 to 6 minutes. Remove the pot from the heat and pour the caramel over the apples, coating them as much as possible (but don't worry if they are not completely coated). Set aside while preparing the cake.

3. Beat the butter, sugar, and brown sugar together. Add the egg yolks, sour cream, and vanilla, and beat until blended.

4. In a separate bowl, sift the flour, baking powder, cinnamon, and salt, and stir this into the butter mixture.

5. In another bowl, whip the egg whites until they hold a soft peak, then fold them into the cake batter in 2 additions (the whites will deflate as you fold them in). Scrape the batter overtop of the apples and spread evenly.

6. Bake the cake for about 50 minutes, until a tester inserted in the centre of the cake comes out clean. Allow the cake to cool for 30 minutes. Run a knife around the inside edge of the cake pan and place a serving plate overtop the pan. Flip the cake over and lift the pan off, revealing the caramel apple top. The cake will keep, well wrapped, for up to 2 days.

CARAMEL APPLE LAYER:

3 apples (Granny Smith, Mutsu, or Cortland), peeled, cored, and each cut in 8 wedges
2 Tbsp (30 mL) water
1 Tbsp (15 mL) lemon juice
1 cup (250 mL) sugar
¼ cup (60 mL) unsalted butter

CAKE:

¼ cup (60 mL) unsalted butter, at room temperature
½ cup (125 mL) sugar
½ cup (125 mL) packed dark brown sugar
4 eggs, at room temperature, separated
⅓ cup (80 mL) sour cream
1 tsp (5 mL) vanilla extract
1¼ cups (310 mL) all-purpose flour
1 tsp (5 mL) baking powder
½ tsp (2 mL) ground cinnamon
¼ tsp (1 mL) salt

note from anna's kitchen
When caramelizing sugar, I like to put the water in the pot first before adding the sugar. This way, it dissolves more evenly and is less likely to crystallize as it starts to boil.

TRES LECHES CAKE

• Makes one 9- × 13-inch (23 × 33 cm) cake | Serves 12 to 16 •

THIS LATIN AMERICAN cake is a moist and simple cake. I have tried many recipes, including a family recipe from a friend in Guatemala, and have come up with this version. The dry cake seems flat and plain until you pour the mixture of condensed milk, evaporated milk, and whipping cream overtop. Watch the cake soak it all in, virtually doubling in size! Because of all of this added dairy, the cake needs to be served from and stored in the pan, but it will feed a crowd. *Tres leches* translates to "three milks" but there are actually four types in this recipe. The more the merrier!

1. Preheat the oven to 325°F (160°C). Grease a 9- × 13-inch (23 × 33 cm) baking pan, and dust the bottom and sides with flour, tapping out any excess flour.

2. Heat the butter and milk over low heat until the butter has melted. Set the mixture aside to cool slightly.

3. Whip the eggs, sugar, and vanilla on high speed using electric beaters or a mixer fitted with the whip attachment until the eggs are doubled in volume, 5 to 7 minutes. Sift the flour, baking powder, salt, and nutmeg. Fold half of the flour mixture into the whipped eggs, then add all of the butter mixture, then fold in the remaining flour mixture. Scrape the batter into the prepared pan.

4. Bake the cake for about 40 minutes, until a tester inserted in the centre of the cake comes out clean.

5. While the cake is baking, prepare the milk mixture. Stir the condensed milk, evaporated milk, whipping cream, and vanilla together. After the cake has come out of the oven and cooled for 10 minutes, poke holes in the cake using a bamboo skewer and slowly pour the milk mixture over the entire surface of the cake (the cake will absorb all of the moisture and swell up). Cool the cake to room temperature, then chill it for at least 3 hours.

6. For the topping, whip the cream until it holds a soft peak. Stir in the icing sugar, skim milk powder, and vanilla, then spread the cream over the surface of the cake. Garnish the top of the cake with toasted coconut (if using), and keep the cake chilled until ready to serve. The cake must be stored and sliced directly from the pan. The cake will keep in the refrigerator for up to 5 days.

CAKE:

½ cup (125 mL) unsalted butter

1 cup (250 mL) milk

4 eggs, at room temperature

2 cups (500 mL) sugar

2 tsp (10 mL) vanilla extract

2 cups (500 mL) all-purpose flour

2 tsp (10 mL) baking powder

½ tsp (2 mL) salt

¼ tsp (1 mL) ground nutmeg

MILK MIXTURE:

1 tin (300 mL) sweetened condensed milk

1 tin (370 mL) evaporated milk

¾ cup (185 mL) whipping cream

1 tsp (5 mL) vanilla extract

TOPPING:

1 cup (250 mL) whipping cream

2 Tbsp (30 mL) icing sugar

1 Tbsp (15 mL) instant skim milk powder

1 tsp (5 mL) vanilla extract

1 cup (250 mL) sweetened, flaked coconut, lightly toasted (optional)

SPRINGTIME LEMON WEDDING CAKE WITH FONDANT

• Makes one 2-tier wedding cake •
Serves 24 as a full dessert and 40 as a tasting portion

THIS SWEET LITTLE wedding cake is so fresh and pretty. A small wedding cake is not just appropriate for a small wedding but also if you are setting up a dessert table and would like a cake to dress the table but not overwhelm it. Before you begin making this cake, review the recipe completely and make sure you have all the necessary tools to get the job done.

1. Preheat the oven to 350°F (175°C). Grease three 9-inch (23 cm) round cake pans, line the bottom of each pan with parchment paper, and sprinkle the sides of the pans with sugar, tapping out any excess. Repeat the process with three 6-inch (15 cm) round cake pans (or a single 3-inch/8 cm tall, 6-inch/15 cm round cake pan).

2. Beat the butter, sugar, and zest at high speed until light and fluffy (this is best accomplished using electric beaters or a large stand mixer fitted with the paddle attachment). In a separate bowl, sift the flour, baking powder, and salt. In another bowl, whisk the buttermilk, egg whites, and vanilla. Alternately add the flour and buttermilk mixtures to the butter mixture in small additions, starting and ending with the flour, and mixing well after each addition. Divide the batter between the pans and spread to level. Bake the three 6-inch (15 cm) cakes for about 20 minutes (if using the tall 6-inch/15 cm pan, bake the cake for about 40 minutes) and the 9-inch (23 cm) cakes for about 30 minutes, until a tester inserted in the centre of the cake comes out clean. Cool the cakes for 20 minutes in the pans, then turn them out to cool completely.

3. Prepare the buttercream and lemon curd recipes and have them on hand for assembly.

4. To finish each cake layer, peel away the parchment paper and place the first cake layer onto a 9-inch (23 cm) cardboard cake board (so that the cake can be easily lifted and moved). Spoon a cupful of buttercream into a piping bag fitted with a plain tip and pipe a ring of buttercream on the top outside edge of the cake. Spoon a generous $\frac{1}{2}$ cup (125 mL) of the lemon curd into the centre of the cake and spread it evenly. Place the second cake layer on top of the curd and repeat the step with the buttercream and lemon curd. Top with the third cake layer. Spread the top and outsides of the cake with the buttercream, making it as straight and level as possible. Chill each cake for at least 2 hours to set the buttercream. Repeat this process with the 6-inch (15 cm) cake placed on a 6-inch (15 cm) cake board.

5. For the assembly, first set aside a small piece (about 6 oz/175 g) of fondant to keep white for the details, then tint the rest of the fondant. Using a

CONTINUED . . .

LEMON CAKE:

¾ cup (185 mL) unsalted butter, at room temperature

2¼ cups (560 mL) sugar

1½ Tbsp (22.5 mL) finely grated lemon zest

3 cups + 3 Tbsp (795 mL) cake and pastry flour

1½ Tbsp (22.5 mL) baking powder

¾ tsp (4 mL) salt

2 cups (500 mL) buttermilk, at room temperature

6 egg whites, at room temperature (save the yolks for the Lemon Curd)

1½ tsp (7.5 mL) vanilla extract

ASSEMBLY:

9-inch (23 cm) round cardboard cake board

1 recipe Lemon Buttercream (page 181)

1 recipe Lemon Curd (page 181)

6-inch (15 cm) round cardboard cake board

2 lb (1 kg) white rolling fondant

Buttercup yellow food colouring paste

Icing sugar, for rolling the fondant

Measuring tape

Small fondant cutter (flower shape)

Royal Icing (page 252), for piping detail

See pages 182–83 for photos of assembly

CONTINUED . . .

toothpick, add a little yellow colouring to a small piece of fondant (about 6 oz/175 g) and knead it to work in the colour. Now knead this small piece into the remaining fondant until it is evenly incorporated, adding colour just a little at a time until the desired tone is achieved. Keep the fondant well wrapped while assembling the cake.

6. Using a clean rolling pin on a work surface dusted with icing sugar, roll a large piece of fondant about $\frac{1}{4}$ inch (6 mm) thick into a circle large enough to cover the 9-inch (23 cm) cake (using a measuring tape to ensure this). The diameter should probably be about 15 inches (38 cm). If you are not pleased with the appearance of the fondant (it should be smooth with no air bubbles visible), you can always reroll it. To cover the cake, roll the fondant up using your rolling pin, carefully lift it over the 9-inch (23 cm) cake, and unroll it to cover. Starting with the top, gently massage the fondant on the cake, working out any air pockets or bumps, and work your way down the sides. Trim away any excess fondant from the bottom edge of the cake. Repeat this step with the 6-inch (15 cm) cake.

7. Lift the 6-inch (15 cm) cake, on its board, onto the 9-inch (23 cm) cake and check that it is centred.

8. Roll out the reserved small piece of white fondant to about $\frac{1}{8}$ inch (3 mm) thick. Cut out little flowers with a fondant cutter and carefully lift them onto a plate to dry for 15 minutes.

9. Spoon a little prepared royal icing into a piping bag fitted with a small, plain piping tip. Pipe a little icing on the back of a flower, and adhere it where the 6-inch (15 cm) cake meets the top of the 9-inch (23 cm) cake. Continue adhering the flowers all the way around the cake, and add a few flowers to the top of the cake if you wish. Pipe a little royal icing in the centre of each flower and let this set for at least an hour.

10. The wedding cake can be prepared and assembled up to a day in advance, but it is best to assemble just the layers up to a day ahead, then finish the fondant and décor the day the cake will be presented. A fondant-covered cake is best if it can sit out at room temperature, which this cake can do for up to 8 hours. If assembling a day ahead, refrigerate the cake but to avoid condensation, let it sit out at room temperature for 2 hours before transporting.

note from anna's kitchen

Since both wedding cakes in this chapter are a modest size, there is no need for elaborate engineering to stack the tiers. Although larger cakes require pieces of wooden dowelling inserted into the lower tiers so they can hold the weight of the tiers stacked on top of them, this size of cake doesn't need this. If you feel that the cake will sit out longer than 8 hours, insert a few wooden dowelling pieces, cut to the height of the entire cake, into the 9-inch (23 cm) tier, only because the frosting may soften.

LEMON BUTTERCREAM
• Makes about 6 cups (1.5 L) •

ALTHOUGH THIS WEDDING cake is covered with a fondant icing, the buttercream layer underneath is essential both for flavour and to create flat sides and tops to the cake layers.

1. Whisk the sugar and egg whites together in a metal bowl. Place the bowl over a pot of simmering water and whisk by hand until the sugar has dissolved and the mixture is hot, about 3 minutes. Remove from the heat.
2. Switch to electric beaters (or a stand mixer) and whip the whites until they have cooled to room temperature (they will more than double in volume), about 6 minutes. While beating, add the butter a little at a time, then mix in the lemon juice and vanilla and beat until the frosting is smooth and fluffy.
3. Use the frosting at room temperature. If you wish to make the frosting ahead of time, chill it to store, but then bring it to room temperature and beat it to make it smooth and spreadable. The frosting will keep in the refrigerator for up to a week.

1½ cups (375 mL) sugar
6 egg whites
2¼ cups (560 mL) unsalted butter, at room temperature
⅓ cup (80 mL) lemon juice
1½ tsp (7.5 mL) vanilla extract

LEMON CURD
• Makes about 2½ cups (625 mL) •

1. Whisk the sugar, lemon juice, lemon zest, egg yolks, and whole eggs together in a metal bowl. Place the bowl over a pot of simmering water and gently whisk the mixture by hand (you do not need to whisk quickly, and can even step away now and again), until thickened to the point that the curd leaves a ribbon on top of itself when the whisk is lifted, about 20 minutes.
2. Remove the curd from the heat and strain it into a bowl. Whisk in the butter until it melts in completely, then chill the curd until it has set, about 2 hours. The curd will keep in the refrigerator for up to a week.

1⅓ cups (330 mL) sugar
1 cup (250 mL) fresh lemon juice
4 tsp (20 mL) finely grated lemon zest
4 egg yolks
2 eggs
1 cup (250 mL) unsalted butter, at room temperature

note from anna's kitchen
Any extra lemon curd can be used as a sauce served alongside the wedding cake.

Assembling Springtime Wedding Cake with Fondant (pages 178–181)

AUTUMN CARROT WEDDING CAKE WITH CREAM CHEESE FROSTING

• *Makes one 2-tier wedding cake* •
Serves 24 as a full dessert and 40 as a tasting portion

*T*HE IDEA OF a carrot cake for an autumn wedding is immensely appealing, and if the bride and groom, or the guests, are huge carrot cake fans, this cake could suit any season. If your cake-decorating skills are not at the master level, this cake style is very forgiving. The use of a leaf tip to create beautiful ribbon-like stripes is easy enough to do, and this technique, along with a generous sprinkling of maple-toasted walnuts to cover the tops of the tiers, hides any imperfections.

1. For the cake layers, preheat the oven to 325°F (160°C). Grease a 9-inch (23 cm) cake pan and a 6-inch (15 cm) cake pan.

2. Sift the flour, baking powder, baking soda, cinnamon, and salt into a large bowl. Stir in the grated carrots. In a separate bowl, whisk the brown sugar, oil, and eggs, and add this to the carrot mixture, stirring until well blended. Scrape the batter into the prepared cake pans, filling them each to the same height. Bake the 6-inch (15 cm) cake for 25 to 30 minutes and the 9-inch (23 cm) cake for 40 to 50 minutes, until a tester inserted in the centre of the cake comes out clean. Cool the cakes for 20 minutes in the pan, then turn them out to cool completely.

3. For the frosting, beat the butter and cream cheese until fluffy, about 3 minutes. Add the icing sugar and vanilla, and beat gently until the sugar is incorporated, then beat more vigorously until the icing is fluffy.

4. To frost the cakes, place the 9-inch (23 cm) cake onto a cake board and slice into 3 horizontal layers. Spread a generous layer of frosting onto the first layer, top with the second, and spread frosting on it before topping with the final layer. Chill the cake while assembling the 6-inch (15 cm) cake in the same manner, then chill both for an hour.

5. Frost the top and sides of each cake, making the frosting as smooth and level as possible. Chill the cakes for another hour while getting ready to assemble.

CARROT CAKE:

3 cups (750 mL) all-purpose flour
1 Tbsp (15 mL) baking powder
1½ tsp (7.5 mL) baking soda
1½ tsp (7.5 mL) ground cinnamon
¾ tsp (4 mL) salt
4½ cups (1.125 L) coarsely grated, loosely packed carrots
1 cup (250 mL) packed light brown sugar
1 cup (250 mL) vegetable oil
6 eggs

CREAM CHEESE FROSTING:

2 cups (500 mL) unsalted butter, at room temperature
3 pkg (8 oz/250 g each) cream cheese, at room temperature
8 cups (2 L) icing sugar, sifted
1 Tbsp (15 mL) vanilla extract

ASSEMBLY:

9-inch (23 cm) round cardboard cake board
6-inch (15 cm) round cardboard cake board
2½ cups (625 mL) walnut pieces
¼ cup (60 mL) maple syrup
Piping bag
Flat leaf tip (as pictured, page 187)

CONTINUED . . .

CONTINUED . . .

6. For the maple-toasted walnuts, preheat the oven to 350°F (175°C) and line a baking tray with parchment paper. Toss the walnut pieces with the maple syrup and spread them evenly on the prepared baking tray. Toast the nuts for about 15 minutes, stirring occasionally, until they are evenly browned. Once the nuts have cooled, the maple syrup will have caramelized on them, and they can be stored in an airtight container until ready to use.

7. To assemble the cake, carefully place the 6-inch (15 cm) tier on top of the 9-inch (23 cm) tier, adjusting to ensure it is centred. Fill a piping bag fitted with a flat leaf tip with cream cheese frosting and pipe vertical lines up the sides of the cake, starting at the bottom and working up. Any rough edges at the top of each cake tier can be smoothed with a small spatula. Generously sprinkle the maple-toasted walnuts over the top of each tier, covering completely. The cake should be stored chilled, but it can sit out on display (indoors and out of direct sunlight) for up to 5 hours. This cake can be baked and assembled up to 2 days in advance of presenting.

Assembling Autumn Wedding Cake with Cream Cheese Frosting

CLASSIC VANILLA CRÈME BRÛLÉE
• *Makes 6 individual crème brûlées* •

A GOOD CRÈME BRÛLÉE is a beautifully simple thing, and the ingredient ratio in this recipe blends richness (without it being too heavy) and a nice set (without it being too eggy). In two words: *just right*.

2½ cups (625 mL) whipping cream

1 vanilla bean, or 1 Tbsp (15 mL) vanilla bean paste

8 egg yolks

6 Tbsp (90 mL) sugar, plus extra for torching

1. Preheat the oven to 325°F (160°C). Place six 6-ounce (180 mL) ramekins into a baking dish with a lip the same height as or taller than the ramekins.

2. Heat 2 cups (500 mL) of the cream with the scraped vanilla seeds and the vanilla bean (or the vanilla bean paste) to just below a simmer. In a medium bowl, whisk the egg yolks, sugar, and remaining ½ cup (125 mL) of the cream. Slowly whisk the hot cream into the yolk mixture until blended. Divide this evenly between the ramekins, and if there any bubbles on the surface of the custards, use the edge of a paper towel to touch them and pull them away (a smooth top to the custards is the goal).

3. Pour boiling water around the ramekins to halfway up the sides, and bake for about 25 minutes, until the outside of the custards are set but the centre still has a little jiggle to it. Cool the custards for 15 minutes in the water bath, then remove them to cool to room temperature before chilling for at least 4 hours.

4. To serve the brûlées, sprinkle the tops of each of the custards with a thin layer of sugar, then carefully melt and caramelize the sugar using a kitchen torch. Add a second thin layer of sugar and repeat—this technique builds a crunchy top that is less likely to burn than if you put on a thick layer of sugar.

note from anna's kitchen

Vanilla is such an important ingredient, especially in such a classic recipe as crème brulée. For more insight into the world of vanilla, refer to page 13.

To scrape the seeds from a vanilla bean, first run a paring knife down the length of the bean to open it. Then use the dull side of the knife and run it along the inside of the bean—the seeds will stick to the knife and be easily transferred to your cream to infuse the flavour.

DULCE DE LECHE CRÈME BRÛLÉE
• Makes 6 individual crème brûlées •

gluten-
FREE

*T*HIS CRÈME BRÛLÉE is for the true caramel fan, as caramelized condensed milk sweetens and enriches the custard itself.

1. Preheat the oven to 350°F (175°C). Lightly grease six 6-ounce (180 mL) ramekins and place them into a baking dish that comes up as high as the dishes.
2. Pour the condensed milk into a heavy-bottomed saucepot and whisk in ½ cup (125 mL) of the whipping cream. Constantly stir the condensed-milk mixture with a silicone spatula over medium heat until it thickens and caramelizes lightly to a golden brown colour, 12 to 14 minutes.
3. Whisk the remaining 1 cup (250 mL) of whipping cream and the light cream into the condensed-milk mixture and bring this to just below a simmer, whisking until the caramelized condensed milk *(dulce de leche)* dissolves into the cream. In a large bowl, whisk the egg yolks, whole egg, and vanilla together. Pour the condensed-milk mixture into the eggs and whisk until evenly blended. Pour this carefully into the ramekins. Pour boiling water around the ramekins so that the water comes at least halfway up the ramekins. Bake the custards for 30 to 35 minutes, until the custards are set at the edges but still jiggle in the middle. Let the custards cool for 20 minutes in the pan, then carefully remove to cool to room temperature before chilling for at least 3 hours.
4. To serve the brûlées, sprinkle the tops of each of the custards with a thin layer of sugar, then melt and caramelize the sugar using a kitchen torch. Add a second thin layer of sugar and repeat—this technique builds a crunchy top that is less likely to burn than if you put on a thick layer of sugar. The brûlées will keep in the refrigerator for up to 2 days.

1 tin (300 mL) sweetened condensed milk
1½ cups (375 mL) whipping cream
1 cup (250 mL) 5% (light half-and-half) cream
6 egg yolks
1 egg
2 tsp (10 mL) vanilla extract
Sugar, for torching

MAPLE CRÈME WITH ALMOND CRACKLE
• *Makes 4 individual crème brûlées* •

gluten-
FREE

*T*HE SUBTLE SWEETNESS of maple really adds a nice touch to this crème brûlée. This is a lighter version of the original crème brûlée, using half-and-half cream and milk instead of whipping cream, but it still has a satisfyingly creamy end result. The step of burning the tops of the desserts is skipped, since a maple-coated almond crackle adds that signature crunchy top layer.

1. Preheat the oven to 325°F (160°C). Arrange four 6-ounce (180 mL) ramekins or other baking dishes in a larger baking dish that has sides that are at least the height of the ramekins.
2. Whisk all of the ingredients together (except the crackle) and pour them into the prepared ramekins.
3. Pour boiling water around the ramekins so that the water comes up to about two-thirds of the height of the ramekins.
4. Bake the crèmes between 35 and 45 minutes, until they are set around the outside but still jiggle a bit at the centre. Allow the custards to cool in the water-filled pan for 10 minutes, then carefully remove them from the water to cool to room temperature before chilling for at least 4 hours.
5. The crackle can be prepared while the crèmes are in the oven. To serve, break the crackle into pieces and place them on top of the crèmes immediately before serving. The brûlées will keep in the refrigerator for up to 2 days.

1¼ cups (310 mL) half-and-half cream
¾ cup (185 mL) milk
⅔ cup (160 mL) pure maple syrup
2 tsp (10 mL) vanilla extract
5 egg yolks
1 egg
Pinch ground cinnamon
1 recipe Nut Crackle (almond) (page 321)

note from anna's kitchen
We love crème brûlée for the crack of the caramelized sugar, but it's much more than that. That cool, barely set cream lying underneath is just as compelling.

Classic Vanilla Crème Brûlée (page 190)
and *Maple Crème with Almond Crackle*
(page 192)

CLASSIC SPANISH FLAN
• *Makes 6 individual crème caramels* •

gluten-FREE

THIS IS SIMILAR to the French crème caramel, except for the little pinch of cinnamon in the recipe. You'll find this refreshing dessert on virtually all menus in Spain.

½ cup (125 mL) + ⅓ cup (80 mL) sugar
1 Tbsp (15 mL) lemon juice
3 eggs
2 cups (500 mL) half-and-half (10%) or light (5%) cream
2 tsp (10 mL) vanilla extract
Pinch ground cinnamon

1. Preheat the oven to 350°F (175°C). Lightly grease six 6-ounce (180 mL) ramekins and place them into a baking dish that comes up as high as the ramekins do.

2. To prepare the caramel layer, pour 2 tablespoons (30 mL) of water into a saucepot and add ½ cup (125 mL) of the sugar and the lemon juice. Bring the sugar to a boil over high heat, without stirring. Boil the sugar until it caramelizes, about 4 minutes—as it cooks, occasionally brush down the sides of the pot with cool water. Carefully spoon this into the prepared ramekins and let it cool for 15 minutes.

3. To prepare the custard, whisk the eggs with the remaining ⅓ cup (80 mL) of sugar, then whisk in the cream, vanilla, and cinnamon. Pour this into the ramekins (expect the cinnamon to float to the top). Pour boiling water around the ramekins so that the water comes at least halfway up the ramekins. Bake the custards for 25 to 30 minutes, until the custards are set at the edges but still jiggle in the middle. Let the custards cool for 20 minutes in the pan, then carefully remove to cool to room temperature before chilling for at least 3 hours.

4. To serve, run a knife or palette knife around the inside edge of each ramekin to loosen the custard. Place a dish overtop the ramekin and invert. Lift away the ramekin and serve. The custards will keep in the refrigerator for up to 2 days.

note from anna's kitchen
This style of custard is altogether different from crème brûlée. Made with whole eggs, these custards set to the point where they can be turned out onto a plate, and since they are made with milk or low-fat cream, they have a silky, almost palate-cleansing texture and taste.

SESAME HONEY CRÈME CARAMEL
• *Makes one 8-inch (20 cm) crème caramel* | *Serves 8* •

gluten-
FREE

A HINT OF SESAME oil adds an unexpected nuttiness to this crème caramel, and the sesame seeds float to the surface as the custard bakes, toasting nicely. Once the crème caramel is inverted, the seeds become almost like a crust at the bottom of the dessert.

½ cup (125 mL) sugar
½ tsp (2 mL) cream of tartar
2 Tbsp (30 mL) water
4 cups (1 L) milk
1 vanilla bean
6 eggs
⅓ cup (80 mL) honey
1½ tsp (7.5 mL) sesame oil
2 Tbsp (30 mL) sesame seeds

1. Preheat the oven to 350°F (175°C).
2. In a saucepot, bring the sugar, cream of tartar, and water up to a boil, and boil over high heat without stirring, occasionally brushing the sides of the pot with water, until the sugar caramelizes, about 3 minutes. Carefully pour the hot sugar into an 8-inch (20 cm) baking dish and swirl to coat the bottom of the dish. After the sugar has cooled, lightly grease the surface of the dish that is not coated with sugar and place the dish into a larger pan, with sides that come up at least to the height of the baking dish.
3. Heat the milk with the seeds scraped from the vanilla bean until the milk is just below a simmer. Whisk the eggs and honey to blend, then slowly pour in the hot milk while whisking. Whisk in the sesame oil and pour the custard into the baking dish (the sesame oil will float to the top of the custard). Sprinkle the sesame seeds over the surface of the custard.
4. Pour boiling water around the baking dish and bake for 50 to 60 minutes, until the custard is set around the outside but still has a jiggle to the middle when moved. Let the custard cool in the water bath for 15 minutes, then remove to cool to room temperature before chilling completely, about 4 hours.
5. To plate and serve, run a knife around the inside edge of the baking dish. Place a large platter with a lip over the dish and quickly invert and lift off the baking dish (about ½ cup/125 mL) of caramel liquid will also come out with the custard as you flip it). Spoon or cut to serve. The custard will keep in the refrigerator for up to 2 days.

GREEN TEA GINGER CRÈME CARAMEL
• Makes 6 individual crème caramels •

gluten-
FREE

*T*HE WARMTH OF fresh ginger plays none too gingerly against the cool sweetness within this chilled crème caramel. In larger measures, ginger can add a chili-like heat to baked goods, but the sweetness of the custard cools it down to create a perfect balance.

1. Preheat the oven to 350°F (175°C).
2. In a saucepot, bring the water, ¾ cup (185 mL) of the sugar, and cream of tartar up to a boil, and boil over high heat without stirring, occasionally brushing the sides of the pot with water until the sugar caramelizes, about 3 minutes. Carefully pour the hot sugar into six 6-ounce (180 mL) ramekins, and swirl to coat the bottom of the dishes. After the sugar has cooled, lightly grease the surface of the ramekins that is not coated with sugar and place them into a larger pan that has sides that come up to at least the height of the ramekins.
3. Heat the milk with the green tea and ginger until just below a simmer. Remove the tea bags, or, if using loose tea, strain out the tea. Whisk the whole eggs, yolks, remaining ⅓ cup (80 mL) of sugar and the vanilla, and slowly pour in the hot milk while whisking. Ladle this into the ramekins. Pour boiling water around the ramekins and bake for 25 to 30 minutes, until the custards are set but still have a little jiggle in the centre. Remove the ramekins from the water after they have cooled for 10 minutes, cool to room temperature, then chill until set, about 3 hours.
4. To serve, run a knife or palette knife around the inside of each dish, place a plate over each, and invert, watching out for the caramel syrup that may run out. Serve on their own or with fresh berries. The custards will keep in the refrigerator for up to 2 days.

3 Tbsp (45 mL) water

¾ cup (185 mL) + ⅓ cup (80 mL) sugar

½ tsp (2 mL) cream of tartar

2½ cups (625 mL) milk

2 bags green tea or 1 Tbsp (15 mL) loose green tea

2 tsp (10 mL) finely grated fresh ginger

2 eggs

3 egg yolks

½ tsp (2 mL) vanilla extract

BAILEYS® CHOCOLATE SOUFFLÉS
• Makes 6 individual soufflés •

ONE SHOULD NEVER pick favourite recipes in cookbooks, but this has to be one of my latest favourite recipes, particularly when I pour caramel sauce with a little added Baileys® onto it.

1. Preheat the oven to 400°F (200°C). Lightly butter six 1-cup (250 mL) soufflé dishes or other 1-cup (250 mL) baking dishes. Sprinkle the inside of the cups with sugar and tap out any excess. Place the dishes onto a baking tray.
2. Whisk the milk, ¼ cup (60 mL) of the sugar, the cornstarch, and vanilla in a small dish, and set aside. Melt the chocolate and butter in a small saucepot over low heat, stirring constantly until melted. Stir in the milk mixture in 2 additions, whisking until evenly blended (the mixture will be a thick paste and may look a little grainy, but that is to be expected—it will smooth out after the whites are folded in). Stir in the Baileys® and keep the chocolate paste warm over low heat, stirring occasionally.
3. Whip the egg whites and cream of tartar until they are foamy, then slowly pour in the remaining 6 tablespoons (90 mL) of sugar and continue to whip until the whites hold a medium peak when the beaters are lifted. Quickly but gently fold a third of the whites into the warm chocolate—they will deflate quite a bit, but this is expected. Fold in the remaining two-thirds of the batter until incorporated, then pour this into the prepared soufflé dishes.
4. Bake the soufflés for 10 to 12 minutes, until the tops take on a dull look, but the inside still looks shiny and soft where a crack may form. Serve immediately.
5. The soufflés are tastiest served with caramel Baileys® sauce poured into the centre. Simply stir 3 tablespoons (45 mL) of Baileys® into the creamy caramel sauce (the sauce should be served at room temperature).

½ cup (125 mL) milk
¼ cup (60 mL) + 6 Tbsp (90 mL) sugar
2 tsp (10 mL) cornstarch
1 tsp (5 mL) vanilla extract
5 oz (150 g) unsweetened chocolate, chopped
2 Tbsp (30 mL) unsalted butter
¼ cup (60 mL) Baileys® Irish Cream liqueur
10 egg whites, at room temperature
½ tsp (2 mL) cream of tartar
1 recipe Creamy Caramel Sauce (page 319) (optional)

notes from anna's kitchen

1. If you don't have 1-cup (250 mL) soufflé dishes, but you have 6-ounce (180 mL) ramekins, tie a collar of parchment paper around each ramekin so that the parchment rises 2 inches (5 cm) above the top of the ramekin. Once the soufflés come out of the oven, untie the strings and carefully peel away the parchment.

2. An accurate oven temperature is critical to a successful soufflé. Although you may set your oven to 400°F (200°C), is it really at 400°F (200°C)? The only way to know is to keep an oven thermometer inside your oven. The digital thermostat may read 400°F (200°C) on your oven panel, but where that is measured from may not always be reliable.

3. When baking a soufflé, be certain not to slam the oven door. For an evenly risen soufflé, make sure the convection fan is off when baking.

4. If planning to make this soufflé for a dinner party, you can get your components ready ahead of time. You can fully prepare step 2 and chill the chocolate base until ready to bake. When ready to assemble, warm the chocolate base over low heat, ensure your egg whites are at room temperature before whipping, then pick up the recipe at step 3.

gluten-free **VARIATION**

Omit the Baileys®, as it is not certified gluten-free.

RASPBERRY SOUFFLÉS
• *Makes 8 individual soufflés* •

dairy- **FREE**   *low-* **FAT**

THIS SIMPLE SOUFFLÉ recipe uses a cooked raspberry syrup as its base. The intensity of the raspberry shines through in this satisfying dessert.

1. Preheat the oven to 375°F (190°C). Grease eight 1-cup (250 mL) soufflé dishes (see note 1 on page 199) and sprinkle them with sugar, tapping out any excess and placing them onto a baking tray.
2. Bring the raspberry puree and sugar up to a boil in a saucepot and boil the mixture without stirring until it reaches 242°F (117°C) on a candy thermometer, about 5 minutes from when the mixture starts to boil.
3. While the raspberry syrup is cooking, whip the whites with the cream of tartar until foamy. Once the syrup reaches temperature, carefully pour it down the side of the mixing bowl (to avoid splashing) into the egg whites while whipping, then increase the speed to high and continue to whip until the whites hold a medium peak when the beaters are lifted. Fold in the lemon juice, vanilla, and Chambord or other raspberry liqueur.
4. Gently spoon the soufflé mix into the prepared cups to fill just halfway and bake for about 20 minutes, until they have doubled in size and are just beginning to turn golden on top. Serve immediately.

¾ cup (185 mL) raspberry purée (about 2 cups/500 mL fresh or thawed frozen raspberries puréed and strained)
1 cup (250 mL) sugar
5 egg whites, at room temperature
½ tsp (2 mL) cream of tartar
1 Tbsp (15 mL) lemon juice
1 tsp (5 mL) vanilla extract
2 Tbsp (30 mL) Chambord or other raspberry liqueur

Omit the Chambord.   *gluten-free* **VARIATION**

note from anna's kitchen
A soufflé is best served with a sauce, and the best way to serve this is to present a soufflé to each guest and have a boat or pitcher of the sauce on the table (for this raspberry soufflé, I recommend Classic Chocolate Sauce; see page 319). Each guest should take a first bite right from the centre of the soufflé, then the sauce can be poured into it so that every bite to follow has a bit of sauce with it.

Baileys® Chocolate Soufflés (pages 198–199)
with *Creamy Caramel Sauce* (page 319)
and *Raspberry Soufflés* (page 200)
with *Classic Chocolate Sauce* (page 319)

CARAMEL SOUFFLÉS
• *Makes 6 individual soufflés* •

gluten-
FREE

*T*HESE ARE VERY much like a crème caramel but in soufflé form and is delicious served with chocolate sauce (page 319).

1. Pour the water, $\frac{1}{3}$ cup (80 mL) of the sugar, and the lemon juice into a small saucepot, and bring to a boil. Boil uncovered, without stirring, occasionally brushing the sides of the pot with water, until the mixture is amber in colour, about 4 minutes. Remove the pot from the heat and carefully whisk in the whipping cream (watch out for steam), stirring until smooth. You can return the pot to a low heat to melt completely, if needed. Cool the caramel to room temperature.

2. Preheat the oven to 425°F (220°C). Lightly butter six 1-cup (250 mL) soufflé or other 1-cup (250 mL) baking dishes (see note 1 on page 199) and sprinkle the inside with sugar, tapping out any excess. Place the cups on a baking tray.

3. Whisk the egg yolks, cornstarch, and vanilla together, and whisk this into the cooled caramel.

4. In a separate bowl, whip the egg whites and cream of tartar at high speed until they are foamy, then slowly pour the remaining $\frac{1}{3}$ cup (80 mL) of sugar into the egg whites while whipping, and continue to whip them until they hold a medium peak when the beaters are lifted. Pour the yolks into the whipped whites and stir gently but quickly until incorporated. Spoon the soufflé batter into the prepared cups and immediately bake for 8 to 10 minutes, until the soufflés double in volume and the tops are an even, rich brown. Serve immediately.

3 Tbsp (45 mL) water
⅔ cup (160 mL) sugar
1 Tbsp (15 mL) lemon juice
½ cup (125 mL) whipping cream
6 egg yolks
1 Tbsp (15 mL) cornstarch
1 Tbsp (15 mL) vanilla extract
7 egg whites
½ tsp (2 mL) cream of tartar

note from anna's kitchen
Soufflés are all about timing. They are light as air and look gorgeous coming out of the oven, but within 10 minutes, they can wilt and melt into themselves. Soufflés are grand and elegant, but plan to serve them when you have time budgeted between the main course and dessert for them to bake.

CREAMY RICE-PUDDING CUSTARDS
• *Makes 6 individual rice puddings* •

gluten-
FREE

To DRESS UP these rice puddings, try sprinkling sugar overtop and torching them in the style of crème brûlée.

2¼ cups (560 mL) milk
1 cinnamon stick
½ vanilla bean or 1½ tsp (7.5 mL) vanilla bean paste
⅓ cup (80 mL) arborio rice
¼ cup (60 mL) raisins (optional)
2 Tbsp (30 mL) unsalted butter
2 egg yolks
⅔ cup (160 mL) sugar
½ cup (125 mL) whipping cream

1. In a heavy-bottomed saucepot, bring the milk, cinnamon stick, and scraped seeds from the vanilla bean (or the vanilla bean paste) up to a simmer. Add the rice and cook at a gentle simmer, uncovered and stirring often, until the rice is al dente, about 20 minutes. Remove from the heat and stir in the raisins (if using) and butter to melt. Remove the cinnamon stick.

2. Preheat the oven to 350°F (175°C). Lightly grease six 6-ounce (180 mL) ramekins and place them in a roasting pan that is taller than the ramekins.

3. Whisk the egg yolks, sugar, and whipping cream in a small dish, and whisk this into the pot of hot pudding. Ladle the rice pudding into the prepared dishes and pour boiling water into the roasting pan so that it comes halfway up the sides of the ramekins. Bake the puddings for about 15 minutes, until the sugar on top has melted completely. The puddings can be served warm or chilled. The puddings will keep in the refrigerator for 3 days.

CROISSANT ORANGE PUDDINGS
• *Makes 6 individual puddings* •

BUTTERY, FLAKY CROISSANTS make a decadent base for these desserts, and you need stale croissants, at least 2 days old. Fresh croissants will collapse under the weight of the custard while stale croissants can hold up.

4 stale plain croissants
3 egg yolks
¼ cup (60 mL) sugar
2 Tbsp (30 mL) orange marmalade
2 tsp (10 mL) finely grated orange zest
1 tsp (5 mL) vanilla extract
¼ tsp (1 mL) ground cinnamon
¾ cup (185 mL) milk
½ cup (125 mL) half-and-half cream
2 Tbsp (30 mL) orange liqueur (optional)

1. Preheat the oven to 325°F (160°C). Grease six 6-ounce (180 mL) ramekins and place them in a baking dish taller than they are.

2. Cut the croissants into large pieces (2-inch/5 cm cubes) and spread them on an ungreased baking tray. Toast the croissant pieces until they are lightly browned and dry, about 15 minutes. Cool them on the tray.

3. In a large bowl, whisk the egg yolks with the sugar and orange marmalade to blend, then whisk in the orange zest, vanilla, and cinnamon. Pour in the milk and cream while whisking. Add the toasted croissant pieces and stir to coat (the croissants will deflate quickly), then spoon into the prepared ramekins.

4. Pour boiling water into the baking dish so that the water comes halfway up the ramekins, and bake the custards for about 40 minutes, until they soufflé and are golden on top. While still warm, brush the tops with orange liqueur (if using) and serve. The puddings are best served directly after baking.

BANANA CHOCOLATE BREAD PUDDING
• *Makes one 9-inch (23 cm) pudding | Serves 12 to 16* •

THIS IS A bread pudding to feed a crowd! A full loaf of banana bread is crumbled into a chocolate custard base, and once baked and chilled, it makes for a decadent dessert.

Like a cheesecake, this dessert is best prepared the day before you wish to serve it.

1. Preheat the oven to 375°F (190°C). Grease a 9-inch (23 cm) springform pan, wrap the bottom in foil, and place the pan in a roasting pan.
2. Cut the banana bread into 1-inch (2.5 cm) cubes and spread the cubes out on an ungreased baking tray. Toast the banana bread until the outsides of the cubes have dried, about 10 minutes. Leave on the tray to cool.
3. Place the chopped chocolate in a bowl. Heat the milk to just below a simmer and pour it over the chopped chocolate. Whisk the mixture until the chocolate has melted.
4. In a separate bowl, whisk the eggs, sugar, and vanilla. While whisking, add the chocolate milk to the eggs, and whisk until evenly blended. Add the banana bread pieces and stir to coat. Let the mixture sit for 10 minutes, stirring occasionally (the banana bread cubes will begin to break up—that is expected). Reduce the oven temperature to 350°F (175°C).
5. Pour the mixture into the prepared pan and pour boiling water into the roasting pan so that it comes halfway up the side of the springform pan. Bake the pudding for 60 to 70 minutes, until a tester inserted in the centre of the pudding comes out clean. Let the cake cool for 15 minutes, then remove it from the water bath before cooling it to room temperature. Chill the pudding in the pan until set, about 5 hours. The bread pudding is best served chilled, and slices into wedges, just like a cake. The pudding will keep, refrigerated, up to 3 days.

1 loaf Basic Banana Chocolate-Chip Bread (page 224)

4 oz (125 g) semisweet chocolate, chopped

3 cups (750 mL) milk

3 eggs

⅓ cup (80 mL) sugar

1 tsp (5 mL) vanilla extract

note from anna's kitchen
On the simpler side of custards, puddings often take less time to make, or use common ingredients on hand; they're a comforting treat at the end of a meal.

CRANBERRY ORANGE CLAFOUTIS

• *Makes 4 individual clafoutis* •

gluten-
FREE

*T*HE BATTER FOR this custard is like a crêpe batter, but when it's baked in a dish, it turns out light, fluffy, and more substantial than a custard. The tart cranberries make this a refreshing ending to a rich meal.

1. Preheat the oven to 375°F (190°C). Grease four 6-ounce (180 mL) ramekins (or other flat baking dishes) and place them onto a baking tray.

2. Stir the sugar, rice flour, orange zest, and cinnamon together. Whisk in the egg, egg yolk, cream, and vanilla until smooth. Divide the batter evenly between the ramekins and sprinkle each with ¼ cup (60 mL) of cranberries.

3. Bake the clafoutis for about 18 minutes, until they are puffed and golden (they will deflate when they come out of the oven). The clafoutis are best served warm and dusted with icing sugar. To serve them warm, either pull them fresh from the oven and allow them to cool for 10 minutes, or prepare them in advance, chill, then reheat for 12 minutes at 300°F (150°C) before serving.

⅓ cup (80 mL) sugar

3 Tbsp (45 mL) brown rice flour

2 tsp (10 mL) finely grated orange zest

Pinch ground cinnamon

1 egg

1 egg yolk

½ cup (125 mL) whipping cream

1 tsp (5 mL) vanilla extract

1 cup (250 mL) fresh or thawed frozen cranberries

Icing sugar, for dusting

LEMON POSSET
• *Makes 6 individual possets* •

egg-
FREE

gluten-
FREE

*T*HIS EGGLESS CUSTARD is set with the acidity of the lemon juice, which thickens the cream without curdling it. Because it is not baked and uses no eggs, the consistency is more fluid than in a traditional set custard. Posset sets just enough so that it can be topped with a few fresh berries and eaten with a spoon, but it does turn fluid once stirred.

2 cups (500 mL) whipping cream
½ cup (125 mL) sour cream (not low-fat)
⅔ cup (160 mL) sugar
1 Tbsp (15 mL) finely grated lemon zest
½ cup (125 mL) lemon juice
1 tsp (5 mL) vanilla extract

1. Whisk the cream, sour cream, sugar, and lemon zest in a small saucepot and over medium-low heat just until the sugar has melted. Remove the pot from the heat and stir in the lemon juice and vanilla.
2. Pour this into 6 serving dishes (glass or ceramic) and let it set for at least 6 hours, up to 24 hours (the longer the posset is left, the more it will set).
3. The possets can be served with fresh berries on top.

note from anna's kitchen
Because this "custard" is not baked, you can pour the posset mixture into pretty or decorative glasses to set.

muffins, coffee cakes, and
other morning goodies

NOTES ON MORNING GOODIES

Muffins

A muffin needs to be filling and fulfilling, and it should be able to double as a breakfast or an afternoon snack.

Coffee Cakes

Coffee cakes have their own special identity, but the name says it all. Great companions to a cup of coffee (tea is acceptable, too, of course), these cakes are also elegant enough to serve for dessert and can be eaten as a late afternoon treat or even at breakfast.

Loaves

A quick loaf is easy to make. It's pretty much the most practical and efficient baked treat you can have.

Scones

A flaky tender scone is a thing of beauty. While they taste rich, scones are not often as butter laden as we may believe. Scones are best enjoyed the day they are baked; unbaked scones freeze exceptionally well, to be baked another day.

Sticky Buns

Sticky buns are all about comfort. It takes time to make them and as you let the dough slowly rise you can anticipate that absolutely mouth-watering aroma of yeast, butter, and cinnamon once they hit the oven. They are worth the effort every single time.

OLD SCHOOL BLUEBERRY MUFFINS
• Makes 18 muffins •

I'VE NAMED THESE "old school" since they are the cake-like sweet and tender muffins that are more of a treat than a functionally nutritious breakfast item (but we love them all the same).

1. Preheat the oven to 375°F (190°C), and grease 2 muffin tins or line 18 cups with paper liners.
2. In a large mixing bowl, whisk the sugar, yogurt, eggs, oil, melted butter, vanilla, and orange zest together. In a separate bowl, sift the flour, baking powder, and salt. Add the flour to the yogurt mixture and stir just until blended. Stir in the blueberries and spoon the batter evenly into 18 muffin cups, then sprinkle the tops with turbinado sugar.
3. Bake the muffins for about 20 minutes, until the tops of the muffins spring back when gently pressed. Cool the muffins for 10 minutes in the tin before removing to cool completely. The muffins will keep for up to 3 days in an airtight container.

1½ cups (375 mL) sugar
1 cup (250 mL) plain yogurt (not low-fat)
2 eggs
¼ cup (60 mL) vegetable oil
¼ cup (60 mL) unsalted butter, melted
1 tsp (5 mL) vanilla extract
1 tsp (5 mL) finely grated orange zest
3 cups (750 mL) all-purpose flour
2 tsp (10 mL) baking powder
1 tsp (5 mL) salt
2 cups (500 mL) fresh blueberries
Turbinado sugar, for sprinkling

KITCHEN SINK MUFFINS
• *Makes 12 muffins* •

dairy-
FREE

*T*HESE MUFFINS EARN their name because they include in them everything but the kitchen sink.

¾ cup (185 mL) sugar
½ cup (125 mL) vegetable oil
2 eggs
1 cup (250 mL) peeled and coarsely grated tart apple, such as Granny Smith
1 cup (250 mL) coarsely grated carrot
⅔ cup (160 mL) drained crushed pineapple
2 tsp (10 mL) finely grated lemon zest
2 Tbsp (30 mL) lemon juice
1 cup (250 mL) whole wheat flour
½ cup (125 mL) rolled oats, plus extra for sprinkling
2¼ tsp (12 mL) baking powder
1 tsp (5 mL) ground cinnamon
¼ tsp (1 mL) salt
½ cup (125 mL) raisins
½ cup (125 mL) unsalted sunflower seeds
½ cup (125 mL) unsweetened, flaked coconut

1. Preheat the oven to 375°F (190°C), and grease or use paper liners to line a muffin tin.
2. In a large bowl, whisk the sugar, oil, and eggs. Stir in the apple, carrot, pineapple, lemon zest, and lemon juice.
3. In a separate bowl, stir the whole wheat flour, oats, baking powder, cinnamon, and salt to combine. Add the flour mixture to the sugar mixture and stir just until blended. Stir in the raisins, sunflower seeds, and coconut. Spoon the batter into the prepared muffin cups.
4. Bake for about 30 minutes, until the muffins spring back when gently pressed. Cool the muffins in the tin for 10 minutes before removing to cool completely. The muffins will keep in an airtight container for up to 3 days.

BRAN AND RAISIN MUFFINS
• *Makes 12 muffins* •

low-
FAT

*H*EALTHY AND WHOLESOME, these bran muffins contain less fat than the typical grocery store versions.

1½ cups (375 mL) wheat bran
½ cup (125 mL) sugar
¼ cup (60 mL) packed light brown sugar
1¼ cups (310 mL) all-purpose flour
1 tsp (5 mL) baking powder
½ tsp (2 mL) baking soda
½ tsp (2 mL) salt
½ tsp (2 mL) ground cinnamon
1 egg
1 cup (250 mL) buttermilk
¼ cup (60 mL) vegetable oil
½ cup (125 mL) boiling water
1 cup (250 mL) raisins

1. Preheat the oven to 350°F (175°C) and line a muffin tin with paper liners, or grease it well.
2. Stir together the bran, sugar, brown sugar, flour, baking powder, baking soda, salt, and cinnamon. In a separate bowl, whisk the egg, then add the buttermilk and oil. Stir this into the bran mixture, then pour it into the boiling water and blend. Stir in the raisins and spoon the batter into the prepared muffin tin.
3. Bake the muffins for 20 to 25 minutes, until the tops of the muffins spring back when gently pressed. Let the muffins cool in the tin for 15 minutes, then remove them to cool completely. The muffins will keep for 3 days stored in an airtight container.

Bran and Raisin Muffins, top left (page 212), *Old School Blueberry Muffins*, top right (page 211), and *Kitchen Sink Muffins*, centre (page 212)

OAT MUFFINS
WITH CRANBERRIES AND PEARS
• Makes 12 muffins •

*T*HESE MUFFINS ARE light and moist. The naturally sweet pear balances with the tart cranberry, but you could replace the cranberry with virtually any fruit you prefer.

1⅓ cups (330 mL) rolled oats, plus extra for sprinkling
1¼ cups (310 mL) plain yogurt (not low-fat or fat-free)
½ cup (125 mL) fancy molasses
½ cup (125 mL) packed light brown sugar
½ cup (125 mL) unsalted butter, melted and cooled
1 egg
½ cup (125 mL) all-purpose flour
½ cup (125 mL) whole wheat flour
1½ tsp (7.5 mL) baking powder
½ tsp (2 mL) baking soda
½ tsp (2 mL) salt
¼ tsp (1 mL) ground cinnamon
¼ tsp (1 mL) ground nutmeg
⅔ cup (160 mL) peeled and diced pears
⅓ cup (80 mL) dried cranberries

1. Preheat oven to 375°F (190°C) and line a muffin tin with paper liners.
2. Stir the oats and yogurt together in a large bowl. Stir in the molasses, brown sugar, melted butter, and egg.
3. In a separate bowl, sift the flours, baking powder, baking soda, salt, cinnamon, and nutmeg. Stir the flour mixture into the oat mixture until blended, then stir in the pears and cranberries and sprinkle with a few oats. Spoon into the muffin cups.
4. Bake for 20 to 25 minutes, until the muffins spring back when gently pressed. Let the muffins cool for 10 minutes in the tin before removing to cool completely. The muffins will keep in an airtight container for up to 3 days.

BANANA COCONUT MUFFINS
• Makes 10 muffins •

*I*F COCONUT ISN'T your thing, substitute the same measure with walnut pieces instead.

¾ cup (185 mL) mashed, ripe bananas (about 2)
½ cup (125 mL) packed golden-yellow sugar
1 egg
1 tsp (5 mL) finely grated lime zest
½ tsp (2 mL) vanilla extract
½ cup (125 mL) unsalted butter, melted and cooled
1¼ cups (310 mL) all-purpose flour
1 tsp (5 mL) baking powder
¼ tsp (1 mL) salt
½ cup (125 mL) sweetened, flaked coconut

1. Preheat the oven to 375°F (190°C) and line a muffin tin with paper liners.
2. Stir the bananas and sugar together, then stir in the egg, lime zest, and vanilla. Stir in the melted butter.
3. In a separate bowl, sift the flour, baking powder, and salt, then add the flour mixture to the banana mixture and stir until combined. Mix in the coconut and spoon the batter into the prepared muffin tin.
4. Bake for 20 to 25 minutes, until the muffins spring back when gently pressed. Let the muffins cool for 10 minutes before removing from the tin to cool completely. The muffins will keep in an airtight container for up to 3 days.

PECAN-TOPPED APPLESAUCE COFFEE CAKE
• Makes one 9-inch (23 cm) coffee cake | Serves 12 to 16 •

*T*HIS LARGE, STICKY cake presents beautifully, and can double as a dessert, if needed.

1. Preheat the oven to 350°F (175°C) and grease a 9-inch (23 cm) springform pan.
2. In a large mixing bowl, whisk the eggs just to blend, then whisk in the applesauce, brown sugar, and oil until smoothly blended. In a separate bowl, sift the flour, baking powder, salt, cinnamon, allspice, and cloves, and stir this into the applesauce mixture until evenly combined. Scrape the batter into the prepared pan and prepare the topping.
3. For the topping, stir the brown sugar, butter, and cinnamon together, then stir in the pecans and the grated apple. Spread this over the cake batter.
4. Bake for 60 to 70 minutes, until a tester inserted in the centre of the cake comes out clean. Cool the cake to room temperature, then remove the cake from the pan before serving. The cake can be stored in an airtight container for up to 3 days.

CAKE:

2 eggs
1½ cups (375 mL) unsweetened applesauce
1½ cups (375 mL) packed light brown sugar
½ cup (125 mL) oil
2½ cups (625 mL) all-purpose flour
2 tsp (10 mL) baking powder
½ tsp (2 mL) salt
½ tsp (2 mL) ground cinnamon
½ tsp (2 mL) ground allspice
¼ tsp (1 mL) ground cloves

TOPPING:

½ cup (125 mL) packed dark brown sugar
¼ cup (60 mL) unsalted butter, melted
½ tsp (2 mL) ground cinnamon
1 cup (250 mL) chopped pecan pieces
1 peeled apple, coarsely grated

CINNAMON STREUSEL COFFEE CAKE
• *Makes one 8-inch (20 cm) square cake* | *Serves 9 to 12* •

*T*HIS IS THE classic coffee cake, with a streusel layer on top of the cake.

1. Preheat the oven to 350°F (175°C). Grease an 8-inch (20 cm) square pan and line the bottom and sides with parchment paper.
2. For the streusel topping, stir the flour, brown sugar, cinnamon, and salt in a small bowl with a fork to combine. Add the melted butter and stir until the mixture is evenly moistened.
3. For the cake, beat the butter and sugar until it is light and fluffy. Add the whole egg and then the egg yolk, and beat well after each addition. Stir in the sour cream and vanilla. In a separate bowl, sift the flour, baking powder, baking soda, and salt. Add the flour mixture to the butter mixture and stir just until blended.
4. Spread the batter into the prepared pan and sprinkle the streusel topping overtop. Bake the cake for about 35 minutes, until a tester inserted in the centre of the cake comes out clean. Allow the cake to cool completely in the pan, then cut into squares as needed to serve. The coffee cake will keep, well wrapped and unrefrigerated, for 3 days.

TOPPING:

¾ cup (185 mL) all-purpose flour
½ cup (125 mL) packed light brown sugar
½ tsp (2 mL) ground cinnamon
Pinch salt
¼ cup (60 mL) unsalted butter, melted

CAKE:

½ cup (125 mL) unsalted butter, at room temperature
¾ cup (185 mL) sugar
1 egg
1 egg yolk
½ cup (125 mL) sour cream
1 tsp (5 mL) vanilla extract
1⅓ cups (330 mL) all-purpose flour
1 tsp (5 mL) baking powder
¼ tsp (1 mL) baking soda
¼ tsp (1 mL) salt

APRICOT YEAST COFFEE CAKE
• *Makes one 9-inch (23 cm) round coffee cake | Serves 12 to 16* •

THIS EUROPEAN-STYLE, YEAST-RAISED coffee cake suits a special occasion, like a holiday or a Sunday brunch. As is the case with most yeast-raised goodies, the cake is best enjoyed within a day of being baked.

1. Stir the milk, water, and yeast together until the yeast has dissolved, then stir in the sugar, egg yolks, and vanilla. Add the flour, salt, and nutmeg, and using a wooden spoon, beaters, or a mixer fitted with the dough-hook attachment, mix the dough until it comes together and looks elastic, about 3 minutes. Add the butter, and keep blending the dough for another 3 minutes—the dough should be sticky and stretchy. Scrape the dough into a lightly oiled bowl, cover the bowl with plastic wrap, and let the dough rise for 1 to 2 hours, until it has doubled in size.

2. Preheat the oven to 350°F (175°C) and grease a 9-inch (23 cm) springform pan.

3. Tip the risen dough into the greased pan and, with floured fingers, gently spread it into the edges of the pan. Arrange the apricot halves over the top of the dough.

4. In a small bowl, stir the sugar, flour, and cardamom or cinnamon together for the topping. Cut in the butter until the mixture is a rough, crumbly texture, and sprinkle this over the apricots. Let the cake sit for 10 minutes.

5. Bake the cake for 30 to 40 minutes, until the edges of the visible cake are golden brown. Cool the cake for at least 20 minutes before slicing. The coffee cake can be stored in an airtight container for up to a day.

CAKE:

½ cup (125 mL) milk,
   at room temperature
¼ cup (60 mL) tepid (105°F/41°C) water
2¼ tsp (11 mL/1 pkg) instant yeast
¼ cup (60 mL) sugar
2 egg yolks
1 tsp (5 mL) vanilla extract
2 cups (500 mL) all-purpose flour
½ tsp (2 mL) salt
¼ tsp (1 mL) ground nutmeg
¼ cup (60 mL) unsalted butter,
   at room temperature

TOPPING:

1 tin (14 oz/398 mL) apricot halves,
   drained
6 Tbsp (90 mL) sugar
3 Tbsp (45 mL) all-purpose flour
¼ tsp (1 mL) ground cardamom
   or ground cinnamon
6 Tbsp (90 mL) cool unsalted butter,
   cut in pieces

note from anna's kitchen
Although I prefer to bake with fresh, seasonal fruits, I make an exception for apricots. Tinned apricots have a great flavour, and they hold their shape in baking. And since the fresh apricot season is so short in Niagara, where I live, I am content to settle for tinned when fresh isn't an option for me.

BLUEBERRY BUCKWHEAT COFFEE CAKE
• Makes one 8-inch (20 cm) square coffee cake | Serves 9 to 12 •

low-
FAT

low-
SUGAR

*T*HIS IS A simple and wholesome cake—it's just 1 inch (2.5 cm) tall, so it's great for a small bite. While the height of this coffee cake may be short, the flavours are big, from the buckwheat, the buckwheat honey, and even the olive oil.

½ cup (125 mL) yogurt
⅓ cup (80 mL) extra virgin olive oil
⅓ cup (80 mL) buckwheat honey
1 egg
¾ cup (185 mL) whole wheat flour
½ cup (125 mL) buckwheat flour
1½ tsp (7.5 mL) baking powder
½ tsp (2 mL) ground cinnamon
¼ tsp (1 mL) salt
1 cup (250 mL) fresh blueberries

1. Preheat the oven to 350°F (175°C) and grease an 8-inch (20 cm) square pan. Line the pan with parchment paper so that it just hangs over the sides of the pan.
2. Whisk the yogurt, olive oil, honey, and egg until blended. In a separate bowl, stir the whole wheat flour, buckwheat flour, baking powder, cinnamon, and salt together, then add this to the honey mixture, stirring until blended. Add the blueberries and combine, then pour the batter into the prepared pan.
3. Bake for 20 to 25 minutes, until a tester inserted in the centre of the cake comes out clean. Cool the cake to room temperature before slicing. The cake can be stored in an airtight container for up to 3 days.

STRAWBERRY CREAM CHEESE COFFEE CAKE
• *Makes one 9-inch (23 cm) coffee cake | Serves 12 to 16* •

THIS CAKE IS rather tall, hence the need for the springform pan. If you don't have a springform pan, prepare the cake in a 9- × 13-inch (3.5 L) pan, but reduce the baking time by 10 to 15 minutes.

1. Preheat the oven to 350°F (175°C) and grease a 9-inch (23 cm) springform pan and place it on a baking tray.
2. In a mixer fitted with the paddle attachment (or using electric beaters), combine the flour and sugar. Add the butter and blend until the mixture is a coarse, crumbly texture.
3. Measure out 1 cup (250 mL) of the mixture into a small bowl and set aside. To the larger bowl, add the baking powder, baking soda, and salt.
4. In a separate bowl, stir together the sour cream, egg, and vanilla, and add to the large mixing bowl, stirring until blended (the batter will be thick). Spread the batter into the prepared pan.
5. For the topping, beat the cream cheese and sugar together until smooth. Stir in the egg and vanilla until blended, then pour the mixture overtop of the cake batter.
6. Stir the strawberry jam to soften. Add the sliced strawberries to the jam and stir to coat, then spread overtop the cream cheese layer. Stir the chopped pecans into the reserved 1 cup (250 mL) of the flour mixture, and sprinkle overtop the strawberries.
7. Bake for about 55 minutes, until a tester inserted into the centre of the cake comes out clear of crumbs. Cool the cake to room temperature, then run a knife or spatula around the outside edge before removing the outside ring. The cake will keep in the refrigerator for up to 2 days.

CAKE:

2½ cups (625 mL) all-purpose flour
¾ cup (185 mL) sugar
¾ cup (185 mL) cool unsalted butter, cut in pieces
1 tsp (5 mL) baking powder
½ tsp (2 mL) baking soda
¼ tsp (1 mL) salt
¾ cup (185 mL) sour cream (not low-fat)
1 egg
1 tsp (5 mL) vanilla extract

TOPPING:

1 pkg (8 oz/250 g) cream cheese, at room temperature
½ cup (125 mL) sugar
1 egg
½ tsp (2 mL) vanilla extract
½ cup (125 mL) strawberry jam
1½ cups (375 mL) sliced fresh strawberries
½ cup (125 mL) chopped pecans

note from anna's kitchen
Strawberries aren't a typical ingredient to bake into desserts (unless accompanied by rhubarb). On their own, their turn soft, lose their bright colour, and can taste flat, but when stirred into jam, as in this recipe, their flavour and colour are maintained.

MORNING GLORY YOGURT LOAF
• *Makes one 9- × 5-inch (2 L) loaf | Serves 12 to 16* •

WITH ITS ORANGE, pineapple, coconut, and yogurt accents, this is a great breakfast loaf.

1. Preheat the oven to 325°F (160°C) and grease a 9- × 5-inch (2 L) loaf pan.
2. Cream the butter and sugar together. Add the eggs to the butter mixture one at a time, blending well after each addition. Stir in the yogurt and orange zest.
3. In a separate bowl, sift the flour, baking powder, salt, and cinnamon, and stir this into the butter mixture. Stir in the peaches (or pineapple, if using), raisins, and coconut. Scrape the batter into the prepared pan.
4. Bake for 60 to 70 minutes, until a tester inserted in the centre of the cake comes out clean. Cool the loaf for 30 minutes, then tap it out of the pan to cool completely on a cooling rack. The loaf will keep, well wrapped and unrefrigerated, for up to 3 days.

6 Tbsp (90 mL) unsalted butter, at room temperature

1 cup (250 mL) sugar

3 eggs, at room temperature

⅔ cup (160 mL) plain yogurt

2 tsp (10 mL) finely grated orange zest

1⅔ cups (410 mL) all-purpose flour

2 tsp (10 mL) baking powder

¼ tsp (1 mL) salt

Pinch ground cinnamon

1 cup (250 mL) peeled and diced fresh peaches, or one tin (14 oz/398 mL) crushed pineapple, well-drained

½ cup (125 mL) raisins

⅓ cup (80 mL) sweetened, shredded coconut

note from anna's kitchen
Even when trying to be healthy and more wholesome in baking, you need to use full-fat sour cream and yogurt in your recipes. For a further explanation, refer to page 13.

BASIC BANANA CHOCOLATE-CHIP BREAD
• Makes one 9- × 5-inch (2 L) loaf | Serves 12 to 16 •

I'VE CONDUCTED AN unscientific survey, and chocolate chips beat walnuts and raisins as the preferred add-in to banana bread, particularly for that first slice when the bread is still a little warm from the oven.

1. Preheat the oven to 350°F (175°C) and grease a 9- × 5-inch loaf (2 L) pan.
2. Beat the butter and brown sugar together until smooth. Stir in the bananas, then stir in the egg and vanilla. In a separate bowl, stir the all-purpose flour, whole wheat flour, baking soda, cinnamon, and salt to combine. Add this to the butter mixture and stir until evenly blended. Add the chocolate chips, then scrape the batter into the prepared pan and spread evenly.
3. Bake the loaf for about an hour, until a tester inserted in the centre of the cake comes out clean. Cool the loaf for 30 minutes in the pan, then turn out to cool completely. The loaf will keep, well wrapped and unrefrigerated, for up to 3 days.

⅓ cup (80 mL) unsalted butter, at room temperature

1 cup (250 mL) packed light brown sugar

3 cups (750 mL) mashed ripe bananas (3 to 4 bananas)

1 egg, at room temperature

1 tsp (5 mL) vanilla extract

¾ cup (185 mL) all-purpose flour

¾ cup (185 mL) whole wheat flour

1 tsp (5 mL) baking soda

¼ tsp (1 mL) ground cinnamon

¼ tsp (1 mL) salt

¾ cup (185 mL) chocolate chips

WHITE CHOCOLATE BLACK PEPPER SCONES
• Makes 10 scones •

*T*HESE SCONES ARE made to be served with strawberry jam. They can even double as shortcake biscuits, to serve with fresh strawberries and whipped cream.

1. Preheat the oven to 400°F (200°C) and line a baking tray with parchment paper.
2. Stir the flour, sugar, baking powder, salt, and pepper to combine. Cut in the butter using a pastry cutter, 2 knives, or your fingertips until the mixture is a rough crumbly texture but pieces of butter are still visible. Stir in the chopped white chocolate to coat with the flour.
3. In a separate bowl, whisk the egg, then whisk in the milk and vanilla. Add the milk mixture to the flour and stir until the dough just begins to come together, then turn it out onto a work surface.
4. Using your hands, flatten and fold the dough 2 or 3 times, until the dough is an even texture. Roll out the dough to just under 1 inch (2.5 cm) in thickness and cut scones with a 2½-inch (6 cm) round cutter, rerolling the dough as needed to get 10 scones.
5. Place the scones 1 inch (2.5 cm) apart on the prepared baking tray and brush the tops with milk. Bake the scones for about 15 minutes, until they have browned evenly.
6. The scones are best served the day they are baked but can be reheated the second day for 5 minutes in a 300°F (150°C) oven to refresh them.

1⅔ cups (410 mL) all-purpose flour

1 Tbsp (15 mL) sugar

2½ tsp (12 mL) baking powder

½ tsp (2 mL) salt

½ tsp (2 mL) finely ground black pepper

6 Tbsp (90 mL) unsalted butter,
cut in pieces and chilled

4 oz (125 g) white chocolate,
chopped or 1 cup (250 mL) of
white chocolate chips

1 egg

6 Tbsp (90 mL) cold milk,
plus extra for brushing

1 tsp (5 mL) vanilla extract

CURRANT SCONES
• Makes 16 scones •

*T*HESE SCONES ARE rich and flaky. As a plainer style of scone, they suit breakfast or tea time and can be topped with any kind of jam.

1. Preheat the oven to 400°F (200°C) and line a baking tray with parchment paper.
2. Stir the flour, sugar, baking powder, salt, zest, and nutmeg to combine.
3. Cut in the chilled butter using a pastry cutter, 2 knives, or your fingers until the mixture is crumbly but pieces of butter are still visible.
4. In a separate bowl, whisk the whole egg and egg yolk, then whisk in the 1 cup (250 mL) of milk. Add to the flour mixture and stir with a wooden spoon until the dough begins to come together, then turn the dough out onto a work surface (the dough will feel a bit sticky).
5. Sprinkle the currants overtop the dough, and work them in by flattening the dough out with your hands and then folding it in half, pressing the currants in at the same time (it takes about 4 or 5 folds to do this; see photo on facing page).
6. Shape the dough into a square and gently roll it out to an 8-inch (20 cm) square, lightly dusting with flour if needed. Cut the dough into 16 square scones, and place them onto the prepared baking tray, leaving 1 inch (2.5 cm) between them.
7. Brush the scones with milk and bake for about 15 minutes, until they are an even golden brown. The scones are best served the day they are baked but can be reheated the second day for 5 minutes in a 300°F (150°C) oven to refresh them.

3 cups (750 mL) all-purpose flour
¼ cup (60 mL) sugar
4 tsp (20 mL) baking powder
½ tsp (2 mL) salt
½ tsp (2 mL) finely grated lemon zest
⅛ tsp (0.5 mL) ground nutmeg
¾ cup (185 mL) unsalted butter, cut in pieces and chilled
1 egg
1 egg yolk
1 cup (250 mL) cold milk, plus extra for brushing scones
½ cup (125 mL) dried currants

Shaping dough for scones

APPLE CHEDDAR WALNUT SCONES
• *Makes 8 scones* •

egg-
FREE

*T*HESE SCONES ARE on the sweet side, but the celery salt and the cheddar cheese add a nice savoury nip.

1. Preheat the oven to 400°F (200°C) and line a baking tray with parchment paper.
2. Stir the flour, sugar, baking powder, celery salt, and cinnamon to combine.
3. Cut in the chilled butter using a pastry cutter, 2 knives, or your fingers until the mixture is crumbly but pieces of butter are still visible. Stir in the cheddar cheese to coat it with the flour mixture.
4. Using the coarse side of a box grater, grate the apple into the flour mixture and stir it in. Stir in the milk until the dough begins to come together, then turn it out on a work surface.
5. Sprinkle the walnuts overtop the dough and work them in by flattening the dough out with your hands and then folding it in half, pressing the walnuts in at the same time (it takes about 4 or 5 folds to do this; see photo on page 227).
6. Shape the dough into a disc and flatten it with your hands until it is about 8 inches (20 cm) across. Cut the dough into 8 wedges and place them onto the prepared baking tray.
7. Brush the tops of the scones with milk and bake for about 16 minutes, until they are a rich golden brown. The scones are best served the day they are baked but can be reheated the second day for 5 minutes in a 300°F (150°C) oven to refresh them.

1⅔ cups (410 mL) all-purpose flour

2 Tbsp (30 mL) sugar

1 Tbsp (15 mL) baking powder

½ tsp (2 mL) celery salt

⅛ tsp (0.5 mL) ground cinnamon

5 Tbsp (75 mL) unsalted butter, cut in small pieces and chilled

2 oz (60 g) coarsely grated old cheddar cheese (about 1 cup/250 mL)

1 tart apple, such as Granny Smith, peeled

⅓ cup (80 mL) cold milk, plus extra for brushing

½ cup (125 mL) chopped walnut pieces, lightly toasted

White Chocolate Black Pepper Scones, top left (page 225),
Currant Scones, top right (page 226), *Cranberry Spelt
Drop Scones*, bottom left (page 230), and *Apple Cheddar
Walnut Scones*, bottom right (page 228)

CRANBERRY SPELT DROP SCONES
• *Makes 12 scones* •

low-
FAT

*T*HESE SCONES ARE wholesome, healthy, *and* tasty, with a crunchy exterior yielding to a softer centre. The spelt flour has a natural nutty taste to it, making the scones taste a little like there are walnuts added. For a sweeter version, you can use dried cranberries in place of the fresh or frozen.

1. Preheat the oven to 375°F (190°C) and line a baking tray with parchment paper.
2. Stir the spelt flour, whole wheat flour, sugar, baking powder, salt, and cinnamon in a large bowl. In a separate bowl, whisk the egg, then add the buttermilk and vegetable oil. Add the liquid to the flour and stir until blended. Stir in the cranberries (if using frozen, they do not need to be thawed).
3. Drop the dough by large spoonfuls (or an ice cream scoop) onto the prepared baking tray, leaving 1 ½ inches (4 cm) between each. Bake the scones for 15 to 18 minutes, until the bottoms have begun to brown. The scones will keep in an airtight container for 2 days.

1 cup (250 mL) spelt flour
1 cup (250 mL) whole wheat flour
7 Tbsp (105 mL) packed demerara
   or dark brown sugar
1 Tbsp (15 mL) baking powder
½ tsp (2 mL) salt
½ tsp (2 mL) ground cinnamon
1 egg
1 cup (250 mL) buttermilk
2 Tbsp (30 mL) vegetable oil
1 cup (250 mL) fresh or frozen cranberries

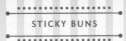

SPECIAL STICKY BUNS
• Makes 6 large sticky buns •

WHAT MAKES THESE sticky buns special is the filling—a cream cheese–brown sugar spread adds a decadently and unexpectedly creamy surprise—truly special.

1. For the dough, stir the milk, yeast, sugar, and egg to blend. Pour this into a stand mixer fitted with the hook attachment, or use a wooden spoon, and blend in the flour, salt, and nutmeg, mixing the dough until it is evenly combined. Add in the butter, mixing until blended (there is no need to knead the dough). Place the dough into a lightly greased bowl, cover with plastic wrap, and set on the counter to rise until it is about 1 1/2 times its original size, about 2 hours.

2. While the dough is rising, prepare the filling. Beat the cream cheese and butter together, then beat in the brown sugar, vanilla, and cinnamon. Set aside.

3. Grease an 8-inch (20 cm) square pan. Turn out the risen dough onto a lightly floured work surface. Roll the dough into a rectangle about 15 inches (38 cm) by 10 inches (25 cm). Spread the cream cheese filling evenly over the dough and roll it up from the long side. Slice into 6 buns and arrange them in the prepared pan. Cover the pan with a tea towel and let sit 30 minutes.

4. Preheat the oven to 350°F (175°C). Uncover the buns and bake them for about 30 minutes, until evenly golden brown. Let the sticky buns cool for 15 minutes.

5. For the glaze, whisk the icing sugar and milk together, and use a fork to drizzle the glaze overtop the sticky buns. The sticky buns are best served warm, but can be served at room temperature for up to a day.

DOUGH:

¾ cup (185 mL) milk,
   at room temperature
2 tsp (10 mL) instant yeast
2 Tbsp (30 mL) sugar
1 egg, at room temperature
2 cups (500 mL) all-purpose flour
½ tsp (2 mL) salt
¼ tsp (1 mL) ground nutmeg
¼ cup (60 mL) unsalted butter,
   at room temperature

FILLING:

½ pkg (4 oz/125 g) cream cheese,
   at room temperature
3 Tbsp (45 mL) unsalted butter,
   at room temperature
1 cup (250 mL) packed light brown sugar
1 tsp (5 mL) vanilla extract
½ tsp (2 mL) ground cinnamon

GLAZE:

½ cup (125 mL) icing sugar, sifted
1 Tbsp (15 mL) milk

WHOLE WHEAT CARROT STICKY BUNS
• Makes 12 sticky buns •

WHILE I WOULD never profess that these sticky buns are healthy, the whole wheat flour adds a nice nutty taste and using grated fresh carrots in the dough makes it moist so less butter is needed than a typical sticky bun. For a sticky bun that would remind you of carrot cake, try replacing the filling below with the cream cheese filling from page 231.

1. Stir the buttermilk, warm water, and yeast in a large bowl or in the bowl of a stand mixer fitted with the dough hook attachment and let sit for 5 minutes. Add the sugar, egg, carrot, whole wheat and all-purpose flours, and salt, and mix at low speed (or with beaters with the hook attachments) until blended. Add the butter, increase the speed, and mix until blended and stretchy-looking, about 4 minutes (the batter will be very soft and sticky). Scrape the dough into a lightly oiled bowl and let it rest in a warm spot until it has doubled in size, about 1½ hours.

2. Prepare the filling by stirring the butter and brown sugar together. Stir in the maple syrup and cinnamon. Grease a muffin tin and spoon a teaspoonful of the filling into the bottom of each cup, reserving the rest of the filling for inside the sticky buns.

3. On a generously floured work surface, turn out the dough. Flour the surface of the dough and roll it to a rectangle about 20 inches (50 cm) by 12 inches (30 cm) (because the dough is so soft, it will roll easily). Spread the reserved filling over the surface of the dough and sprinkle it with raisins and walnut pieces. Roll up the dough from the long side and slice into 12 buns. Place each bun into a muffin cup. Cover the pan with a tea towel and let the dough rise for another 45 minutes.

4. Preheat the oven to 350°F (175°C). Bake the sticky buns for about 30 minutes, until the tops have browned evenly and the dough appears fully cooked when you separate the layers to look. Let the buns sit for 5 minutes, then turn the muffin tin onto a baking tray to tip them out. The sticky buns are best served warm or at room temperature. The sticky buns will keep in an airtight container for a day.

DOUGH:

1 cup (250 mL) buttermilk,
   at room temperature
¼ cup (60 mL) warm water (105°F/41°C)
2¼ tsp (11 mL/1 pkg) instant yeast
5 Tbsp (75 mL) packed light brown sugar
1 egg, at room temperature
1½ cups (375 mL) loosely packed, coarsely
   grated carrot
1¾ cups (435 mL) whole wheat flour
1¾ cups (435 mL) all-purpose flour
½ tsp (2 mL) salt
2 Tbsp (30 mL) unsalted butter,
   at room temperature

FILLING:

⅓ cup (80 mL) unsalted butter,
   at room temperature
⅔ cup (160 mL) packed light
   brown sugar
⅓ cup (80 mL) pure maple syrup
1 Tbsp (15 mL) ground cinnamon
½ cup (125 mL) raisins
½ cup (125 mL) walnut pieces

note from anna's kitchen

If you plan on serving any of these sticky bun recipes for a breakfast or brunch, you do not need to get up at 5 a.m. to start baking. Prepare the recipe the evening before through step 3, but after putting the dough in the muffin cups, cover the tin with plastic wrap and refrigerate overnight. The next morning, pull the tin from the fridge 45 minutes before baking as instructed in step 4.

CHOCOLATE CRANBERRY STICKY BUNS
• *Makes 12 sticky buns* •

*T*HESE CAKE-LIKE STICKY buns are better suited for dessert than breakfast.

1. For the starter, stir all the ingredients together and set aside while preparing the base.
2. For the base, using electric beaters or in a stand mixer fitted with the paddle attachment, cream the butter and sugar until fluffy. Add the eggs, one at a time, blending well after each addition. Stir in the vanilla.
3. In a separate bowl, sift the flour, cocoa, cinnamon, and salt. Add the dry ingredients to the butter mixture alternately with the buttermilk, starting and ending with the dry ingredients and blending well and scraping the bowl after each addition. Stir in the starter and add the dried cranberries and chocolate chips (the dough will be wet and sticky). Place the dough in a large, lightly oiled bowl, cover with plastic wrap, and let rise, refrigerated, overnight.
4. Prepare the filling by creaming the butter until fluffy, then beat in the icing sugar and cocoa. Grease a muffin tin.
5. On a generously floured work surface, turn out the dough. Flour the surface of the dough and roll it to a rectangle about 20 inches (50 cm) by 12 inches (30 cm) (because the dough is so soft, it will roll easily). Spread the filling over the surface of the dough and sprinkle it with the remaining dried cranberries. Roll up the dough from the long side and slice into 12 buns. Place each bun into a muffin cup. Cover lightly and let rise for 1 hour.
6. Preheat the oven to 350°F (175°C).
7. Whisk the egg with the water, brush buns with the egg mixture, and bake for about 50 minutes until they are cooked through, when you peek between the layers of dough. Let the buns cool completely in the pan. These sticky buns will keep in an airtight container for up to 2 days.

STARTER:

¾ cup (185 mL) milk,
 at room temperature
2 Tbsp (30 mL) sugar
1 Tbsp (15 mL) dry instant yeast
¼ cup (60 mL) cocoa powder, sifted
¼ cup (60 mL) all-purpose flour

BASE:

¾ cup (185 mL) unsalted butter,
 at room temperature
½ cup (125 mL) sugar
3 eggs, at room temperature
2 tsp (10 mL) vanilla extract
4 cups (1 L) all-purpose flour
⅓ cup (80 mL) cocoa powder
1 tsp (5 mL) ground cinnamon
1 tsp (5 mL) salt
1½ cups (635 mL) buttermilk,
 at room temperature
½ cup (125 mL) dried cranberries
1 cup (250 mL) dark chocolate chips

FILLING:

½ cup (125 mL) unsalted butter,
 at room temperature
⅔ cup (160 mL) icing sugar, sifted
2 Tbsp (30 mL) cocoa powder, sifted
½ cup (125 mL) dried cranberries

FOR BRUSHING:

1 egg
2 Tbsp (30 mL) water

HOT CROSS STICKY BUNS
• *Makes 12 sticky buns* •

*H*OT CROSS BUNS are a springtime favourite, and when a classic hot cross bun dough is rolled and filled like a sticky bun, it doubles its satisfaction quotient.

1. For the dough, stir the milk, sugar, yeast, lemon zest, and vanilla in a stand mixer or by hand and let sit for 5 minutes. Add the flour, salt, nutmeg, cinnamon, currants, and citrus peel and blend. Using a hook attachment, knead until elastic, but the dough should still stick to the bottom of the bowl (or, if kneading by hand, stir until stiff, then turn out onto a lightly floured surface and knead until elastic but still sticky). Place in a large, lightly oiled bowl, cover with plastic and set in a warm, draft-free place for 1½ hours.

2. Prepare the filling by stirring the butter and brown sugar together. Stir in the maple syrup and cinnamon. Grease a 9- × 13-inch (23 × 33 cm) pan, and spread half of the filling on the bottom, reserving the rest of the filling for inside the sticky buns.

3. On a generously floured work surface, turn out the dough. Flour the surface and roll it to a rectangle about 20 inches (50 cm) by 12 inches (30 cm) (because the dough is so soft, it will roll easily). Spread the reserved filling over the surface of the dough. Roll up the dough from the long side and slice into 12 buns. Place the buns into the pan, leaving space to expand between them. Cover the pan with a tea towel, or wrap the pan in plastic wrap and chill overnight.

4. The next morning, preheat the oven to 350°F (175°C).

5. Bake the buns for 40 to 45 minutes, until they are a rich golden colour. While the buns are baking, prepare the hot glaze.

6. For the hot glaze, stir the sugar, lemon juice, and water in a small pot over medium heat until the sugar has dissolved. When the buns just come out of the oven, poke holes in them with a bamboo skewer and brush them repeatedly with the glaze, allowing the glaze to soak in. Let the buns cool in the pan.

DOUGH:

2¼ cups (560 mL) milk,
   at room temperature
½ cup (125 mL) sugar
1 Tbsp (15 mL) dry instant yeast
1½ tsp (7.5 mL) finely grated lemon zest
1 tsp (5 mL) vanilla extract
4½ cups (1.125 L) all-purpose flour
1 tsp (5 mL) salt
½ tsp (2.5 mL) ground nutmeg
¼ tsp (1 mL) ground cinnamon
1¼ cups (310 mL) dried currants
¾ cup (185 mL) diced Candied Citrus Peel
   (page 321)

FILLING:

⅓ cup (80 mL) unsalted butter,
   at room temperature
⅔ cup (160 mL) packed light brown sugar
⅓ cup (80 mL) pure maple syrup
1 Tbsp (15 mL) ground cinnamon

GLAZE:

½ cup (125 mL) sugar
2 Tbsp (30 mL) lemon juice
2 Tbsp (30 mL) water

Chocolate Cranberry Sticky Buns, top left (page 233), *Hot Cross Sticky Buns,* top right (page 234), *Whole Wheat Carrot Sticky Buns,* bottom left (page 232), and *Special Sticky Buns,* bottom right (page 231)

NOTES ON HOLIDAY DESSERTS

The holiday season is a perfect time to bake, and to bake with family and friends, not just for them. The desserts and treats in this chapter are intended to really impress and feed a larger group. Plus, they can be made ahead of time, so you can get into the other holiday activities that fill up your schedule.

GINGERBREAD DARK CHOCOLATE TRIFLE
• *Makes one 12-cup (3 L) trifle* | *Serves 12 to 16* •

*T*HE GINGERBREAD CAKE in this trifle makes it so tender and moist that it doesn't require brushing with syrup or spirits to soften it. The dark chocolate sauce sets up like a truffle filling among the silky custard and gingerbread layers—very festive indeed.

1. For the cinnamon custard, bring the milk and cinnamon up to a simmer over medium heat. In a bowl, whisk the egg yolks, cornstarch, brown sugar, and vanilla. Slowly pour the hot milk into the egg mixture, whisking constantly until all of the milk has been added. Over medium heat, whisk until the custard thickens and becomes glossy, about 5 minutes.

2. Remove from the heat and stir in the butter to melt. Strain into a bowl and cover the surface of the custard directly with plastic wrap. Chill completely.

3. For the chocolate sauce, heat the condensed milk and chocolate over low heat, stirring until melted. Whisk in the water and set aside.

4. When ready to assemble, whip the cream to soft peaks. Fold half of the whipped cream into the custard, and stir the sugar into the remaining half of the whipped cream and chill for topping.

5. To assemble, slice the gingerbread in half, then make ½-inch (1 cm) slices from each half. Arrange a layer of sliced gingerbread at the bottom of a 12-cup (3 L) trifle dish. Dollop a third of the chocolate sauce over the gingerbread and spread. Dollop a third of the cinnamon custard over the chocolate sauce and spread. Cover the custard with a layer of the gingerbread, and repeat the process 2 more times, ending with cinnamon custard. Chill until ready to serve.

6. To serve, spread the reserved whipped cream over the trifle and garnish with chocolate shavings and cinnamon.

CINNAMON CUSTARD:

3 cups (750 mL) 2% milk

1 tsp (5 mL) ground cinnamon

4 large egg yolks

½ cup (125 mL) cornstarch

½ cup (125 mL) packed light brown sugar

1 tsp (5 mL) vanilla extract

2 Tbsp (30 mL) unsalted butter

DARK CHOCOLATE SAUCE:

1 tin (300 mL) sweetened condensed milk

3 oz (90 g) unsweetened chocolate, chopped

½ cup (125 mL) water

ASSEMBLY:

1 cup (250 mL) whipping cream

1 tsp (5 mL) sugar

1 recipe Classic Gingerbread Cake (page 132), cooled

Chocolate Shavings (page 321), for garnish

Cinnamon, for garnish

PEAR, GRAND MARNIER, AND WHITE CHOCOLATE TRIFLE
• Makes one 8-cup (2 L) trifle | Serves 12 •

*I*F YOU DON'T have a trifle bowl (typically a flat-sided, footed bowl), you can use just about any glass bowl. What counts is that you can see the trifle and all its lovely layers.

1. Preheat the oven to 350°F (175°C), and line the bottom and sides of an 8-inch (20 cm) square pan with parchment paper.

2. Whip the eggs and sugar at high speed until they have doubled in volume and they hold a ribbon when the beaters are lifted, about 5 minutes. Beat in the vanilla extract (or paste, if using). Sift the flour over the eggs and quickly fold it in. Scrape the batter into the prepared pan and level.

3. Bake the cake for 18 to 20 minutes, until the top of the cake is an even golden brown and the cake springs back when gently pressed. Cool the cake to room temperature (the cake can be baked a day ahead and stored, wrapped in plastic wrap).

4. To prepare the white chocolate cream, heat the milk and scraped seeds from the vanilla bean (or paste, if using) over medium heat. Whisk the egg yolks, sugar, and cornstarch in a small bowl. Place the white chocolate and butter in a larger bowl, and ready a strainer overtop of the bowl. Once the milk comes to just below a simmer, when bubbles just begin to appear on the surface, slowly whisk half of it into the egg mixture, then pour the warmed egg mixture into the pot, whisking it over medium heat until it just begins to bubble, about 4 minutes. Pour the hot custard through the strainer over the white chocolate and butter, let it sit for a minute, then whisk until the chocolate and butter have melted. Stir in the Grand Marnier. Place a piece of plastic wrap directly onto the surface of the custard, cool to room temperature, and chill it completely.

TRIFLE SPONGE:
3 eggs, at room temperature
½ cup (125 mL) sugar
½ tsp (2 mL) vanilla extract or vanilla bean paste
¾ cup (185 mL) all-purpose flour

WHITE CHOCOLATE CREAM:
1½ cups (375 mL) milk
½ vanilla bean or 1½ tsp (7.5 mL) vanilla bean paste
4 egg yolks
¼ cup (60 mL) sugar
3 Tbsp (45 mL) cornstarch
3 oz (90 g) white chocolate, chopped
3 Tbsp (45 mL) unsalted butter
2 Tbsp (30 mL) Grand Marnier

POACHED PEARS:
2 Bartlett or Anjou pears
2 cups (500 mL) water
1 cup (250 mL) sugar
1 navel orange peel on, sliced
2 Tbsp (30 mL) Grand Marnier

ASSEMBLY:
⅓ cup (80 mL) red currant jelly
Chocolate Shavings (white) (page 321)

CONTINUED . . .

CONTINUED . . .

5. Peel the pears, cut them in half, and core out the centres using a melon baller or teaspoon. Place these in a saucepot with the water, sugar, and orange slices. Place a cover directly onto the pears (this can be a lid just a little smaller than the pot, or a disc of parchment paper)—this allows the poaching liquid to simmer over the entire surface of the pears, which have a habit of floating on top of the liquid. Simmer the pears until they yield easily when pierced with a knife—depending on the ripeness of the pears, this can take 8 to 20 minutes. Cool the pears in the liquid and spoon them into a bowl using a slotted spoon. Drizzle the Grand Marnier over the pears and chill them until ready to assemble.

6. To assemble, slice the sponge cake horizontally using a serrated (bread) knife. Stir the red currant jelly to soften it, and spread this over the surface of the middle of the cake. Place the top layer over the jam and trim away a scant ½ inch (1 cm) off of the edges of the cake. Slice the cake in half, then slice each half into 12 cake "fingers." Arrange these fingers around the inside of an 8-cup (2 L) glass trifle bowl so that the jam layer shows outward. Arrange any remaining slices in the bottom of the bowl. Drain the chilled pears, reserving the liquid, and brush the liquid onto the cake. Slice the pears thinly and arrange them in the bottom of the bowl. Stir the chilled custard to soften it and pour it overtop of the pears. Chill until ready to serve. Garnish with white chocolate curls before spooning the trifle into serving dishes.

ICEWINE FRUIT AND CREAM TRIFLE
• *Makes one 10-cup (2.5 L) trifle | Serves 10 to 12* •

*T*HIS TRIFLE IS the closest to a traditional fruit and cream trifle. If icewine is not available, you can replace it with sweet Marsala wine or sweet sherry.

1. For the icewine fruits, simmer all the fruits with the sugar and icewine, uncovered, until they are tender and the liquid has reduced by half, about 20 minutes. Cool, then chill until ready to assemble the trifle.
2. For the topping, whip the cream to soft peaks and stir in the sugar and icewine. Chill until ready to assemble.
3. For the cream filling, whip the cream to soft peaks and stir in the vanilla extract. Chill. Place a pot with 2 inches (5 cm) of water on medium heat and bring it to a simmer. In a metal or glass bowl, whisk together the egg yolks, sugar, and icewine. Place over the pot of simmering water and whisk constantly until the mixture has doubled and holds a ribbon when you lift the whisk. Remove from the heat.
4. Beat in the mascarpone cheese or cream cheese (using electric beaters is fine), and if the mixture is still warm, chill until at least room temperature. Fold in the vanilla cream filling. Set this aside until ready to assemble.
5. For the ladyfinger base, mix the water, sugar, and icewine until the sugar has dissolved.
6. To assemble, dip the ladyfingers in the liquid base just for a moment, to let them soak but not get soggy. Line the bottom of a 10-cup (2.5 L) trifle bowl, or a decorative casserole dish, completely with half of the soaked ladyfingers. Spread half of the cream filling over the ladyfingers and spoon half of the fruit overtop. Repeat with the second half of the ladyfingers, cream filling, and fruit. Spread the whipped cream topping over the trifle and chill until ready to serve.

ICEWINE FRUITS:

2 Bartlett pears, peeled and diced

2 peaches, peeled and diced

3 red or black plums, pitted and diced

3 apricots, pitted and diced

1 cup (250 mL) sugar

½ cup (125 mL) icewine

TOPPING:

1 cup (250 mL) whipping cream

2 tsp (10 mL) sugar

2 Tbsp (30 mL) icewine

CREAM FILLING:

1 cup (250 mL) whipping cream

1 Tbsp (15 mL) vanilla extract

5 large egg yolks

½ cup (125 mL) sugar

⅓ cup (80 mL) icewine

1 tub (1 lb/450 g) mascarpone cheese, or 2 pkg (8 oz/250 g each) cream cheese, at room temperature

LADYFINGER BASE:

1½ cups (375 mL) water

⅓ cup (80 mL) sugar

½ cup (125 mL) icewine

1 large package ladyfinger biscuits

APPLE CRISP AND BOURBON-CREAM TRIFLE
• Makes one 12-cup (3 L) trifle | Serves 12 to 16 •

*N*OT A TYPICAL trifle, this holiday dessert is made by layering chilled apple crisp with a bourbon-spiked pastry cream and toasted pecans.

1. Bring the cream and milk to a simmer in a saucepot. In a separate bowl, whisk the egg yolks, brown sugar, cornstarch, and vanilla. While whisking, slowly pour in the hot cream, then pour the entire mixture back into the pot. Whisk the custard over medium heat until it has thickened and just begins to bubble, about 3 minutes. Pour the cooked custard through a strainer into a bowl, and stir in the butter. Place a piece of plastic wrap directly over the surface of the pastry cream and chill completely. Once chilled, stir in 3 tablespoons (45 mL) of bourbon.

2. Whip the cream until it holds soft peaks. Fold 1 cup (250 mL) of the whipped cream into the pastry cream. Stir the sugar, vanilla, and 2 tablespoons (30 mL) of bourbon into the remaining whipped cream.

3. To assemble, spoon half of the chilled apple crisp into a 12-cup (3 L) trifle bowl and sprinkle with bourbon. Top the crisp with half of the pastry cream and sprinkle with half of the pecans. Top this with the remaining apple crisp, sprinkle with bourbon, and top with the remaining pastry cream and pecans. Spread the whipped cream overtop and dust lightly with cinnamon. Chill until ready to serve.

PASTRY CREAM:

½ cup (125 mL) half-and-half cream

½ cup (125 mL) milk

4 egg yolks

¼ cup (60 mL) packed light brown sugar

2½ Tbsp (37.5 mL) cornstarch

2 tsp (10 mL) vanilla extract

2 Tbsp (30 mL) unsalted butter

3 Tbsp (45 mL) bourbon

WHIPPED CREAM:

1½ cups (375 mL) whipping cream

2 Tbsp (30 mL) sugar

1 tsp (5 mL) vanilla extract

2 Tbsp (30 mL) bourbon, plus extra for sprinkling

ASSEMBLY:

1 recipe Classic Fruit Crisp, made with apples (page 124), chilled

1½ cups (375 mL) lightly toasted pecan halves

Ground cinnamon, for garnish

HAZELNUT LATTE YULE LOG
• *Makes one 10-inch (25 cm) Yule log | Serves 12* •

*H*AZELNUTS ADD A festive dimension to this Yule log. The chocolate mousse doubles as a filling and a frosting, and it has just enough coffee flavour to accent the hazelnut taste, but it is not overwhelming.

1. Preheat the oven to 350°F (175°C) and line a 15½- × 10½-inch (39 × 26 cm) jelly roll pan with parchment paper.

2. Pulse the hazelnuts, flour, and salt in a food processor until the nuts are finely ground.

3. Whisk the eggs and sugar in a large metal or glass bowl, and place the bowl over a pot of gently simmering water. Whisk until the mixture has warmed to about 105°F (41°C). Whip this mixture at high speed until it is pale yellow and the mixture leaves a ribbon when the beaters are lifted, about 7 minutes. Beat in the vanilla. While beating at medium speed, quickly sprinkle in the nut mixture, blending only until incorporated. Spoon about a cup of the batter into a dish with the hazelnut or vegetable oil, and stir to blend it in. Add this back to the larger batter and fold in by hand. Pour the batter into the prepared pan and spread evenly.

4. Bake the cake for about 15 minutes, until the cake springs back when gently pressed in the centre. Let the cake cool for just 5 minutes.

5. While the cake is still warm, dust the surface of it with icing sugar and run a knife around the outside edge of the cake to loosen it. Place a clean tea towel over the cake, then place a cutting board or second baking tray over the cake and invert the cake so that it tips out onto the board, and lift off the original pan. Carefully peel away the parchment paper, dust the cake surface with icing sugar, and place a second tea towel over the cake. From the shorter side, roll the cake up and let the cake cool completely in the tea towels. This step will set the jelly roll "memory" so that the cake will not crack or split when filled.

6. To prepare the latte mousse, heat the cream, skim milk powder, and instant coffee in a saucepot to just below a simmer, and pour it over the chocolate. Let it sit for one minute, then whisk until the chocolate is completely melted. Cool the mixture to room temperature, then chill it completely, about 2 hours.

7. Whip the chilled latte cream until it holds a soft peak, then stir in the hazelnut liqueur or brandy, then the vanilla.

8. To assemble the Yule log, gently unroll the cooled cake and remove the tea towels. Spread half of the latte mousse over the surface of the cake and roll it up. Carefully lift the cake onto the desired serving platter and spread the remaining half of the mousse over the top and ends. If the mousse starts to set as you spread it, stir in a little more fluid cream to loosen it up. Dust the Yule with a little cocoa powder and chill it until ready to serve. The Yule log will keep in the refrigerator for up to 2 days.

SPONGE CAKE:

½ cup (125 mL) toasted, peeled hazelnuts
½ cup (125 mL) cake and pastry flour
¼ tsp (1 mL) salt
6 eggs
⅔ cup (160 mL) sugar
1 tsp (5 mL) vanilla extract
3 Tbsp (45 mL) hazelnut oil
   or vegetable oil
Icing sugar for dusting

LATTE MOUSSE:

1½ cups (375 mL) whipping cream
1½ Tbsp (22.5 mL) instant skim milk
   powder
1 Tbsp (15 mL) instant coffee granules
5 oz (150 g) semi-sweet chocolate,
   chopped
2 Tbsp (30 mL) hazelnut liqueur or brandy
1 tsp (5 mL) vanilla extract
Cocoa powder, for dusting

note from anna's kitchen
For a tip on toasting nuts, see page 54.
   Yule logs are a roulade cake, essentially a jelly roll but with more interesting fillings. The key to making a nice Yule log that doesn't crack is to roll the sheet cake while it is still warm and pliable. Once cooled, it can be gently unrolled, filled, and re-rolled without cracking.

CHOCOLATE RASPBERRY YULE LOG
• Makes one 10-inch (25 cm) Yule log | Serves 12 •

*T*HE MARSHMALLOW-LIKE MAPLE Meringue Frosting that covers this Yule log is reminiscent of snow—perfect for the holiday season.

1. Preheat the oven to 350°F (175°C) and line a 15½- × 10½-inch (39 × 26 cm) jelly roll pan with parchment paper.

2. Heat the milk and butter until the butter has melted. Keep warm.

3. Whisk the eggs and sugar in a large metal or glass bowl, and place the bowl over a pot of gently simmering water, whisking until the mixture has warmed to about 105°F (41°C). Whip this mixture at high speed until it is pale yellow and the mixture leaves a ribbon when the beaters are lifted, about 5 minutes. Beat in the vanilla.

4. Sift the flour, cocoa, and salt into a bowl, then, while beating at medium speed, quickly sprinkle the flour mixture into the egg mixture, blending just until incorporated. Spoon about 1 cup (250 mL) of the batter into the warm milk mixture, and add this to the batter and fold in by hand. Pour the batter into the prepared pan and spread evenly (the batter will be quite fluid).

5. Bake the cake for about 15 minutes, until the cake springs back when gently pressed in the centre. Let the cake cool for just 5 minutes.

6. While the cake is still warm, dust the surface of it with icing sugar and run a knife around the outside edge of the cake to loosen it. Place a clean tea towel over the cake, then place a cutting board or second baking tray over the cake and invert the cake so that it tips out onto the board, and lift off the original pan. Carefully peel away the parchment paper, dust the cake surface with icing sugar, and place a second tea towel over the cake. From the shorter side, roll the cake up and let the cake cool completely in the tea towels. This step will set the jelly roll "memory" so that the cake will not crack or split when filled.

7. When the cake has cooled, prepare the Maple Meringue Frosting recipe and assemble the cake while the frosting is still warm. Unroll the cake and remove the tea towels. Stir the raspberry jam to soften it, then spread it over the surface of the cake. Spread half of the frosting over the jam and roll the cake up. Carefully lift the cake onto the desired serving platter and spread the remaining frosting over the entire surface of the cake. Top the cake with fresh berries and chocolate shavings, and chill until ready to serve. The cake will keep in the refrigerator for up to 3 days.

CAKE:

¼ cup (60 mL) milk

3 Tbsp (45 mL) unsalted butter

5 eggs

¾ cup (185 mL) sugar

1 tsp (5 mL) vanilla extract

¾ cup (185 mL) cake and pastry flour

⅓ cup (80 mL) cocoa powder

¼ tsp (1 mL) salt

Icing sugar, for dusting

FILLING:

1 recipe Maple Meringue Frosting (page 152)

¾ cup (185 mL) raspberry jam

1 cup (250 mL) fresh raspberries

Chocolate Shavings (dark), for garnish (page 321)

VERY FRUITY MINI WHISKEY FRUITCAKES
• Makes 12 mini fruitcakes •

dairy-
FREE

*T*HESE FRUITCAKES ARE for those who like the intensity of a boozy, fruit-laden fruitcake. Baked as little loaves, they package up nicely for gifting.

1. Stir the raisins, dates, apricots, figs, cranberries, almonds, and pecans with the cinnamon, ginger, cloves, and nutmeg, and stir in the whisky. Cover and let sit for at least 4 hours, up to a day.
2. Preheat the oven to 300°F (150°C) and grease twelve 2¼ × 4 × 1¼-inch (5.5 × 10 × 3 cm) mini loaf pans. Sift the flour, baking powder, and salt over the fruit, and stir until incorporated.
3. Cut the orange into quarters, remove seeds, and purée in a food processor (peel and all) with the brown sugar. Add the eggs and vanilla, and purée. Pour this over the fruit and stir until blended. Spoon and pack the batter into the prepared pans.
4. Bake the fruitcakes for about 40 minutes, until a tester inserted into the centre of the cake comes out clean. Brush the fruitcakes with a little whisky while in the tins, then cool completely. Remove the cakes from the tins and brush 2 more times with whisky before wrapping to store. The cakes should sit for 5 days before eating, and can store for up to 4 weeks.

2 cups (500 mL) raisins
1 cup (250 mL) chopped pitted dates
1 cup (250 mL) chopped dried apricots
1 cup (250 mL) chopped dried figs
1 cup (250 mL) chopped dried cranberries
1 cup (250 mL) sliced almonds
1 cup (250 mL) pecan halves
1 tsp (5 mL) ground cinnamon
1 tsp (5 mL) ground ginger
¼ tsp (1 mL) ground cloves
¼ tsp (1 mL) ground nutmeg
1 cup (250 mL) whisky, plus extra
   for brushing
1¼ cups (310 mL) all-purpose flour
½ tsp (2 mL) baking powder
½ tsp (2 mL) salt
1 whole orange
1 cup (250 mL) dark brown sugar
4 eggs, at room temperature
1 Tbsp (15 mL) vanilla extract

LIGHT FRUITCAKE RING
• Makes one 8-cup (2 L) Bundt cake | Serves 20 to 24 •

*T*HIS FRUITCAKE IS light in colour and mild tasting, and it is more like a coffee cake or loaf cake than a traditional fruitcake. Rather than candied fruit that has been dyed red and green, this cake contains naturally dried fruits that add a rich depth of flavour, and the little bit of chocolate really works with the rum.

1. Stir the pecans, prunes, figs, dates, apricots, citrus peel, and chocolate with the rum. Cover and let sit for an hour.
2. Preheat the oven to 325°F (160°C) and grease an 8-cup (2 L) Bundt pan.
3. Sift the flour, baking powder, cloves, and salt, and stir this into the fruit. Whisk the sugar, honey, milk, egg yolks, and vanilla, then stir this into the fruit mixture. Whip the egg whites until they hold a medium peak when the beaters are lifted, and fold this into the cake batter in 2 additions (the whites will deflate somewhat, but that is normal).
4. Bake the cake for about an hour, until a tester inserted in the centre of the cake comes out clean. Cool the cake for 20 minutes in the pan, then turn it out to let it cool completely.
5. While still warm, brush the surface of the cake with rum. Once cooled, brush the cake again with rum. Wrap and store the cake for 5 days before slicing. If the fruitcake is well wrapped, it will keep for up to 2 weeks, or can be frozen for up to 3 months.

¾ cup (185 mL) pecan pieces
½ cup (125 mL) chopped pitted prunes
½ cup (125 mL) chopped dried figs
½ cup (125 mL) chopped pitted dates
½ cup (125 mL) chopped dried apricots
⅓ cup (80 mL) diced Candied Citrus Peel (page 321)
3 oz (90 g) bittersweet chocolate, chopped
⅓ cup (80 mL) amber rum, plus extra for brushing cake
2¼ cups (560 mL) all-purpose flour
2½ Tbsp (37.5 mL) baking powder
¼ tsp (1 mL) ground cloves
¼ tsp (1 mL) salt
¾ cup (185 mL) sugar
2 Tbsp (30 mL) honey
1 cup (250 mL) milk
2 eggs, separated
1 tsp (5 mL) vanilla extract

QUAINT GINGERBREAD HOUSE
• *Makes 1 gingerbread house about 9 × 5 inches (23 × 12 cm)* •
and 7½ inches (19 cm) tall

*A*GINGERBREAD HOUSE TAKES a little time and planning, but it doesn't have to be overly difficult and it should be a task that you share with others. This is a modestly proportioned abode, so it won't completely take over the dining room table.

1. Preheat the oven to 325°F (160°C) and line 3 baking trays with parchment paper.
2. On a lightly floured surface, roll out the first disc of gingerbread cookie dough into a rectangle about 20 inches (50 cm) by 10 inches (25 cm) and ¼ inch (6 mm) thick. Place the top of your loaf pan onto the dough and cut around the edge of the loaf pan to cut out two 9- × 5-inch (23 × 12 cm) rectangles—these are your 2 roof pieces. Place these onto a baking tray and bake for about 20 minutes, until they begin to brown around the edges. The gingerbread pieces should become firm after they cool, but if they still feel soft, you can return them to the oven to bake another 5 to 7 minutes.
3. Repeat step 2, but this time use the bottom part of the loaf pan to trace two 8- × 4-inch (20 × 10 cm) rectangles from the dough—these are the long sides to your house. Place these on the next baking tray and bake for just under 20 minutes, until they begin to brown around the edges.
4. Make a template for the 2 end pieces of the house (see note on page 254). Repeat step 2, but now cut out 2 end pieces to the house using the template you drew. Place these on the third baking tray and, if you wish, cut out 8 small rectangles from the remaining dough to be window shutters. Bake the small rectangles for about 12 minutes and the end pieces for about 18 minutes, until they just begin to brown around the edges. Let all the house pieces cool completely before assembling.
5. For the royal icing, whip the egg whites with electric beaters or in a mixer fitted with the paddle attachment just to loosen them. Add the icing sugar, corn syrup, and lemon juice, and beat first on low speed to blend, then on high until the royal icing is white and fluffy, about 5 minutes. Keep the icing well covered while assembling the gingerbread house (it can be stored in a resealable bag at room temperature—do not refrigerate).

STRUCTURE:

2 recipes Maple Gingerbread Cutout cookie dough (page 48), shaped into 3 discs, wrapped, and chilled

ROYAL ICING:

2 egg whites
2 cups (500 mL) icing sugar, sifted
1 Tbsp (15 mL) white corn syrup
1 tsp (5 mL) lemon juice

ASSEMBLY:

9- × 5-inch (2 L) loaf pan, ideally with angled sides
Ruler
Piping bag
Small plain tip
Icing sugar, for dusting

CONTINUED . . .

CONTINUED . . .

6. First, paint the décor on each piece of the gingerbread house—this is easiest to do before the house gets assembled. Fill a piping bag fitted with a plain tip with royal icing. Pipe a roof design on the 2 largest pieces, and pipe window frames and any other designs on the long side pieces, adhering the shutters on an angle using the royal icing. Pipe doors and other desired details on the end pieces. Let the icing dry for at least 2 hours.

7. Next, assemble the sides of the house. Pipe royal icing on each edge and stick the side pieces together. You may wish to carefully prop a book against each side to hold it in place as it dries for 2 hours.

8. Lastly, place the roof on the house. Pipe royal icing around the top edges of the assembled sides of the house and place each roof piece on top. Pipe a line of royal icing to join the 2 roof pieces together and let this dry for 2 hours. Stacking a couple of books under the roof edges will hold them in place as they dry.

9. Once dried, the gingerbread house can be moved to a presentation board and dusted with icing sugar, or you can add additional candy items to it, if you wish. The gingerbread house will keep, uncovered, for up to a week and still be edible, and it will keep for up to a month if it's used only for décor.

note from anna's kitchen

Creating a gingerbread house design that does not require an elaborate set of templates to draw and trace took a little thinking. In searching around the kitchen, I found that a basic straight-sided loaf pan offered the perfect template base, since a 9- × 5-inch (2 L) loaf pan has a wider top than its bottom and can be used as a template for the roof and sides of the house. Only the ends of the house need a paper template. To create these end pieces, trace the end of your loaf pan onto a piece of paper—it will be 5 inches (12 cm) on top, 4 inches (10 cm) on the bottom, and will slope along the sides. Find the centre of the top side, measure a point 3½ inches (9 cm) straight up from the centre, and draw lines from this point to the two ends of the top line to form a triangle. Now you have a template to cut out and trace, and the end pieces will fit with the side and roof pieces.

Replacing Dairy

Compared to replacing eggs or wheat flour in a recipe, replacing milk, butter, and other dairy products is likely the easiest of the replacement challenges. But there are some products that work better than others, or may have other virtues that make them a viable choice for you.

The recipes that use vegetable oil in this chapter have been specially designed and tested to use it instead of a solid fat. Typically, vegetable oil cannot replace butter in a conventional recipe with similar results. The type of vegetable oil you wish to use is up to you, but any neutral-tasting oil is fine.

Replacing Cow's Milk

Instead of cow's milk, use one of the following:

ALMOND MILK This has a nice body to it and a modest fat content, making it the preferred dairy-free, measure-for-measure milk replacement in a recipe. If you are baking for someone with nut allergies, then this cannot be used.

SOY MILK Not quite as rich as almond milk, it does bake acceptably well into muffins, cakes, and other treats.

RICE MILK This is the least-favoured baking alternative to milk, as it tends to be very thin in consistency and lacks the fat that gives baked goods structure and tenderness.

Replacing Butter

Instead of butter, use one of the following:

VEGETABLE MARGARINE The selection in the world of margarines is much improved, including many unhydrogenated options. Using unhydrogenated margarine in place of butter takes a delicate hand, since it will work itself into dough much faster than butter. Select a product with a natural taste, and, like butter, bake using unsalted margarine.

VIRGIN COCONUT OIL This is becoming more popular and also more available, though is quite costly. Different than the hydrogenated coconut oil you get with your movie theatre popcorn, virgin coconut oil is naturally solid (not hydrogenated), making it behave similarly to butter in baking. Like butter, it is also high in saturated fat, but this is the lesser of two evils when compared to hydrogenated fat (a trans fat). Virgin coconut oil does have a coconut taste to it, so it can impact that final taste of your baked items.

VEGETABLE SHORTENING Cheap and accessible, this option is also laden with trans fat. The addition of extra hydrogen atoms to fat molecules changes a liquid fat to a solid fat, but also changes the way our body processes it, increasing our bad cholesterol (LDL) and lowering our good cholesterol (HDL).

WHETHER YOU ARE lactose intolerant or baking for someone who is, you'll find these treats easily accessible, with similar methods to traditional baking and proportions of ingredients that seamlessly take the place of dairy products.

Recipes in other chapters of the book that are dairy-free:

MAPLE RAISIN SCONES
• Makes 8 large scones •

*dairy-*FREE   *egg-*FREE   *low-*FAT

*T*HESE SCONES ARE easy to make, and you can change up the raisins with pecans or walnuts.

1. Preheat the oven to 375°F (190°C) and line a baking tray with parchment paper.
2. Stir the flour, baking powder, cinnamon, ginger, and salt together.
3. In a separate bowl, whisk the ¾ cup (185 mL) of almond or soy milk, ½ cup (125 mL) of the maple syrup, and the vegetable oil.
4. Make a well in the centre of the flour and pour in the liquid. Stir the mixture until it becomes too hard to do, then turn the dough out onto a work surface, work in the raisins, and knead the dough just until it comes together.
5. Shape the dough into a disc about 8 inches (20 cm) across and cut into 8 wedges. Place the scones onto the baking tray, leaving 2 inches (5 cm) between them. Stir the remaining 1 tablespoon (15 cm) of almond or soy milk and 1 tablespoon (15 cm) of maple syrup together, and brush the tops of the scones.
6. Bake for 20 to 25 minutes, until the tops and bottoms of the scones are golden brown. Serve warm or at room temperature.
7. The scones are best enjoyed the day they are baked, but the dough or the baked scones can be frozen (do not refrigerate).

3 cups (750 mL) all-purpose flour

2 tsp (10 mL) baking powder

1 tsp (5 mL) ground cinnamon

1 tsp (5 mL) ground ginger

¼ tsp (1 mL) salt

¾ cup (185 mL) + 1 Tbsp (15 mL) almond or soy milk

½ cup (125 mL) + 1 Tbsp (15 mL) pure maple syrup

3 Tbsp (45 mL) vegetable oil

½ cup (125 mL) raisins

note from anna's kitchen
I like the visual impact that Thompson raisins can make, but I do like baking with golden raisins, which are not as sweet.

dairy-
FREE

egg-
FREE

*T*HESE TERRIFICALLY TART squares are a snap to make, and they're immensely satisfying. Silken or soft tofu replaces the need for egg, and when I taste-tested these with my mother, she preferred them to the original dairy-laden squares I've been making for years!

1. Preheat the oven to 350°F (175°C). Grease an 8-inch (20 cm) square pan and line it with parchment paper so that the paper comes up the sides of the pan.

2. Stir 1 cup (250 mL) of the flour, the sugar, and the lemon zest to blend. Cut in the margarine (or coconut oil or shortening) until the mixture is a rough, crumbly texture, then stir in the remaining $1/3$ cup (80 mL) of flour and press this into the prepared pan. Bake the base for about 20 minutes, until the edges begin to brown. While cooling, prepare the filling.

3. For the filling, in a food processor, purée the tofu, margarine (or coconut oil or shortening), and sugar until smooth. Add the almond or soy milk, lemon zest, lemon juice, cornstarch, and baking powder, and pulse until smooth. Pour the batter over the crust (it is all right if the crust is still warm) and bake for 20 to 25 minutes, until the squares show signs of bubbles at the edges and are set but with a little jiggle. Cool the pan to room temperature, then chill completely before slicing into squares. The squares can be stored refrigerated for up to 3 days.

BASE:

1⅓ cups (330 mL) all-purpose flour
¼ cup (60 mL) icing sugar
1 tsp (5 mL) finely grated lemon zest
½ cup (125 mL) dairy-free margarine or virgin coconut oil

FILLING:

8 oz (250 g) silken or soft tofu
3 Tbsp (45 mL) dairy-free margarine, virgin coconut oil, or vegetable shortening
½ cup (125 mL) sugar
¼ cup (60 mL) almond or soy milk
2 tsp (10 mL) finely grated lemon zest
½ cup (125 mL) fresh lemon juice
2 Tbsp (30 mL) cornstarch
1 tsp (5 mL) baking powder

THIS PIE REPLICATES a key lime pie with its tart but creamy filling. The crust tastes exactly like a graham cracker crust because it uses the key ingredients in graham crackers: whole wheat flour, honey, and a touch of cinnamon, but of course without the dairy or eggs.

CRUST:

1½ cups (375 mL) whole wheat flour
¼ cup (60 mL) vegetable oil
3 Tbsp (45 mL) packed dark brown sugar
3 Tbsp (45 mL) honey
Pinch ground cinnamon
Pinch salt

FILLING:

12 oz (360 g) silken or soft tofu
1 cup (250 mL) sugar
1 Tbsp (15 mL) finely grated key lime or lime zest
½ cup (125 mL) key lime or lime juice
2 tsp (10 mL) vanilla extract

GARNISH:

1 cup (250 mL) fresh raspberries

1. Preheat the oven to 350°F (175°C) and lightly grease a 9-inch (23 cm) pie plate.
2. Stir the flour, oil, sugar, honey, cinnamon, and salt together until it is a rough, crumbly texture. Press into the prepared pan (it will be very crumbly) and bake for 15 minutes, then cool while preparing the filling.
3. For the filling, purée the tofu with the sugar, lime zest, lime juice, and vanilla until smooth, and pour into the cooling crust (it's all right if the crust is still a little warm). Bake for about 25 minutes, until there are a few bubbles visible just around the edge of the pie and the filling still has a little jiggle to it. Cool the pie to room temperature, then chill until set, at least 3 hours.
4. To serve, garnish the edge of the pie with fresh raspberries. The pie will keep in the fridge for up to 2 days.

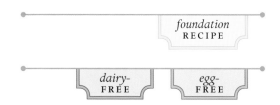
USING VEGETABLE OIL in place of butter in pie dough is not a new technique, but it does take a delicate hand so that the dough does not get overworked. The baking powder adds a little lift to the dough, and although the pastry won't have quite the flakiness of a butter pastry, it will have the melt-in-your-mouth appeal and the structure to hold any filling.

2⅓ cups (580 mL) all-purpose flour
1 Tbsp (15 mL) sugar
1 tsp (5 mL) salt
¼ tsp (1 mL) baking powder
½ cup (125 mL) vegetable oil
½ cup (125 mL) cold almond or soy milk

1. Stir the flour, sugar, salt, and baking powder together by hand.
2. Pour in the oil and almond or soy milk at once, and mix quickly, just until the dough comes together—do not over mix (the dough should have streaks of oil through it). Wrap and set aside for 40 minutes before rolling. The dough should be made on the same day you use it. It does not refrigerate or store well if made in advance.

note from anna's kitchen

If you would prefer to use virgin coconut oil as your fat in a dairy-free pie crust recipe, you can follow the Double-Crust Pie Dough recipe on page 82 and add 2 tablespoons (30 mL) of water to the dough (but do not omit the egg).

BUTTERLESS BUTTER TARTS
• Makes 12 butter(less) tarts •

dairy-
FREE

egg-
FREE

ᴇ VEN WITHOUT THE butter and eggs, the filling in these tarts comes out gooey and soft, with that good little syrupy drip hiding at the bottom. The tops of the tarts will bake up with a smoother surface than a traditional tart, but otherwise they are virtually the same.

1. Preheat the oven to 375°F (190°C) and lightly grease a muffin tin.
2. Shape the pie dough into 2 logs. Cut each log into 6 pieces. Roll out each piece of dough on a floured work surface to just over 4 inches (10 cm) across, and cut out 4-inch (10 cm) circles with a cookie cutter. Line each muffin cup with the pastry.
3. In a food processor, purée the brown sugar, corn or maple syrup, oil, tofu, vinegar, and vanilla until smooth. Sprinkle a few raisins or walnut pieces into each muffin cup, and pour an equal amount of the filling into each (about three-quarters full).
4. Bake the tarts for about 20 minutes, until the crust has turned a golden brown and the filling bubbles around the outside. Cool the tarts completely before removing.
5. The tarts can be stored in an airtight container for up to 3 days.

1 recipe Dairy-Free, Egg-Free Double-Crust Pie Dough (page 263)
¾ cup (185 mL) packed dark brown sugar
¾ cup (185 mL) corn syrup or pure maple syrup
⅓ cup (80 mL) vegetable oil
5 oz (150 g) silken or soft tofu
1 Tbsp (15 mL) white vinegar
1 tsp (5 mL) vanilla extract
⅓ cup (80 mL) golden raisins or walnuts

note from anna's kitchen:
You can use 2 whole eggs in place of the tofu for a version that is only dairy-free, but extend the baking time by 5 minutes.

dairy-
FREE

THIS VARIATION ON a butterscotch cream pie is satisfyingly creamy, though there is not a drop of cream in sight. Using almond milk is definitely preferred, since its subtle almond taste complements the creamy caramel filling.

1. On a lightly floured surface, roll out the dough to ⅛ inch (3 mm) thick. Line a 9-inch (23 cm) pie shell with dough, and trim and cinch the edges. Chill for 20 minutes.

2. Preheat the oven to 375°F (190°C). Line the pie shell with aluminum foil and weight with pie weights, rice, or dried beans. Bake for 18 to 20 minutes, then remove the foil and weights and bake for 10 to 12 more minutes, until the centre of the pie shell is dry and the edges are lightly browned. While the pie is hot from the oven, whisk the egg white to loosen it and brush this over the surface of the pie shell (this creates a barrier to prevent the crust from going soggy). Allow to cool.

3. Bring the sugar, cream of tartar, and water up to a boil in a medium saucepot over high heat. Without stirring, boil the sugar, uncovered, and occasionally brush the sides of the pot with water until the sugar turns a light amber colour, about 6 minutes. Remove the pot from the heat and whisk in 1 cup (250 mL) of the almond milk, watching out for the steam that rises. Return the pot to low heat, whisk in the remaining almond milk a little at a time until it has all been incorporated. If any caramelized sugar remains on the whisk, keep stirring until melted.

4. Increase the heat of the caramel milk to medium. In a bowl, whisk the egg yolks, maple syrup, cornstarch, and vanilla. Once simmering, slowly pour the caramel milk into the egg mixture while whisking. Pour the entire mixture back into the pot and whisk over medium heat until thickened and bubbling, about 4 minutes. Remove from the heat and strain into a bowl. Cover the custard with a piece of plastic wrap directly on the surface of the custard and cool for 30 minutes. After this time, spoon the custard into the cooled pie shell and place the plastic wrap directly on the surface of the custard again and chill just until set, about 2 hours.

5. Prepare and finish the meringue recipe as instructed for the Lemon Meringue Pie, including pulling out the filled pie from the fridge in advance of making the meringue so that the meringue won't weep or slide. The pie can be stored in the refrigerator for up to 2 days.

½ recipe Dairy-Free, Egg-Free Double-Crust Pie Dough (page 263)
1 egg white

FILLING:
1 cup (250 mL) sugar
½ tsp (2 mL) cream of tartar
3 Tbsp (45 mL) water
2½ cups (625 mL) almond milk
6 egg yolks
⅓ cup (80 mL) pure maple syrup
6 Tbsp (90 mL) cornstarch
1 Tbsp (15 mL) vanilla extract
1 recipe Italian Meringue (page 92)

DAIRY-FREE CHOCOLATE LAYER CAKE
• *Makes one 8-inch (20 cm) cake | Serves 8 to 10* •

dairy-
FREE

egg-
FREE

*N*ow you can have your cake and eat it, too! Cold almond milk stirred with vinegar is the key to this rich-tasting and moist cake made without dairy *or* eggs. I like to use balsamic vinegar, as it complements the chocolate taste, has a subtle sweetness, and enriches that deep chocolate colour.

1. Preheat the oven to 350°F (175°C). Grease two 8-inch (20 cm) cake pans. Line the bottom of each pan with parchment paper, then dust the sides with flour, tapping out any excess.

2. Sift the flour, sugar, cocoa, baking powder, baking soda, and salt into a large bowl. In a separate bowl, whisk the almond or soy milk, oil, vinegar, and vanilla. Make a well in the flour and pour in the liquids, mixing well by hand or with electric beaters. Beat the batter for a minute until it is smooth, then divide it between the 2 cake pans, spreading evenly. Bake the cakes for 25 to 30 minutes, until a tester inserted in the centre of the cake comes out clean. Cool the cakes in the pan for 30 minutes, then turn them out onto a rack to cool completely.

3. For the frosting, beat the margarine with the brown sugar and vanilla until smooth. Beat in the cocoa and then half of the icing sugar. Add 3 tablespoons (45 mL) of the almond or soy milk, then beat in the remaining icing sugar, adding the remaining 1 tablespoon (15 mL) of almond or soy milk at the end to make the icing a spreadable consistency.

4. Place one cake layer onto a plate and spread an even layer of frosting overtop. Place the second cake layer on the first and cover the top and sides with frosting, spreading to smooth. There should be about ¾ cup (185 mL) of frosting left for piping patterns or designs if desired. The cake can be left at room temperature until ready to serve, with any leftovers wrapped and stored on the counter. The cake will keep at room temperature for 2 days.

CAKE:

1½ cups (375 mL) all-purpose flour

1 cup (250 mL) sugar

¼ cup (60 mL) Dutch process (alkalized) cocoa powder

1 tsp (5 mL) baking powder

½ tsp (2 mL) baking soda

¼ tsp (1 mL) salt

1 cup (250 mL) chilled almond or soy milk

6 Tbsp (90 mL) vegetable oil

1 Tbsp (15 mL) balsamic vinegar

1 tsp (5 mL) vanilla extract

FROSTING:

½ cup (125 mL) dairy-free margarine

3 Tbsp (45 mL) packed dark brown sugar

1 tsp (5 mL) vanilla extract

½ cup (125 mL) Dutch process (alkalized) cocoa powder, sifted

2½ cups (625 mL) icing sugar, sifted

3 to 4 Tbsp (45 to 60 mL) almond or soy milk

FESTIVE FRUITCAKE
• *Makes one 9- × 5-inch (2 L) fruitcake* | *Serves 12 to 16* •

dairy- FREE   *egg-* FREE

A FRUITCAKE SHOULD BE about just that: the fruit! Soaking the fruit in orange juice keeps the fruitcake moist and sweet, and eliminates the need for spirits.

1. Preheat the oven to 350°F (175°C) and grease a 9- × 5-inch (2 L) loaf pan.
2. Bring the water and orange juice up to a boil, pour over the raisins, citrus peel, and dried cherries, and stir. Cool the mixture to room temperature, stirring occasionally.
3. Stir the sugar and oil into the fruit, then sift the flour, baking powder, cinnamon, nutmeg, cloves, and salt overtop and stir in. Scrape the batter into the prepared pan and spread to level. Bake the fruitcake for 45 to 50 minutes, until a tester inserted in the centre of the cake comes out clean. Cool the cake for 20 minutes in the pan, then turn it out onto a rack to cool completely. The fruitcake will keep, well wrapped, for up to 2 weeks, or it can be frozen for up to 3 months.

1½ cups (375 mL) water
1 cup (250 mL) orange juice
2 cups (500 mL) Thompson raisins
1½ cups (375 mL) Candied Citrus Peel (page 321)
½ cup (125 mL) dried cherries
1 cup (250 mL) sugar
2 Tbsp (30 mL) vegetable oil
2½ cups (625 mL) all-purpose flour
1½ tsp (7.5 mL) baking powder
½ tsp (2 mL) ground cinnamon
½ tsp (2 mL) ground nutmeg
½ tsp (2 mL) ground cloves
½ tsp (2 mL) salt

FLUFFY FROSTED CARROT CAKE
• *Makes one 9-inch (23 cm) cake* | *Serves 12* •

dairy-
FREE

*T*HIS RECIPE IS like a traditional carrot cake, which typically is made using vegetable oil, so few adjustments had to be made to make it dairy-free. The Maple Meringue Frosting (page 152) replaces the need for a cream cheese frosting, and it keeps the cake fresh for days.

1. Preheat the oven to 325°F (160°C). Grease a 9-inch (23 cm) cake pan.

2. Sift the flour, baking powder, baking soda, cinnamon, and salt into a large bowl. Stir in the grated carrots. In a separate bowl, whisk the brown sugar, oil, and eggs, and add this to the carrot mixture, stirring until well blended. Stir in the raisins or walnuts (if using) and scrape the batter into the prepared cake pan. Bake the cake for 40 to 50 minutes, until a tester inserted in the centre of the cake comes out clean. Cool the cake for 20 minutes in the pan, then turn it out to cool completely.

3. Prepare the Maple Meringue Frosting recipe, and use the frosting while it is still warm. Cut the cake in half horizontally and place one cake layer on a platter. Spread a cupful of frosting over the cake and top with the second cake layer. Spread the remaining frosting on the top and sides of the cake. Garnish the edge of the cake with walnut halves, if you wish. Let the cake set for an hour and store unwrapped until sliced. The cake will keep for up to 4 days.

2 cups (500 mL) all-purpose flour

2 tsp (10 mL) baking powder

1 tsp (5 mL) baking soda

1 tsp (5 mL) ground cinnamon

½ tsp (2 mL) salt

3 cups (750 mL) coarsely grated, loosely packed carrots

⅔ cup (160 mL) packed light brown sugar

⅔ cup (160 mL) vegetable oil

4 eggs

½ cup (125 mL) raisins or walnut pieces (optional)

1 recipe Maple Meringue Frosting (page 152)

Walnut halves, for garnish (optional)

NOTES ON EGG-FREE BAKING

Replacing Eggs

To REPLACE EGGS in a baking recipe, you first need to look at the nature of the recipe to determine the best solution.

A large egg is 2 ounces (¼ cup/60 mL by volume), so you must compensate for this amount of liquid in a recipe. Some options for replacing eggs include:

BAKING POWDER PLUS MOISTURE In many loaves and muffins, an additional ½ teaspoon (2 mL) of baking powder plus ¼ cup (60 mL) of milk, yogurt, or applesauce can replace a single egg. Often 1 to 2 teaspoons (5 to 10 mL) of vinegar is needed to truly coax the leavening to life and to thicken ingredients so that they rise and bind at the appropriate time as your cake bakes in the oven.

GROUND FLAXSEED PLUS MOISTURE In loaves, but especially in cookies, 1 tablespoon (15 mL) of ground flaxseed plus 3 to 4 tablespoons (45 to 60 mL) of applesauce can replace the moisture usually provided by eggs. The flaxseed gives some structure, fat, and added fibre.

SILKEN OR SOFT TOFU These types of tofu can replace eggs in mixtures that are blended in a food processor, such as a cheesecake or even a cake batter. It is best to weigh the tofu, as measuring by volume can be difficult.

EGGS OFFER STRUCTURE and richness to desserts, so finding suitable alternatives can be an adventure.

Recipes in other chapters of this book that are egg-free:

Plus Sauces and Garnishes (pages 318 to 321)

BANANA WALNUT BREAD
• *Makes one 9- × 5-inch (2 L) loaf* •
Cuts into 12 to 16 slices

dairy- **FREE**   *egg-* **FREE**

THIS BANANA BREAD recipe is moist and lovely—no missing the eggs or dairy here!

1½ cups (375 mL) mashed ripe bananas (about 3 medium-sized bananas)
⅓ cup (80 mL) packed light brown sugar
⅓ cup (80 mL) vegetable oil
⅓ cup (80 mL) almond or soy milk
1⅔ cups (410 mL) all-purpose flour
2 tsp (10 mL) baking powder
½ tsp (2 mL) baking soda
¼ tsp (1 mL) salt
1 cup (250 mL) walnut pieces

1. Preheat the oven to 350°F (175°C) and grease a 9- × 5-inch (2 L) loaf pan.
2. Whisk the mashed bananas, brown sugar, oil, and almond or soy milk together.
3. In a separate bowl, sift the flour, baking powder, baking soda, and salt.
4. Add the dry mixture to the banana mixture and stir until evenly blended. Stir in the walnut pieces, scrape the batter into the prepared pan, and spread to level.
5. Bake the banana bread for 45 to 50 minutes, until a tester inserted in the centre of the loaf comes out clean. Cool the loaf for 20 minutes in the pan, then turn out to cool completely.
6. The banana bread will keep for up to 3 days at room temperature, or you can freeze it for up to 3 months. Do not refrigerate.

APPLESAUCE RAISIN MUFFINS
• *Makes 12 muffins* •

dairy- **FREE**   *egg-* **FREE**

THESE MUFFINS ARE tender and moist, and they keep well for days.

1½ cups (375 mL) unsweetened applesauce
¾ cup (185 mL) packed light brown sugar
6 Tbsp (90 mL) vegetable oil
1½ cups (375 mL) all-purpose flour
2 tsp (10 mL) baking powder
¾ tsp (4 mL) ground cinnamon
¼ tsp (1 mL) ground allspice
¼ tsp (1 mL) salt
1 cup (250 mL) regular rolled oats
¾ cup (185 mL) Thompson raisins

1. Preheat the oven to 350°F (175°C) and line a muffin tin with large paper liners.
2. Whisk the applesauce, brown sugar, and oil together.
3. In a separate bowl, sift the flour, baking powder, cinnamon, allspice, and salt. Add this to the applesauce and stir to blend. Stir in the oats and raisins, and spoon the batter into the muffin cups.
4. Bake the muffins for about 30 minutes, until a tester inserted in the centre of a muffin comes out clean. Let the muffins cool for 20 minutes in the pan, then remove to cool completely. The muffins will keep in an airtight container for up to 4 days.

note from anna's kitchen

You may be tempted to use whole wheat flour in place of all-purpose in this recipe, to make the muffins even more wholesome, and although you can replace up to 50 percent of the all-purpose flour in a traditional recipe with whole wheat flour, it will prove unsatisfactory here. The fibre of the whole grain (the bran and germ) in whole wheat flour can shorten the gluten (protein) strands that hold air from baking powder, which makes the muffins dense, and in this case they'd be even more dense since there are no eggs in the recipe.

EGG-FREE CHOCOLATE CHIP COOKIES
• *Makes about 2 dozen small cookies* •

THESE COOKIES ARE based on the Chocolate Chip Cookies on page 18 but are adapted for dietary needs—and they're still just as yummy and soft inside.

½ cup (125 mL) butter
½ cup (125 mL) packed light brown sugar
¼ cup (60 mL) unsweetened applesauce
1 tsp (5 mL) vanilla extract
1¼ cups (310 mL) all-purpose flour
2 Tbsp (30 mL) cornstarch
1 Tbsp (15 mL) ground flaxseed
½ tsp (2 mL) baking soda
½ tsp (2 mL) salt
1 cup (250 mL) chocolate chips or chunks

1. Preheat the oven to 350°F (175°C) and line a baking tray with parchment paper.
2. Cream the butter and brown sugar together until smooth, then stir in the applesauce and vanilla.
3. In a separate bowl, stir the flour, cornstarch, flaxseed, baking soda, and salt together. Add this to the butter mixture and stir until blended, then stir in the chocolate chunks. Scoop teaspoonfuls of dough onto the baking tray, leaving 1½-inches (4 cm) between each cookie, and press the cookies down a little.
4. Bake the cookies for 11 to 13 minutes, until they just begin to brown. Cool the cookies on the tray and store in an airtight container for up to 3 days.

dairy-free **VARIATION**

Use dairy-free margarine in place of the butter, and dairy-free chocolate chips.

EGG-FREE BERRY COBBLER
• *Serves 6 to 8* •

THE CRUST OF this cobbler has the expected crunchy cap, which yields to a soft, cake-like centre baked over the colourful berries.

2 cups (500 mL) peeled and diced cooking apples, such as Granny Smith or Mutsu
1½ cups (375 mL) fresh or frozen raspberries
1½ cups (375 mL) fresh or frozen blueberries
3 Tbsp (45 mL) + ⅓ cup (80 mL) sugar
1¼ cups (310 mL) all-purpose flour
2 tsp (10 mL) baking powder
⅓ cup (80 mL) cool unsalted butter, cut in pieces
¾ cup (185 mL) sour cream
1 tsp (5 mL) vanilla extract

1. Preheat the oven to 350°F (175°C).
2. Toss the diced apples, raspberries, and blueberries with 3 tablespoons (45 mL) of the sugar and spread into an 8-cup (2 L) baking dish.
3. Stir the flour, the remaining ⅓ cup (80 mL) of sugar, and the baking powder together. Cut in the butter until the mixture is a rough, crumbly texture. In a separate bowl, stir the sour cream and vanilla together, and add it to the flour, mixing until well blended. Break the dough into pieces over the fruit, leaving gaps in between for the topping to expand as it bakes. Bake for 25 to 30 minutes, until the fruit is bubbling at the edges and the topping is lightly browned. Let the cobbler cool for 15 minutes, then serve with ice cream. The cobbler will keep in the refrigerator for up to 3 days.

BLUEBERRY COCONUT CUSTARD MINI TARTS
• Makes 18 mini tarts •

dairy-
FREE

egg-
FREE

COCONUT MILK MAKES a richly decadent custard filling, replacing any need for eggs when using cornstarch for thickening.

1 recipe Key Lime Pie crust (page 263)

1 tin (398 mL) coconut milk

1 vanilla bean or 1 Tbsp (15 mL) vanilla bean paste

½ cup (125 mL) sugar

¼ cup (60 mL) cornstarch

1 cup (250 mL) fresh blueberries

1. Preheat the oven to 350°F (175°C) and lightly grease a 24-cup mini muffin tin.

2. Prepare the graham crust and press it into the bottom and sides of the muffin cups. Bake for 10 minutes, then cool to room temperature.

3. Pour the coconut milk into a saucepot and scrape in the seeds of the vanilla bean (or stir in the vanilla bean paste). In a bowl, stir the sugar and cornstarch together and whisk into the coconut milk, then turn the heat to medium and whisk until the mixture comes to a simmer and thickens, about 6 minutes. Scrape the custard into a bowl, cover the surface of the custard with plastic wrap, and allow to cool to room temperature.

4. Once cooled, spoon the coconut filling into the mini tart shells and top each with 3 blueberries. Chill for at least 2 hours in the tin before popping them out to serve.

5. The tarts will keep in the refrigerator for up to 3 days.

note from anna's kitchen

You can make the coconut filling up to a day ahead of time and chill it before filling your tart shells. But before using the filling, it's best to purée it in a food processor or use an immersion blender to make it smooth.

dairy-
FREE

egg-
FREE

FLUFFY, SWEET, AND moist, these cupcakes are a hit at birthday parties. Added sprinkles or coloured sugars can tailor these cupcakes to suit any party theme.

1. Preheat the oven to 350°F (175°C) and line 2 muffin tins with medium paper liners.

2. Sift the flour, sugar, baking powder, baking soda, and salt into a large bowl. In a separate bowl, whisk the almond or soy milk with the oil, lemon juice, and vanilla. Make a well in the centre of the flour and pour in the liquids. Whisk vigorously until well blended (the batter will be quite fluid). Pour the batter into the paper-lined muffin tins, filling the cups two-thirds of the way full.

3. Bake the cupcakes for about 25 minutes, until a tester inserted in the centre of one comes out clean. Let the cupcakes cool in the tin, then remove them before frosting.

4. Beat the margarine with half of the icing sugar, until blended, then beat in the almond or soy milk and the vanilla. Add the remaining icing sugar and beat until the frosting is smooth and fluffy, about 3 minutes. Pipe or spread the frosting onto the cupcakes and store at room temperature. The cupcakes will keep in an airtight container for up to 2 days.

CUPCAKES:

2¼ cups (560 mL) all-purpose flour
1¾ cups (435 mL) sugar
2 tsp (10 mL) baking powder
½ tsp (2 mL) baking soda
¼ tsp (1 mL) salt
1½ cups (375 mL) almond or soy milk
½ cup (125 mL) vegetable oil
1 Tbsp (15 mL) lemon juice
2 tsp (10 mL) vanilla extract

FROSTING:

1 cup (250 mL) dairy-free margarine
7 cups (1.75 L) icing sugar, sifted
½ cup (125 mL) almond or soy milk
2 tsp (10 mL) vanilla extract

note from anna's kitchen
While many cake and cupcake recipes call for a fair bit of sugar, this recipe requires more than the average. The sugar adds more than just sweetness here. Since the recipe is egg-free, the sugar also adds moisture and tenderness. With less sugar, the cupcakes would be dry and crumbly.

WARM CHOCOLATE CHERRY PUDDING CAKE
• Serves 8 •

egg-
FREE

Pudding cakes were a popular dessert in the '70s, and after they devolved into a packaged pudding-mix concoction, they faded out of fashion. In looking at the original versions made from scratch, I discovered that many were egg-free, so they can suit a special diet. This pudding cake comes together like a simple cake batter and is topped with a sugar crumble and finished with a pour of boiling water. As the dessert bakes, the batter separates, producing a cake layer on top and hiding a soft and pudding-like sauce underneath. It is best served warm while that pudding sauce is gooey and soft.

1. Preheat the oven to 350°F (175°C) and grease an 8-cup (2 L) baking dish.
2. Sift the flour, sugar, 2 tablespoons (30 mL) of the cocoa, the baking powder, and salt into a large bowl. Add the milk, oil, and vanilla, and stir to blend well (the batter will be thick). Stir in the chocolate chips and dried cherries. Scrape this mixture into the prepared dish and spread the batter evenly.
3. Stir the brown sugar and remaining ¼ cup (60 mL) of the cocoa to combine, and sprinkle evenly over the cake batter. Pour the boiling water directly over the entire surface of the cake.
4. Bake for about 40 minutes, until the cake bubbles around the entire outside. Let sit for 10 minutes before serving. The pudding is best eaten just after baking, but any remaining portions can be reheated, loosely covered, in the microwave for 20 seconds. Reheating in the oven is not recommended.

1 cup (250 mL) all-purpose flour
⅔ cup (160 mL) sugar
2 Tbsp (30 mL) + ¼ cup (60 mL) cocoa powder
2 tsp (10 mL) baking powder
½ tsp (2 mL) salt
½ cup (125 mL) milk
2 Tbsp (30 mL) vegetable oil
1 tsp (5 mL) vanilla extract
½ cup (125 mL) chocolate chips
½ cup (125 mL) coarsely chopped dried cherries
⅔ cup (160 mL) packed dark brown sugar
1¾ cups (435 mL) boiling water

note from anna's kitchen
The batter can be prepared ahead and chilled. Just pull it out of the refrigerator 30 minutes before baking the cake and then sprinkle with the sugar before pouring the boiling water overtop.

CHOCOLATE ORANGE CHEESECAKE
• *Makes one 9-inch (23 cm) cheesecake | Serves 10 to 12* •

egg-
FREE

SINFULLY RICH AND dense, this cheesecake will never crack in the centre since eggs are usually the culprit behind that problem.

1. Preheat the oven to 350°F (175°C). Grease a 9-inch (23 cm) springform pan and line the bottom with parchment paper.

2. Pulse the oats, brown sugar, cocoa, and salt in a food processor, then pour in the melted butter, pulsing until evenly combined. Press this into the bottom of the prepared pan and bake for 10 minutes. Cool the crust while making the filling.

3. Purée the cream cheese and sugar in a food processor until smooth, scraping the bowl with a spatula. Add the orange zest and tofu and purée well, again scraping the bowl. Purée in the sour cream and vanilla, and blend in the melted chocolate. Scrape the filling into the cooled crust, and spread evenly (it will not move or change as it bakes).

4. Bake the cheesecake for 20 minutes, until the filling bubbles slightly and loses its shine at the edges, but the centre remains shiny. Cool the cheesecake to room temperature, then chill for at least 4 hours before serving. The cheesecake will keep in the refrigerator for up to 5 days.

CRUST:

1 cup (250 mL) rolled oats

⅓ cup (80 mL) packed dark brown sugar

3 Tbsp (45 mL) cocoa powder

Pinch salt

¼ cup (60 mL) unsalted butter, melted

FILLING:

2 pkg (8 oz/250 g each) cream cheese, at room temperature

1 cup (250 mL) sugar

1 Tbsp (15 mL) finely grated orange zest

4 oz (120 g) silken or soft tofu

⅔ cup (160 mL) sour cream

1 tsp (5 mL) vanilla extract

5 oz (150 g) bittersweet chocolate, chopped

gluten-free desserts

The Gluten-Free Challenge

OMITTING WHEAT FLOURS and other grains that contain gluten in baking recipes is a challenge. It is the gluten, or protein, in the grain that gives traditional baked goods their structure: cakes and muffins hold their shape when baking powder is activated, and the gluten makes cookie and pie dough stick together when they are rolled and baked.

I wish there were a magic answer, a single ingredient that could be substituted for wheat flour in all recipes, but there isn't. There are pre-mixed gluten-free flour blends on the market, but results can vary depending on the recipe you use the blend in.

In this chapter, I steer around using flour altogether. Instead, I focus on the strengths of other ingredients to make the recipes their best. I also include some traditional items, made by blending ingredients that are alternatives to wheat flour and best suit the recipes.

I do not specify "gluten-free" for baking powder, vanilla extract, or icing sugar, as these products are generally considered gluten free. However, if you have a serious gluten intolerance, you should purchase certified gluten-free versions of these products, which are available at health-food stores, to use in your baking.

Maintaining Flavour and Structure

The two main areas affected by replacing wheat flour with a gluten-free option are flavour and structure. Wheat flour has a distinctive yet familiar taste, one that you may not notice until you have to replace it with something else. Gluten gives baked goods their strength. It is the element that holds in air as baking powder or eggs rise as they bake. Replacing it with other ingredients that give strength can be accomplished, with similar (though not identical) results.

Combining ingredients can help to maintain flavour and structure, by giving baked goods body and strength and by helping them bond.

BODY

A ground legume, seed, or other product is needed to replace the body of wheat flour. Some gluten-free flours are described below. There are many others, but they are not as readily available or as neutral-tasting as these. Of course, experimenting is really the best way to determine your own preference.

Rice Flour The most readily available and easy to work with. Whether brown or white, this is the most neutral (or familiar) in taste. It can sometimes lend a moderately sandy texture to baked goods.

Legume Flours (Chickpea, Soybean) A common ingredient in gluten-free, all-purpose blends. This has a fine texture but a distinctive taste, stronger than rice flour.

Sorghum Flour Has a pleasant taste and a finer texture than rice flour, but has a grey colour.

Potato Flour Made of dried, ground potato, this has a pleasant, pale yellow colour, and works well when blended with rice flour. It absorbs liquids nicely, contributing to a well-textured baked item. This is not interchangeable with potato starch.

STRENGTH

Starches are added to gluten-free mixes to give baked goods the ability to hold together.

Tapioca Starch The preferred starch to use in gluten-free blends. This has a stronger hold than other starches and virtually no taste (which is why I prefer adding tapioca to my fruit pies).

Cornstarch The most commonly available and affordable starch, but with the least power to hold goods together.

Potato Starch Sits between cornstarch and tapioca starch in terms of strength.

BONDING

Natural gums thicken combined ingredients, allowing them to hold in air and making baked goods lighter in texture. They are most useful in cake and loaf recipes, but not needed in cookie recipes.

Guar Gum From the guar bean, this has eight times the thickening power of cornstarch and is very stable. It gives baked goods resilience, that familiar stretch that also helps to keep in the air as baked goods rise and set during baking. This is generally quite affordable and used in small measure (just 1 to 2 teaspoons/5 to 10 mL in a cake recipe).

Xantham Gum Produced from the fermentations of simple sugars. Be sure to purchase gluten-free xanthan gum, as it can be derived from wheat. Like guar gum, this offers the resilience that is needed in baking, but it is a little more potent and a little more costly.

YOUR LEVEL OF tolerance for ground grain and seed products shapes your dietary requirements, which must be medically determined and abided by. The recipes in this chapter avoid all grains and flours that contain glutens. Some recipes use alternatives to wheat flour—usually a combination of rice flour, a starch, and sometimes a gum. Other recipes use the structural support of other ingredients such as eggs, ground nuts, and chocolate to achieve familiar and tantalizing results.

Recipes in other chapters of the book that are gluten free:

The above recipes do not use oats as the sole grain or flour. Some people with gluten intolerance can consume oats if the oats are certified gluten free (point of origin and processing determines this), some cannot. If you can consume oats, you may enjoy the following recipes, which use oats as the sole grain or flour:

CARROT ALMOND MACAROONS
• *Makes about 2 dozen macaroons* •

gluten-**FREE**   low-**FAT**

*T*HESE COOKIES HAVE a little more substance to them than a traditional French almond *macaron*, and they aren't as sticky sweet as a coconut macaroon.

1. Preheat the oven to 350°F (175°C) and line 2 baking trays with parchment paper.

2. Stir the almonds and carrots with $\frac{1}{4}$ cup (60 mL) of the sugar and 1 egg white. Whip the remaining 2 egg whites with the cream of tartar until foamy, then slowly pour in the remaining $\frac{1}{4}$ cup (60 mL) of sugar and continue whipping until the whites hold a stiff peak. Fold the whites into the carrot mixture in 2 additions. Spoon generous tablespoonfuls of batter onto the prepared baking trays, leaving $1\frac{1}{2}$ inches (4 cm) between each cookie.

3. Bake the cookies for 15 to 20 minutes, until they have lightly browned and are dry to the touch. Cool the cookies completely on the baking trays before removing. The cookies will keep in an airtight container for up to 3 days.

1½ cups (375 mL) ground almonds
1 cup (250 mL) loosely packed, coarsely grated carrots
½ cup (125 mL) sugar
3 egg whites, at room temperature
¼ tsp (1 mL) cream of tartar

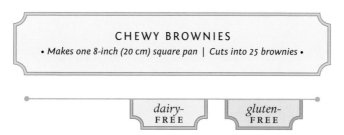

CHEWY BROWNIES
• *Makes one 8-inch (20 cm) square pan | Cuts into 25 brownies* •

dairy-
FREE

gluten-
FREE

THIS IS ONE of those recipes in which working without gluten actually proves advantageous. The texture of these brownies is dense and chewy, and they have a nice, shiny top to them.

1. Preheat the oven to 350°F (175°C). Grease and line an 8-inch (20 cm) square pan with parchment so that the paper comes up the sides of the pan.
2. Stir the sugar, cocoa, and oil together until moistened.
3. Add the eggs and vanilla, and whisk to blend.
4. Add the rice flour, cornstarch, and salt, and stir until incorporated. Stir in the walnut pieces. Scrape the batter into the prepared pan and spread evenly.
5. Bake the brownies for about 25 minutes, until they lose their shine and when a tester inserted in the centre comes out clean. Cool the brownies to room temperature before slicing. The brownies will keep in an airtight container for up to 2 days.

1¼ cups (310 mL) sugar

¾ cup (185 mL) Dutch process (alkalized) cocoa powder, sifted

½ cup (125 mL) vegetable oil

3 eggs

1 tsp (5 mL) vanilla extract

½ cup (125 mL) brown rice flour

2 Tbsp (30 mL) cornstarch

½ tsp (2 mL) salt

½ cup (125 mL) walnut pieces

HAZELNUT CINNAMON COFFEE CAKE
• Makes one 8-cup (2 L) Bundt cake | Serves 12 to 16 •

gluten-
FREE

To bake a gluten-free cake that is as close as possible in texture to a wheat flour cake, you need to use a combination of rice flour for body, potato flour for fine texture, tapioca starch for tenderness and hold, and xanthan gum to hold in the leavening.

1. Preheat the oven to 350°F (175°C) and grease an 8-cup (2 L) Bundt pan.
2. In a small bowl, stir the brown sugar, hazelnuts, lemon juice, and cinnamon, and set aside.
3. In a large bowl, stir the rice flour, potato flour, tapioca starch, xanthan, baking powder, and salt together.
4. In a separate bowl, whisk the sugar and eggs together, then whisk in the buttermilk and vanilla.
5. Pour the liquids into the dry mixture and whisk just until blended. Spoon two-thirds of the batter into the prepared Bundt pan and sprinkle the brown sugar crumble over the batter, then swirl it into the batter a bit with a butter knife. Top with the remaining batter and run a knife through the cake to swirl the crumble a bit.
6. Bake the cake for about 45 minutes, until a tester inserted in the centre of the cake comes out clean. Cool the cake in the pan for 30 minutes, then turn it out to cool completely.
7. The cake will keep, well wrapped, for 2 days, or it can be frozen for up to 3 months. Do not refrigerate.

⅔ cup (160 mL) packed dark brown sugar

½ cup (125 mL) lightly toasted chopped hazelnuts

1 Tbsp (15 mL) lemon juice

1 tsp (5 mL) ground cinnamon

1½ cups (375 mL) brown rice flour

⅔ cup (160 mL) potato flour (not potato starch)

¼ cup (60 mL) tapioca starch

2 tsp (10 mL) xanthan gum

2 tsp (10 mL) baking powder

¼ tsp (1 mL) salt

1½ cups (375 mL) sugar

3 eggs

1¾ cups (435 mL) buttermilk

2 tsp (10 mL) vanilla extract

HONEY ALMOND SHORTBREAD
• Makes about 2 dozen cookies •

egg-
FREE

gluten-
FREE

LIKE MOST TRADITIONAL shortbread recipes, this one, made using ground almonds, improves as it sits in the cookie tin for a day or two.

1. Preheat the oven to 325°F (160°C) and line 2 baking trays with parchment paper.
2. Beat the butter until light and fluffy. Add the icing sugar, honey, and almond extract, and beat 2 minutes more.
3. Stir in the rice flour, ground almonds, guar gum, and salt, and stir until the dough comes together. Spoon the dough by teaspoonful and shape into balls. Place them onto the prepared baking tray, leaving a 1-inch (2.5 cm) gap between them.
4. Bake the shortbread cookies for 12 to 15 minutes, until they just begin to brown on the bottom. Cool the cookies on the baking tray before removing. The cookies will keep in an airtight container for up to 4 days.

⅔ cup (160 mL) unsalted butter,
   at room temperature
¼ cup (60 mL) icing sugar, sifted,
   plus extra for dusting
3 Tbsp (45 mL) honey
⅛ tsp (0.5 mL) almond extract
1 cup (250 mL) brown rice flour
½ cup (125 mL) ground almonds
1 tsp (5 mL) guar gum
¼ tsp (1 mL) salt

GLUTEN-FREE PIE CRUST
• Makes one 9-inch (23 cm) pie crust •

gluten-
FREE

I HAVE FOUND THAT sorghum flour works best in a gluten-free pie crust recipe for taste and for ease in rolling. Although the crust may crack a little when rolling and baking, it will bake together nicely, and it can be easily sliced and lifted out of a pie plate.

1. Stir the rice flour, sorghum flour, tapioca starch, sugar, salt, and spices to combine. Cut in the butter until the whole mixture has a rough, crumbly texture but there are a few larger bits of butter visible.
2. In a small dish, whisk the eggs, water, and vanilla. Add this to the flour mixture, and stir until the dough comes together.
3. Shape the dough into a disc, wrap it, and chill for just 15 minutes (to chill the butter).

⅔ cup (160 mL) rice flour (white or brown)
½ cup (125 mL) sorghum flour
½ cup (125 mL) tapioca starch
2 Tbsp (30 mL) packed dark brown or demerara sugar
½ tsp (2 mL) salt
½ tsp (2 mL) ground cinnamon
¼ tsp (1 mL) ground nutmeg
½ cup (125 mL) cool unsalted butter, cut in pieces
2 eggs
1 Tbsp (15 mL) cold water
1 tsp (5 mL) vanilla extract

notes from anna's kitchen
1. Rice flour is quite neutral in colour and taste. Sorghum flour has a mild nutty taste and is more of a dove colour.
2. I intentionally selected the rice flour, sorghum, and tapioca for their workability and taste, and because of their affordability—some gluten-free elements can be costly.
3. Unlike traditional flour pastry dough that has to rest to relax the glutens in the flour before being rolled out, gluten-free pastry dough needs to chill to set the butter and to allow the rice and sorghum flours to absorb some of the liquid for easier rolling. You may find the crust crumbles just a bit as you roll it and lift it, but once baked, it holds together very well and slices into portions nicely.

RASPBERRY PEACH GALETTE
• *Makes one 9-inch (23 cm) pie | Serves 6 to 8* •

gluten-
FREE

A GALETTE IS A free-form tart, typically baked on a baking tray, but I like baking this, rustically folded, in a pie plate to hold in all those luscious peach and berry juices.

1. Preheat the oven to 375°F (190°C). Lightly dust a 9-inch (23 cm) pie plate with rice flour.
2. Prepare the filling by stirring all of the filling ingredients together until evenly blended.
3. Dust a rolling surface with rice flour for rolling and gently roll out the pastry (dusting your rolling pin and the dough as needed) to a diameter of about 14 inches (35 cm), and lift it into the pie plate. Spoon the fruit filling into the shell. Gently fold the edges of the pastry (about 2 inches/5 cm) over the fruit filling—it usually takes about 6 folds. Whisk the egg and water together, brush the top of the pastry with the egg wash, and sprinkle with turbinado or demerara sugar. Bake the galette for about 45 minutes, until the crust has browned evenly and the fruit filling is bubbling. Cool for about an hour before slicing. The tart can be served warm, at room temperature, or chilled, and it will keep in the refrigerator for up to 2 days.

1 recipe Gluten-Free Pie Crust (page 295), chilled
2 cups (500 mL) fresh or thawed frozen raspberries
3 peaches, peeled and diced
⅔ cup (160 mL) packed dark brown or demerara sugar
1 Tbsp (15 mL) tapioca starch
½ tsp (2 mL) vanilla extract
¼ tsp (1 mL) ground allspice

FOR BRUSHING:
1 egg
1 Tbsp (15 mL) water
Turbinado or demerara sugar, for sprinkling

sugar-free
VARIATION

To make this recipe sugar-free, simply eliminate the brown sugar from the crust (no replacement), and replace the brown sugar in the filling with ½ cup (125 mL) of agave syrup.

BANANA ORANGE LOAF
• *Makes one 9- × 5-inch (2 L) loaf | Cuts into 16 to 20 slices* •

dairy-
FREE

gluten-
FREE

THIS RECIPE MAKES a tall loaf, so it cuts into lots of servings. It also freezes well, so you can wrap up half of the baked loaf to freeze and save for a later date.

1. Preheat the oven to 350°F (175°C) and grease a 9- × 5-inch (2 L) loaf pan.
2. Whisk the eggs in a large bowl. Whisk in the bananas, orange juice, oil, brown sugar, and zest until combined. In a separate bowl, sift the rice flour, potato flour, xanthan gum, baking powder, cinnamon, and salt, then stir this into the banana mixture. Stir in the raisins, then scrape the batter into the prepared loaf pan.
3. Bake for 50 to 60 minutes, until a tester inserted in the centre of the cake comes out clean. Cool the cake completely in the pan before turning out to serve or store. The loaf will keep, well wrapped, for up to 3 days, or can be frozen for up to 3 months.

2 eggs
1½ cups (375 mL) puréed ripe bananas
   (2 to 3 bananas)
1 cup (250 mL) orange juice
½ cup (125 mL) vegetable oil
⅔ cup (160 mL) packed light brown sugar
2 tsp (10 mL) finely grated orange zest
2 cups (500 mL) brown rice flour
½ cup (125 mL) potato flour
2 tsp (10 mL) xanthan gum
2 tsp (10 mL) baking powder
1 tsp (5 mL) ground cinnamon
½ tsp (2 mL) salt
⅔ cup (160 mL) golden raisins

note from anna's kitchen
In this recipe, it is important to purée the bananas in a food processor or with an immersion blender as opposed to simply mashing them with a fork. The banana purée lends moisture and helps make a nicely textured loaf.

LEMON ALMOND POUND CAKE
• *Makes one 9-inch (23 cm) cake | Serves 12 to 16* •

*E*GGS GIVE THIS cake its structure so that it holds together without gluten. The texture and taste of this cake are very much like those of a conventional pound cake, and it has a fantastically tart lemon taste.

1. Preheat the oven to 375°F (190°C). Grease a 9-inch (23 cm) round springform pan and coat it with sugar, tapping out any excess.

2. Beat the butter, ¾ cup (185 mL) of the sugar, and the lemon zest using electric beaters or a stand mixer fitted with the paddle attachment. Add the egg yolks two at a time, beating well after each addition. Beat in the vanilla, then pour in the lemon juice while mixing.

3. In a separate bowl, whip the egg whites until they are foamy, then add the remaining ¼ cup (60 mL) of sugar, whipping until the whites hold a medium peak. In another bowl, stir the ground almonds, potato flour, and salt. Add 1 cup (250 mL) of the almond mixture to the butter mixture and stir by hand. Fold in half of the whites, then gently stir in the remaining ground almond mixture. Fold in the remaining whites and scrape the batter into the prepared pan, spreading evenly.

4. Bake the cake for 10 minutes at 375°F (190°C), then reduce the oven temperature to 325°F (160°C) and bake for about 30 more minutes, until a tester inserted in the centre of the cake comes out clean. Cool the cake completely in the pan before turning it out to serve. The cake will keep for 3 days at room temperature or it can be frozen.

½ cup (125 mL) unsalted butter, at room temperature

1 cup (250 mL) sugar

1½ Tbsp (22.5 mL) finely grated lemon zest

6 eggs, at room temperature, separated

2 tsp (10 mL) vanilla extract

¾ cup (185 mL) freshly squeezed lemon juice, at room temperature

1 cup (250 mL) ground almonds

⅔ cup (160 mL) potato flour (not potato starch)

¼ tsp (1 mL) salt

notes from anna's kitchen

1. It is important that all of your ingredients are at room temperature in this recipe, including the lemon juice, so that the batter does not seize or appear curdled. Should the batter take on that appearance when mixing, have no fear—it bakes up beautifully in the end.

2. Like many dense cakes, this pound cake actually improves after it has been frozen and thawed. You can freeze a cake like this for up to 3 months.

CHOCOLATE PAVLOVAS
• Makes 8 individual Pavlovas •

gluten-
FREE

Chocolate Pavlovas are typically softer than their plain meringue cousins. These Pavlovas bake up with a pale chocolate exterior, but when you crack into the centre, you have a rich, almost brownie-like interior.

1. Preheat the oven to 275°F (140°C). Cut 2 sheets of parchment paper to fit 2 baking trays. Trace 4 circles, each 4 inches (10 cm) across, onto each sheet using a marker, then place the sheets onto the baking trays, marker side down (so that the ink does not transfer onto the Pavlovas).

2. Whip the egg whites and cream of tartar until they are foamy, then slowly add the sugar and continue whipping at high speed until the whites hold a stiff peak when the beaters are lifted (the whites will be thick and glossy). Sift the cocoa and cornstarch over the whites and fold in, then quickly fold in the vinegar and vanilla.

3. Dollop a generous cupful of the meringue onto each circle drawn onto the parchment. Gently press an indent into the centre of each, but don't spread or work the meringue too much.

4. Bake the Pavlovas for 75 to 90 minutes, until they are dry on the outside. Let the Pavlovas cool to room temperature, then store in an airtight container until ready to serve.

5. Serve the Pavlovas with a dollop of Crème Fraîche (page 320) on top of each, and sprinkle with fresh berries. The Pavlovas will keep, unassembled, in an airtight container for up to a day.

6 egg whites, at room temperature
½ tsp (2 mL) cream of tartar
1½ cups (375 mL) sugar
3 Tbsp (45 mL) Dutch process (alkalized) cocoa powder
2 tsp (10 mL) cornstarch
1 Tbsp (15 mL) balsamic vinegar
1 tsp (5 mL) vanilla extract
1 recipe Crème Fraîche (page 320)
4 cups (1 L) mixed fresh berries

WALNUT POPPY SEED CAKE
• Makes one 9-inch (23 cm) cake | Serves 16 •

gluten-
FREE

THIS IS A European-style cake—a very simple one-layer torte that is best served with a dollop of cream or fresh berries.

1. Preheat the oven to 350°F (175°C). Grease a 9-inch (23 cm) springform pan and sprinkle the bottom and sides with sugar, tapping out any excess.
2. Pulse the walnuts, poppy seeds, and 1/3 cup (80 mL) of the sugar in a food processor until finely ground.
3. Beat the butter and 1/3 cup (80 mL) of the sugar until light and fluffy. Add the egg yolks and vanilla, and beat until well blended.
4. In a separate bowl, whip the egg whites until foamy, then slowly pour in the remaining 1/3 cup (80 mL) of sugar and whip until the whites hold a soft peak. Fold the whites into the butter mixture. Fold in the ground nuts and poppy seeds until incorporated. Spoon about 1/3 cup (80 mL) of this batter into the cream and then fold this into the batter. Pour the batter into the prepared pan and bake for about 45 minutes, until a tester inserted in the centre of the cake comes out clean. Cool the cake to room temperature (it will sink a little as it cools), then chill it completely before removing from the pan and serving. The cake will keep for up to 3 days in the refrigerator.

1¼ cups (310 mL) walnut pieces
¾ cup (185 mL) poppy seeds
1 cup (250 mL) sugar
⅔ cup (160 mL) unsalted butter,
   at room temperature
5 eggs, at room temperature, separated
1 tsp (5 mL) vanilla extract
½ cup (125 mL) whipping cream

note from anna's kitchen
If you have access to ground poppy seeds from an Eastern European grocery store, those are preferred (and can be used in the same measure), but the recipe works deliciously well with whole poppy seeds, too.

STEAMED CHOCOLATE FIVE-SPICE PUDDING CAKE
• Makes 8 individual cakes •

*T*HESE ARE FESTIVELY spiced individual desserts, in the same family as sticky toffee pudding but with an intense chocolate taste. Steaming the pudding ensures that the cakes are moist, and they are best served warm. A spoonful of Vanilla Cranberry Compote (page 320) would add an extra festive flair.

4 oz (125 g) bittersweet chocolate, chopped
½ cup (125 mL) unsalted butter, at room temperature
½ cup (125 mL) sugar
2 tsp (10 mL) finely grated orange zest
5 eggs, at room temperature, separated
1 tsp (5 mL) vanilla extract
¾ cup (185 mL) ground almonds
1 tsp (5 mL) Chinese Five-spice powder
Cocoa powder, for dusting

1. Preheat the oven to 350°F (175°C). Grease eight 6-ounce (180 mL) ramekins and then sprinkle them with sugar, tapping out the excess. Place the dishes into a roasting pan that has an outside edge that is taller than the ramekins.

2. Melt the chocolate in a metal or glass bowl placed over a pot of barely simmering water, stirring until it has melted. Set aside.

3. Beat the butter, ¼ cup (60 mL) of the sugar, and the orange zest until it is fluffy, then beat in the egg yolks and vanilla. Beat in the melted chocolate. Stir the almonds and the five-spice powder together, and add this to the batter, mixing until blended.

4. In a separate bowl, whip the egg whites until foamy, then slowly pour in the remaining ¼ cup (60 mL) of sugar while whipping, continuing to whip until the whites hold a soft peak. Fold the whites into the batter until well incorporated and ladle this mixture into the prepared ramekins. Pour boiling water into the roasting pan so that the water comes halfway up the sides of the dishes. Cover the roasting pan with foil and bake the puddings for 45 minutes, until they spring back when gently pressed. Let the puddings sit, still covered, for 15 minutes.

5. To serve, run a spatula or knife around the inside edge of each dish and invert it onto a dessert plate. Dust with cocoa and serve warm.

6. Alternatively, the cakes can be prepared a day ahead and warmed in their dishes in a water bath (as they were baked) for 15 minutes at 325°F (160°C).

note from anna's kitchen
Chinese five-spice powder is a blend of star anise, cloves, cinnamon, Szechuan pepper, and fennel seed that matches very well with chocolate. The spice blend adds sophistication without being overwhelming, but if you prefer a basic chocolate dessert, it can be omitted.

low-fat and/or
low-sugar desserts

NOTES ON LOW-FAT AND/OR LOW-SUGAR BAKING

THE DESSERTS IN this chapter are designed to please the palate without using excessive fat or sugar. Instead of using substitutions, these recipes have been designed to use ingredients and methods that are satisfying on their own.

Recipes in other chapters of the book that are low in fat and/or low in sugar:

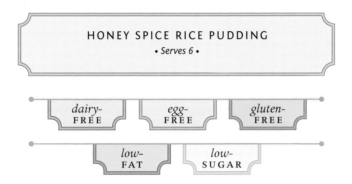

HONEY SPICE RICE PUDDING
• Serves 6 •

*dairy-*FREE *egg-*FREE *gluten-*FREE

*low-*FAT *low-*SUGAR

$\mathcal{S}$ HORT-GRAIN RICE IS key to this recipe. The starch that an arborio or a sushi rice lets out as it cooks thickens the milk, giving it a pleasing richness without adding any fat.

1. Bring the rice milk or almond milk up to a simmer with the cinnamon, cardamom, and star anise. Stir in the rice and cook it, covered and at a gentle simmer, stirring occasionally until the rice is tender, about 20 minutes.

2. Stir in the honey and remove the star anise. Ladle the rice pudding into serving dishes and chill until ready to serve. The pudding will be quite fluid when warm, but it will set once chilled. The pudding will keep in the refrigerator for up to 3 days.

3⅓ cups (830 mL) rice milk
  or almond milk
½ tsp (2 mL) ground cinnamon
½ tsp (2 mL) ground cardamom
1 whole star anise
⅔ cup (160 mL) short-grain rice
  such as arborio or sushi rice
¼ cup (60 mL) honey

MOIST AND TENDER PUMPKIN MUFFINS
• Makes 12 muffins •

low-
FAT

*P*UMPKIN PURÉE IS a fantastic ingredient to use in low-fat and low-sugar baking. Outside of its nutritive benefits (it has alpha and beta carotene, vitamins C and E, potassium, and magnesium, and is high in fibre), pure pumpkin purée adds moisture and a natural sweetness to many recipes.

1. Preheat the oven to 375°F (190°C), and lightly grease or line a muffin tin with large paper liners.
2. Stir the whole wheat flour, all-purpose flour, baking powder, baking soda, salt, nutmeg, and allspice in a large mixing bowl.
3. In a separate bowl, whisk the pumpkin, sugar, buttermilk, egg whites, and vegetable oil.
4. Pour the liquids into the dry mixture and stir just until blended. Spoon the batter into the muffin cups and bake for 20 to 25 minutes, until a tester inserted in the centre of a muffin comes out clean. Cool the muffins for 20 minutes before removing from the tin. The muffins can be stored in an airtight container for up to 3 days or frozen for up to 3 months. Do not refrigerate.

1 cup (250 mL) whole wheat flour

⅔ cup (160 mL) all-purpose flour

1½ tsp (7.5 mL) baking powder

1 tsp (5 mL) baking soda

½ tsp (2 mL) salt

½ tsp (2 mL) ground nutmeg

¼ tsp (1 mL) ground allspice

1½ cups (375 mL) pure pumpkin purée

⅔ cup (160 mL) packed demerara or dark brown sugar

⅔ cup (160 mL) buttermilk

2 egg whites

3 Tbsp (45 mL) vegetable oil

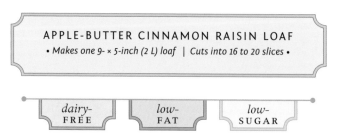

APPLE-BUTTER CINNAMON RAISIN LOAF

• *Makes one 9- × 5-inch (2 L) loaf* | *Cuts into 16 to 20 slices* •

dairy-
FREE

low-
FAT

low-
SUGAR

*L*IKE PUMPKIN PURÉE, apple butter gives moisture and sweetness to baked goodies. Be certain to buy pure apple butter, which is made only of apples that have been slowly cooked down to concentrate their taste and sweetness. Because of this natural sweetness, no sugar is needed in this recipe.

1. Preheat the oven to 325°F (160°C) and grease a 9- × 5-inch (2 L) loaf pan.
2. In a large bowl, whisk the apple butter, apple or orange juice, and eggs. Stir in the grated apple.
3. In a separate bowl, stir the flour, baking powder, cinnamon, allspice, baking soda, and salt. Add this to the apple-butter mixture, and stir just until evenly blended. Stir in the raisins and scrape the batter into the prepared pan, spreading to level.
4. Bake the loaf for 45 to 50 minutes, until a tester inserted in the centre of the loaf comes out clean. Cool the loaf in the pan for 20 minutes, then turn it out to cool completely before slicing. The loaf will keep, well wrapped, for up to 3 days. The loaf can be frozen for up to 3 months, but do not refrigerate.

1 cup (250 mL) pure apple butter

½ cup (125 mL) apple or orange juice

2 eggs

1 medium apple, any variety, peeled and coarsely grated

2 cups (500 mL) whole wheat flour

1 Tbsp (15 mL) baking powder

½ tsp (2 mL) ground cinnamon

¼ tsp (1 mL) ground allspice

¼ tsp (1 mL) baking soda

¼ tsp (1 mL) salt

¾ cup (185 mL) raisins

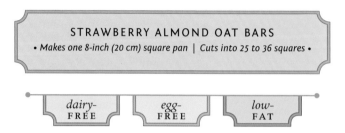

STRAWBERRY ALMOND OAT BARS
• Makes one 8-inch (20 cm) square pan | Cuts into 25 to 36 squares •

dairy-
FREE

egg-
FREE

low-
FAT

*A*LMOND BUTTER GIVES these bars a deliciously toasty taste, and it works wonderfully with a strawberry preserve. A low-sugar preserve will work just fine here.

1. Preheat the oven to 350°F (175°C). Line an 8-inch (20 cm) square baking pan with parchment paper so that the paper hangs over the sides a little.
2. Stir the flour, oats, and sugar to combine.
3. In a separate bowl, stir the almond butter, oil, and orange juice. Add this to the flour mixture and combine until the mixture is a rough, crumbly texture.
4. Press half of the mixture into the prepared pan and spread the strawberry preserves overtop. Crumble the remaining oat mixture over the preserves and gently press.
5. Bake the bars for about 35 minutes, until they brown just around the edges. Cool the bars, then chill before slicing. The bars will keep in the refrigerator for up to 4 days.

1¼ cups (310 mL) whole wheat flour

1½ cups (375 mL) regular rolled oats

½ cup (125 mL) packed demerara or dark brown sugar

⅔ cup (160 mL) pure almond butter, well-stirred

3 Tbsp (45 mL) vegetable oil

2 Tbsp (30 mL) orange juice

1 cup (250 mL) strawberry preserves (can be low-sugar)

HIGH-FIBRE BAKED APPLES
• Makes 4 baked apples •

| dairy-FREE | egg-FREE | low-FAT | low-SUGAR |

THE COMBINATION OF oats with bran, wheat germ, and flaxseed gives the crumble on top of these apples a wonderfully nutty taste.

1. Preheat the oven to 375°F (190°C).
2. Peel the apples halfway down and scoop out the core, but do not scoop through the bottom of each apple. Place the apples in a baking dish and fill the centre of each with 1 tablespoon (15 mL) of raisins.
3. Stir the oats, oat bran, flaxseed, wheat bran, wheat germ, cinnamon, and cloves together. Add the maple syrup and oil, and stir to coat. Press the mixture into the centre and on top of each apple.
4. Bake the apples for about 25 minutes, until the crumble browns just a little and the apples are tender. Let the apples cool for 10 minutes before serving. The apples can be made and chilled up to a day ahead, but should be served warm. They can be reheated in a 325°F (160°C) oven for 10 to 15 minutes.

4 McIntosh apples
4 Tbsp (60 mL) raisins
⅔ cup (160 mL) regular rolled oats
2 Tbsp (30 mL) oat bran
2 Tbsp (30 mL) ground flaxseed
1 Tbsp (15 mL) wheat bran
1 Tbsp (15 mL) wheat germ
½ tsp (2 mL) ground cinnamon
¼ tsp (1 mL) ground cloves
3 Tbsp (45 mL) maple syrup
1 Tbsp (15 mL) vegetable oil

note from anna's kitchen
You can easily double the oat crumble portion of this recipe and spread it over diced apples to make a high-fibre apple crisp. The baking time will be about the same.

CREAMY MOCHA PUDDING
• Makes 4 individual servings •

egg-FREE   gluten-FREE   low-FAT   low-SUGAR

*A*DDING COFFEE TO chocolate makes the chocolate taste richer without using too much coffee, sugar, or fat.

1. In a small saucepot over medium heat, bring the milk, sugar, chopped chocolate, and coffee powder to a simmer, whisking until the chocolate has melted and the coffee powder dissolves into the milk.

2. In a small bowl, whisk the cool coffee with the cornstarch and vanilla. Gradually whisk the cornstarch mixture into the hot milk. Whisk this over medium heat until it returns to a simmer and thickens, about 4 minutes.

3. Pour the pudding into 4 small serving dishes and place plastic wrap over each dish, so that it touches the pudding directly (this will prevent a skin from forming). Refrigerate the pudding until chilled, about 3 hours. To serve, remove the plastic wrap and dust lightly with cocoa powder. The pudding will keep in the refrigerator for up to 3 days.

2 cups (500 mL) 1% milk

¼ cup (60 mL) sugar

2 oz (60 g) unsweetened chocolate, chopped

1 Tbsp (15 mL) instant coffee powder

¼ cup (60 mL) brewed coffee, at room temperature

3½ Tbsp (52.5 mL) cornstarch

1 tsp (5 mL) vanilla extract

Cocoa powder, sifted, for garnish

sauces and garnishes

SAUCES

THIS IS A classic selection of sauces that can accompany any number of desserts. Think fruit sauces with creamy desserts or cake, and chocolate or caramel sauces with fruit desserts, or you can layer common flavours together.

VANILLA CRÈME ANGLAISE
• *Makes just over 1 cup (250 mL)* •

1 cup (250 mL) half-and-half cream
2 egg yolks
2 Tbsp (30 mL) sugar
1 tsp (5 mL) vanilla extract or vanilla bean paste

1. Heat the cream to just below a simmer.
2. In a small bowl, whisk the egg yolks, sugar, and vanilla. While whisking, slowly pour the hot cream into the egg yolks and return the entire mixture to the pot. Over medium heat, stir the custard with a wooden spoon or silicone spatula until it coats the spoon or spatula, about 3 minutes. Pour the custard sauce through a strainer, cool to room temperature, and chill until ready to serve. The sauce will keep in the refrigerator for up to 3 days.

CLASSIC CHOCOLATE SAUCE
• *Makes about 1 cup (250 mL)* •

THIS CHOCOLATE SAUCE is thick and rich and is best served warmed.

¼ cup (60 mL) whipping cream
3 oz (90 g) bittersweet chocolate, chopped
3 Tbsp (45 mL) unsalted butter
2 Tbsp (30 mL) packed light brown sugar
2 Tbsp (30 mL) corn syrup
⅛ tsp (0.5 mL) salt
1 Tbsp (15 mL) brandy (optional)

1. Stir the cream, chocolate, butter, brown sugar, corn syrup, and salt together in a heavy-bottomed saucepot over medium-low heat until melted and smooth.

2. Remove the sauce from the heat and stir in the brandy, if using, and serve warm or at room temperature, or chill for later use. The chocolate sauce will keep in the refrigerator until the best-before date of the cream.

CREAMY CARAMEL SAUCE
• *Makes about 1¼ cups (310 mL)* •

3 Tbsp (45 mL) water
2 tsp (10 mL) lemon juice
⅔ cup (160 mL) sugar
¾ cup (185 mL) whipping cream

1. Pour the water and lemon juice into a small, heavy-bottomed saucepot and add the sugar. Without stirring, bring the sugar to a boil over high heat. Continue to boil the sugar, occasionally brushing the sides of the pot with water, until it turns a rich amber colour. Remove the pot from the heat, and slowly and carefully whisk in the cream (watch out for steam).
2. Let the caramel sauce cool in the pot, then serve at room temperature for a great satiny texture, but store in the refrigerator. The caramel sauce will keep in the refrigerator until the best-before date of the cream.

note from anna's kitchen

Caramel sauce suits flavour additions such as 2 tablespoons (30 mL) of Baileys® liqueur, Grand Marnier, Kahlúa, or whisky, as well as 1 teaspoon (5 mL) of vanilla plus 2 tablespoons (30 mL) of butter to make a butterscotch sauce. Any of these additions can be made after the cream has been added, while the sauce is still warm.

RASPBERRY COULIS
• *Makes about 1 cup (250 mL)* •

1½ cups (375 mL) fresh or thawed frozen raspberries
3 Tbsp (45 mL) sugar, or to taste

Purée the raspberries and sugar, then strain through a fine sieve. Chill until ready to serve. The coulis will keep in the refrigerator for up to 4 days.

MANGO COULIS
• Makes about 1 cup (250 mL) •

1 ripe mango
2 Tbsp (30 mL) sugar

Peel and dice the mango. Purée it with the sugar, and chill until ready to serve (there is no need to strain). The coulis will keep in the refrigerator for up to 4 days.

VANILLA CRANBERRY COMPOTE
• Makes about 2 cups (500 mL) •

2 cups (500 mL) fresh or frozen cranberries
½ cup (125 mL) water
1 vanilla bean or 1 Tbsp (15 mL) vanilla bean paste
1 tsp (5 mL) finely grated orange zest
⅔ cup (160 mL) sugar

1. Bring the cranberries, water, scraped seeds from the vanilla bean (or bean paste, if using), and orange zest up to a simmer over medium heat. Simmer the cranberries for 5 minutes, then add the sugar and simmer for 10 more minutes, stirring occasionally.
2. Remove the compote from the heat, cool to room temperature, then chill until ready to serve. The compote will keep in the refrigerator for up to 2 weeks.

RASPBERRY COMPOTE
• Makes about 1½ cups (375 mL) •

⅓ cup (80 mL) sugar
1½ tsp (7.5 mL) cornstarch
2 cups (500 mL) fresh or frozen raspberries
¼ tsp (1 mL) allspice

Stir the sugar and cornstarch together, and add this to a saucepot with 1 cup (250 mL) of the raspberries. Bring this to a simmer over medium heat, stirring occasionally. Once fully simmering, remove from the heat and stir in the remaining 1 cup (250 mL) of raspberries. Chill until ready to serve, but this compote is best served at room temperature (pull it from the fridge 1 hour before serving). The compote will keep in the refrigerator for up to 5 days.

CRÈME FRAÎCHE
• Makes about 1 cup (250 mL) •

1 cup (250 mL) whipping cream
1 Tbsp (15 mL) buttermilk

1. Stir the whipping cream and buttermilk together, and pour the mixture into a plastic or glass container (a mason jar or resealable plastic container will work well). Place this container into a bowl and fill the bowl with hot tap water, just to the level of the cream. Place this in a warm, draft-free place to culture for 24 to 48 hours (the outside heat and humidity will impact the length this takes—more heat and humidity lessens the time).
2. Check the fragrance for a fresh citrus aroma, and chill the crème fraîche without stirring until set, about 3 hours.
3. To use, spoon off the crème fraîche and dispose of the liquid whey at the bottom. The crème fraîche will keep in the refrigerator until the best-before date of the cream.

CHANTILLY CREAM
• Makes about 2 cups (500 mL) •

CHANTILLY CREAM IS simply whipped cream with added vanilla. To make Chantilly cream that holds its volume, so that you can whip it hours ahead of serving, even a day ahead, check out the tip on page 11.

1 cup (250 mL) whipping cream
1 Tbsp (15 mL) sugar
1 tsp (5 mL) vanilla extract or vanilla bean paste

Whip the cream until the cream holds a soft peak when the beaters are lifted. Stir in the sugar and vanilla, and chill until ready to serve, up to an hour ahead.

GARNISHES

ITH A FEW simple tricks, finishing and garnishing desserts becomes a snap.

CHOCOLATE SHAVINGS
• As desired •

1 block (4 oz/125 g or greater) dark, milk, or white chocolate

Use a vegetable peeler to shave chocolate, and sprinkle over tarts, cakes, or cupcakes as desired.

note from anna's kitchen

White chocolate is softer than milk chocolate, and milk chocolate is softer than dark chocolate. When shaving softer chocolates, you will get larger shavings—even curls from white chocolate. All of the chocolates are equally appealing and tasty.

NUT CRACKLE
• Makes about ½ cup (125 mL) •
Enough to garnish 1 cake or tart, or 6 individual desserts

⅓ cup (80 mL) sliced or chopped nuts (almonds, hazelnuts, walnuts, or pecans)
3 Tbsp (45 mL) pure maple syrup

1. Preheat the oven to 325°F (160°C). Line an 8-inch (20 cm) cake pan with aluminum foil and grease it well.
2. Sprinkle the foil with the nuts, then pour the maple syrup overtop, stirring just slightly. Bake this for about 18 minutes, until the syrup is bubbling vigorously. Let the crackle cool completely, and store at room temperature until ready to serve.
3. To serve, peel the foil away from the crackle and break it into pieces to use. The crackle will keep in an airtight container for up to a week.

CANDIED CITRUS PEEL
• Makes about 1½ cups (375 mL) •

2 whole oranges or lemons
1 cup (250 mL) sugar, plus extra for coating

1. Using a paring knife, score a circle on each citrus at the top and bottom of the fruit. Score down the citrus in 4 or 5 places, and remove the peel. Cut the peel into julienne strips.
2. Bring a small pot of water up to a boil and add the citrus peel. Let the peel boil for 1 minute, then drain away the water (this step draws out the bitterness from the peel).
3. Bring the sugar and 1 cup (250 mL) of water up to a simmer, and add the blanched citrus peel. Gently simmer the peel until it becomes translucent, about 10 minutes. Remove the pot from the heat and let the citrus cool in the syrup.
4. Strain out the peel (and reserve the syrup for other uses), and spread it out on a parchment-lined baking tray to dry a little. Toss the peel in a little extra sugar, or leave plain. The candied peel will keep in an airtight container for up to 2 weeks (do not refrigerate).

notes from anna's kitchen

1. A piece of candied orange or lemon peel can add polish to a simple chocolate torte, or add a festive kick to a fruit dessert, or top a crème caramel.
2. The reserved syrup has a nice citrus essence to it. Use the syrup to poach pears, sweeten tea, iced tea, or coffee, or to brush over a pound cake.

ACKNOWLEDGMENTS

THERE ARE SO many people to recognize and appreciate here, it could almost be its own book, but I appreciate that you, kind reader, wish to get into the kitchen and get baking, so I shall be succinct.

I'd like to express my thanks to those who shared this journey by referencing our five senses—without all five senses, food would not be the pleasure that it is.

Taste

To friends and family who taste-tested my recipes and gave me their honest feedback, so that I could grow and learn. This includes the love of my life, Michael, his daughter, Mika, my parents, our friends Mike and Tina (kind enough to volunteer to taste anything chocolate), and the many Facebooks fans who tested and tasted and shared their results.

Smell

A special thanks goes to Lisa Rollo, who tested every single recipe in this book, which is why she deserves credit all on her own under the sense of fragrance. It takes a sensitive and astute cook to recognize when something is ready from the oven by following their nose. In addition to being a good friend, she helped to make this book what it is. My heartfelt thanks to you, Lisa.

Sight

Photographer Ryan Szulc and prop stylist Madeleine Johari deserve thanks for making these baked delights look as appealing in images as they do in real life. Our photo days are cool, calm, and collected, and together we learned that eating olives while surrounded by a buffet of sweets keeps you from snacking when you shouldn't.

And a shout out to the editorial graphics team at Whitecap Books. It takes many sets of eyes and a shared vision to translate a simple Word document into something that goes beyond mere printed pages.

Sound

To Robert McCullough, my dear friend. I listened to you, and here it is. It has taken many phone conversations and "meetings" over lunch for me to listen, and after almost 10 years, here is the book. I wish you continued success as you venture forth.

Touch

And I thank you, my dear readers and supporters. You have touched my heart and, I hope, your own. You keep me inspired, trying new techniques, playing with new ingredients, and on my toes. I hope to continue our adventures together.